About t

Fred Beckey has achieved enduring recognition as the most imaginative, persistent, and thorough explorer and mountain investigator of the Cascade Range wilderness. His intimate knowledge of the topography has been gained through many years of personal encounter, including the ascent of hundreds of peaks—many of them first ascents—in all parts of the range, and the study of an untold number of maps and aerial photographs.

This knowledge is reflected in his other books, *Mountains of North America, The Range of Glaciers: Exploration and Survey of the Northern Cascades,* and his *Cascade Alpine Guide* Series.

In addition to becoming a legendary personality, Beckey has earned a reputation as a student of human history. He has also carefully perused the body of natural history, ecology, glaciology, and geology, and added his own contributions. Beckey has served as an advisor to the Washington State Board on Geographic Names, and has indirectly contributed many feature names in the Cascades.

Through keeping abreast of published literature, seeking out and interviewing other climbers and explorers, and investigating documents in various libraries throughout North America, Beckey has become widely acknowledged as the authority on Cascade Range history. Many of his findings have been published in the literature of the region.

THE MOUNTAINEERS, founded in 1906, is a nonprofit outdoor activity and conservation club, whose mission is "to explore, study, preserve, and enjoy the natural beauty of the outdoors. . . ." Based in Seattle, Washington, the club is now the third-largest such organization in the United States, with 15,000 members and four branches throughout Washington State.

The Mountaineers sponsors both classes and year-round outdoor activities in the Pacific Northwest, which include hiking, mountain climbing, ski-touring, snowshoeing, bicycling, camping, kayaking and canoeing, nature study, sailing, and adventure travel. The club's conservation division supports environmental causes through educational activities, sponsoring legislation, and presenting informational programs. All club activities are led by skilled, experienced volunteers, who are dedicated to promoting safe and responsible enjoyment and preservation of the outdoors.

The Mountaineers Books, an active, nonprofit publishing program of the club, produces guidebooks, instructional texts, historical works, natural history guides, and works on environmental conservation. All books produced by The Mountaineers are aimed at fulfilling the club's mission.

If you would like to participate in these organized outdoor activities or the club's programs, consider a membership in The Mountaineers. For information and an application, write or call The Mountaineers, Club Headquarters, 300 Third Avenue West, Seattle, Washington 98119; (206) 284-6310.

Send or call for our catalog of more than 300 outdoor titles:
The Mountaineers Books
1001 SW Klickitat Way, Suite 201
Seattle, WA 98134
1-800-553-4453

CHALLENGE OF THE NORTH CASCADES

Seth Mary,
Here's some old tales to help
inspire new adventures.
May your recovery be speedy
& complete. —Tom

CHALLENGE OF THE NORTH CASCADES

BY FRED BECKEY

Maps by Dee Molenaar

THE
MOUNTAINEERS

Published by
The Mountaineers
1001 S.W. Klickitat Way, Suite 201
Seattle, Washington 98134

0 9 8 7 6
5 4 3 2 1

Published simultaneously in Canada by Douglas & McIntyre, Ltd., 1615 Venables Street, Vancouver, B.C. V5L 2H1

Published simultaneously in Great Britain by Cordee, 3a DeMontfort Street, Leicester, England, LE1 7HD

Manufactured in the United States of America

Maps by Dee Molenaar
Cover design by Watson Graphics
Book design by Allen L. Auvil
Cover photograph: *Climbers approaching Nooksack Tower.* Photo by Dee Molenaar.
Insert: *Fred Beckey stemming an open chimney on Rocket Peak.* Photo by Bob and Ira Spring.
Frontispiece: *Mt. Baker at sunset, from the Nooksack River. Author led first ascent of the ice ridge on the north wall, a safe route that since has become a North Cascades classic. (See Chapter 13.)* Photo by Ed Cooper.

Library of Congress Cataloging-in-Publication Data
Beckey, Fred., 1921–
    Challenge of the North Cascades / by Fred Beckey ; maps by Dee Molenaar.—[2nd ed.]
        p. cm.
    ISBN 0-89886-479-8
    1. Hiking—Washington (State)—Guidebooks. 2. Hiking—Cascade Range—Guidebooks. 3. Washington (State)—Guidebooks. 4. Cascade Range—Guidebooks. I. Title.
GV199.42.W2B43   1996   96-7616
796.5'22'09797—dc20   CIP

TO MY MOTHER

*Boston Peak and Boston Glacier, above Skagit Queen Creek. The contrasts
of the North Cascades are here shown in the intricate relationships of
rugged crests, adorning ice, and the mantle of fringing meadows and
forests. (See Chapter 3.) Aerial photo by Austin Post, U.S. Geological
Survey.*

Foreword

Climbers are notorious gossips. When they're not talking about climbs past and planned, they're talking about other climbers. Even before my wife and I joined The Mountaineers in 1948, a close friend had filled us with anecdotes from the careers of the living legends who had created the Climbing Course in 1934 and years following, and in the decade before World War II had raised Northwest mountaineering to a new level of technical respectability.

Nobody was more talked about in those days than Fred Beckey. His electric quality stimulated some, jolted others. In an age of many strange and wonderful heroes, his exploits made a special kind of tumult.

From several of my Climbing Course teachers who earlier had been his teachers, I heard how they had instantly spotted his exceptional ability and drive. (I recall a certain move on Monitor Rock of which it was said, "The only one who's ever done it is Beckey.") In Fred's novice year of 1939, one of the leading Mountaineer climbers of the era, Lloyd Anderson, encouraged his talent by inviting him on a difficult, pioneering ascent. But that same summer he independently organized and led other first ascents, and the next season became in his own right one of the most energetic explorers of the North Cascades. It was in the British Columbia Coast Range, though, that Fred startled his teachers and contemporaries. Mt. Waddington, which dominates a rough white wilderness, had been attempted 17 times

Author on the Index Town Wall, the Town Crier route. (See Chapter 12.) Photo by David Beckstead.

and climbed only once—until the teenage Beckey brothers arrived in 1942 and made the second ascent.

After war-time service Fred resumed high roaming—from the Cashmere Crags, where his weekend romps popularized "cragging," to the aiguilles of the Bugaboos to super-Alpine ranges of Alaska. Meanwhile he was busy in another role that brought a new kind of fame: publication in 1949 of *Climber's Guide to the Cascade and Olympic Mountains of Washington* was perhaps one of the most influential events in the annals of North Cascades travel. "Beckey's Bible," as we called it, shaped the alpine lives of all us new and eager Climbing Course students; as copies trickled through the Northwest and across the nation, strangers from out of state began to join our inner circle of home folk in kicking the snow, scrambling the rock.

This book is concerned solely with the North Cascades portion of Fred's career. (For others, see "Chronology of Climbs: 1936–68.") Through the years since 1939, when he emerged from the Boy Scouts into The Mountaineers, he has visited many ranges in North America and the world, but always has returned regularly to his home hills. His ascents span a long stretch of Cascades history—from olden days when the U.S. Forest Service scarcely knew how to hold a timber sale, because nobody wanted to buy public trees, to modern times when a host of entrepreneurs covets resources of the last remaining scraps of wildlands.

Portions of the North Cascades have been placed in various administrative classifications—Wilderness Area, National Recreation Area, and National Park—which will help keep some of the country something like the way it was when Fred began climbing there 30 years ago. However, a much larger part of the range remains wide-open to loggers, miners, highway engineers, dam-builders, and other apostles of civilization. The stories Fred tells here suggest how much has been lost, how much requires perseverance if it is to be saved.

October 1968   Harvey Manning

Preface

to the Second Edition

Since *Challenge of the North Cascades* was first published in the late 1960s, both the population of the Pacific Northwest and the public's interest in mountaineering have increased dramatically. An unmistakable presence on the horizon, the North Cascade Range has been irrevocably etched into the region's consciousness. Our respect for the North Cascades is linked to their early history—in times when most valleys did not have roads or trails, and most peaks were not yet scaled. Today it is easy to take for granted a quick weekend visit to the Cascade Pass region, where in 1882 (only 113 years ago), the nearest outposts, attainable only by trail, horse, or boat, were Fort Okanogan and a Native American village at the site of present-day Marblemount. Today roads reach high on both flanks of the pass. Access to the wilderness Picket Range has not much changed, but in British Columbia, where at the turn of the century it required a pack-train trek to reach Chilliwack Lake, this heartland body of water is now only two hours from Vancouver by car.

Once the army explorers, government topographers, railroad and wagon-road surveyors had finished their work and chosen a route for what became the North Cascades Scenic Highway, the once-remote crags and peaks of the Washington Pass area quickly became a mecca for climbers. Elsewhere in the range, it is common in the summer to sight numerous mountaineering parties on the ice slopes of Mount Shuksan, and a parade of roped teams on the glaciers of Mount Baker.

Inroads into this dynamic landscape continue to occur: a freeway has been built across Snoqualmie Pass, and logging and private development have increased, accompanied by the associated road building. But with greater environmental awareness on the part of the public, these inroads are facing stronger opposition than in the past. The establishment of Glacier Peak, Pasayten, and other small Wilderness Areas, the North Cascades National Park and Recreation Area, and the recent Skagit River Provincial Park in British Columbia hold some promises in maintaining the region's integrity.

Even the growth in mountaineering has had an effect. Not that long ago, when, with a few companions, I took up the challenge of scaling unknown granite spires in the Enchantment Lakes area of the Stuart Range, it was a surprise to see hikers, and there were no other climbers. Now the Snow Lakes Trail parking lot is regularly overfilled with cars, and the Forest Service is using a permit system as a management device to limit visitors and protect the integrity of the fragile terrain. As wilderness hiking and rock climbing have become more mainstream in our culture, and more people are competing for the same turf, there are new challenges to keeping the North Cascades intact for recreational needs. In an age of accelerating high technology in the sciences and communication, it is important to keep the natural environment intact from intrusions. Both hikers and mountaineers would do well to decentralize: engage in some creativity, seek approaches and peaks that are little known.

Although our knowledge of these majestic mountains is perhaps greater than ever, thanks to easier access, numerous guidebooks, and increased information networking, the challenges they present to the mountaineer are no less compelling today than they were for me when I first confronted them.

January 1996   Fred Beckey

Preface

This book is not just a story of physical adventure and obstacle, but retells some of the historic climbs in the North Cascades and shows what climbers have accomplished in our mountains. A considerable acknowledgement is due my many climbing companions, who are partly responsible for the book being written. Some of the accounts will perhaps strike a strong nostalgic note for people who climbed through these times. For new alpine travelers, they will provide insight into events and personalities.

No recent attempt has been made to deal comprehensively with the exhaustive record of mountaineering in the Cascades and the relationships there between men and mountains. Much of this history has been written, but is locked up in climbing journals, technical works, and obscure treatises. While seeking to include as many as possible of the more interesting pioneer climbs, it has plainly been out of the question for me to treat all of them, much less to describe how men came to this sport of freedom and adventure in the Pacific Northwest. My reporting sometimes has a tone of personal involvement, sometimes of detachment; I naturally have emphasized my own trips because those are the ones I know best. A complete and objective chronicle of travel in the North Cascades from the earliest times to the present would be of great value and is long overdue.

By the late 1930s, when I became involved in alpine adventure, many trying climbs had been made in the Cascades, and reading and hearing about them gave me inspiration.

There were the early climbs by C. E. Rusk, and in particular his 1921 ascent of the Rusk Glacier and "Castle" on the east face of Mt. Adams. On Mt. Rainier the 1935 north face routes of Liberty Ridge and Ptarmigan Ridge, and the 1937 ascent of Sunset Amphitheater, stood out as superb accomplishments.

The influence of writers such as Edmond Meany was constructive, and helped dispel the widespread opinion among the misinformed that the sport is a mild form of lunacy. Climbers gravitated naturally to the Cascades, and after the interest aroused by summer outings of The Mountaineers, exploration went rapidly. In 1928 H. P. Wunderling and C. L. Anderson climbed the south face of The Tooth, a creditable effort for those days. Earlier, in 1915, the conquerors of Huckleberry wrote their wills before completing the ascent. Chimney Rock in 1930 required barefoot rock work on the hardest pitches by Art Winder, Forest Farr, and Lawrence Byington. The west ridge of Mt. Stuart was done in 1935, the first of the more interesting variants on that major peak.

The Index North Peak ascent by Chute and party in 1929 was so remarkable that a decade passed before it was believed. After Bonanza's first ascent in 1937 by a Mazama party, Larry Penberthy and H. Altenfelder completed several new routes, projects little-known until much later. The ascent of Goode in 1936 received more immediate attention, as did the many firsts by Herman Ulrichs, whose route on Silver Star was perhaps his finest completed climb.

Farther north, the early explorations of the Picket Range, such as the Strandberg-Degenhardt climbs, and the firsts of Fury and Challenger, are covered in the text. The notable climb of Shuksan's Hanging Glacier by Otto Trott and Andy Hennig was due to experience gained in Europe. The Canadian ascents of American Border Peak and Slesse opened up serious climbing along the boundary. And, in the rolling pine-woods country of Idaho's panhandle, the men who first reached the top of that lightning-rod, Chimney Rock, prematurely showed the nerve of a later generation of rock specialists.

In the 1940s and 1950s, standards of difficulty steadily rose. The new technical competence, new ideas, new equipment, and the increase in the number of climbers, and the example of other climbing areas, all contributed to the surge. But as has been said of the Alps, regardless of the climbs that get done the Cascades will never be "climbed out."

Although the several regions of the Cascades are often equated in popular fancy, perhaps because the stately procession of volcanos gives a poetic and unifying charm, in reality they differ enormously. Towering above forest, desert, and water, their ramparts rise from three states and British Columbia. However, the principal peaks (excluding volcanos) lie north of Glacier Peak. Between there and where the range falls away to the Fraser River, the organization of crests and valleys is complex; some gregarious groupings on the eastern slope, such as the Methow, Pasayten, and the Stuart Range farther south, rise higher than the main divide. "Challenge" by definition means "disturbingly provocative, enticing," an invitation to discovery. Here the dimensions of challenge are many.

Today, challenges to the integrity of our mountain environment are coming with increasing pace. Hopefully new concepts of preservation will make man critical of burgeoning proposals to "dominate" nature and will allow the bulk of our mountain regions to remain in a permanent wilderness condition. A civilization which values its environmental and esthetic resources certainly can do no other. It is to be hoped the momentum toward destroying our natural wonders in the Pacific Northwest will be halted, and that the tenuous protection of "recreation area" will be firmed by the new North Cascades National Park. Management of the Cascades that is wilderness-oriented will in the long run provide "the greatest good for the greatest number."

Many episodes in the book acknowledge indebtedness to the companionship and inspiration of others. More directly I wish to express thanks for assistance by members of the Literary Fund Committee, especially Harvey Manning. Peggy Ferber's devoted typing simplified manuscript preparation and is much appreciated. A number of people submitted photographs for consideration; Tom Miller and Austin Post helped invaluably in the final selection.

October 1968   Fred Beckey

Northern faces of Mt. Stuart, with their contrasts of granite and ice. Author made first complete ascent of the prominent buttress dividing the walls, and also the first climb through the Ice Cliff Glacier (on left) and its crowning rock headwall. Aerial photo by Austin Post, U.S. Geological Survey.

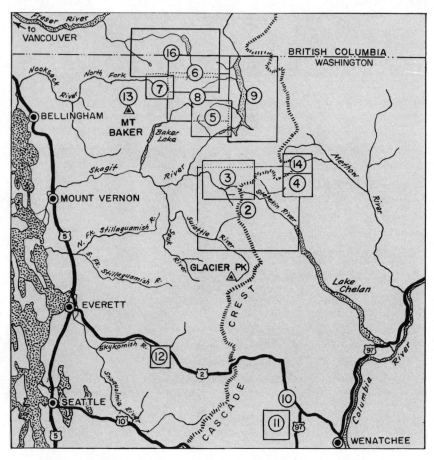

Areas covered by chapter maps are enclosed in boxes, the chapter numbers circled therein.

Chapters 10 and 13 fall within the area covered by the key map, but do not have chapter maps. Chapters 1 and 15 do not have maps either.

Each chapter map shows *only* the travel routes *used* by the author for climbs described in that chapter. Other roads and trails are omitted.

The travel routes, whether by road, trail, or off-trail, are shown *as they were at the time of the author's visits.* Since then new roads and trails may have been built.

The author's automobile travel is shown by parallel dashed lines, trail travel by single dashed lines, and off-trail travel by dotted lines.

2

Contents

1

Discovery of a Challenge

When I first experienced the depths of the Cascade forest empire, the spectacle of the nearby peaks made a permanent impression on me. Mountains struck me as the ultimate manifestation of solitude and scenic grandeur. Though most of my boyhood adventure was spent on the beaches, the water, and among lowland forests, I always was especially excited when my parents planned such trips as a hike to Skyscraper Mountain on Mt. Rainier's Wonderland Trail, or an excursion on the old Everett and Monte Cristo Railroad, which in the early 1930s still ran a pleasure tour to the old mining mecca of Monte Cristo.

The story of these early years is one of self-doubt and self-reliance, the excitement and ecstasy of every moment of fresh adventure and chance for bravery. When I was 13, with the inducement of a sunny day near Olympic Hot Springs, I scrambled up Boulder Peak alone—much to the concern of my parents. For my own good they saw to it I joined the Boy Scouts in West Seattle, where I soon became more versed in the arts of woodcraft and camping. In Troop 288's Comet Patrol, under the inspiration of Leon Allers, I went on hikes ranging from Lake Hancock to Mt. Si, after the latter of which I made the diary notation "I solemnly believe that a man who hasn't his heart in climbing will never make a true climber." A number of short

Mt. Despair, the author's first ascent, from across the deep and jungled valley of Goodell Creek. Photo by Ed Cooper.

summer hikes and scrambles and winter ski tours introduced me to more serious efforts.

The first of these, in 1937, was a Scout trip with the Rangers of Camp Parsons under Jack Morrison; we covered an estimated 75 miles and climbed The Brothers and two other peaks between the Hamma Hamma and Dosewallips Rivers. After one night, while sleeping in the Duckabush valley, I recorded in my diary, "a bear sniffed at us." With just one companion I spent a week in the high country of the Olympics, climbing minor peaks and ridges beyond Flapjack Lakes. My first real winter adventure was a 4-day ski trip to Anderson Pass, a long trail-breaking excursion through the snowy solitude of Olympic forests. In 1938 I joined the Parsons climb of Mt. Olympus, my most thorough alpine experience to that time. With our nailed boots and alpenstocks, wildlife stayed at some distance from our group.

Scouting had its alpine limitations, of course, and through the suggestion of Scout leaders, as well as Ome Daiber, who endorsed me, I joined The Mountaineers in the fall of 1938 as a junior member. I hoped to go on a club climb of Big Four, which I remembered vividly from early trips on the Monte Cristo Railroad, but was turned down because the trip was an "experience climb" for Climbing Course students. After a winter of weekend ski-touring which included trail-breaking for the cross-country Patrol Race from Snoqualmie Lodge to Meany Ski Hut, in Spring 1939 I took the Climbing Course.

Lectures in the clubrooms were augmented with practice trips in the field, ranging from technique sessions at Monitor Rock in West Seattle to weekend practice trips in the Snoqualmie Pass area. I learned fundamentals of snow climbing in Commonwealth Basin and basic rock techniques on Guye and Lundin Peaks. Among a number of climbers assisting with lectures and trips, the ones whose inspiration I remember most include Jack Hossack, George MacGowan, Lyman Boyer, Burge Bickford, and Lloyd Anderson. On most practice sessions, as well as climbs, one rope-leader was assigned to two or three or four students; after another year the students who continued in the Course would become rope-leaders. Trip-leaders, naturally, were those who had gained some years of experience.

One of the main benefits of the Course was an opportunity to meet others interested in private climbs; through Scouting and the Course I met such other enthusiasts as Jim Crooks, Ed Kennedy, John James, Bob Craig, Bob Lee, Wayne Swift, Dwight Watson, and Dave Lind. Sometimes students and instructor friends would team to attempt a climb. On one venture, with Ed Kennedy and Burge Bickford, I tried Mt. Constance; my diary notations said we had to retreat because we were "so numbed by the combined elements of rain, wind, and cold temperature." Bickford was my leader on my first volcano—Baker—and Lloyd Anderson on my first first ascent, Mt. Despair—not far from the then rather-unknown Picket Range. Anderson's invitation introduced me to an awareness of the potential of the North Cascades and the value of a serious experience with a small, self-reliant team in the alpine wilderness. In doing 35 summits that year (1939) I learned the importance of getting into condition and the need to study routefinding.

My first out-of-state mountain adventure came that same year when my brother Helmy and I joined an Austrian friend, Ernst Kassowitz, for a trip to Wyoming's Tetons. Our Model-A Ford filled with food and equipment took 4 days to make the drive from Seattle. In an equal number of climbing days we scaled most of the main peaks and on the trail met my first climbing hero—Paul Petzoldt, well-known for his efforts on K2.

Later that summer three friends and I hiked from Snoqualmie Pass to the Stevens Pass Highway. The real objective of the trip into the Dutch Miller Gap area was not hiking, however, but Bear's Breast Mountain. We had never read or heard of anyone climbing it, and upon reaching the summit "we shouted with joy at finding no cairn." The route had a few obstacles, ranging from a volley of rocks knocked down by goats to the ascent of an unknown chimney and brushing loose rock off an insecure ledge traverse. As a tune-up we had climbed Little Big Chief—apparently another first ascent, though we didn't know it at the time. Once out to the highway we split into two groups to hitchhike home. Quoting from my diary, "Joe Barto and I made about 30 miles that evening, but were forced to spend the night sleeping near the roadside. We awoke in the morning to find farmers working near us and hastily left."

An attempt on Chimney Rock with John James did not fare so well. Traveling light, we made a bivouac at 6000 feet with only a stone windbreak and a fire to combat the elements—including enough raindrops to urge us back to Salmon La Sac. A logging truck took us to Cle Elum, from where we had a smoky freight train ride on a flatcar via the Stampede Tunnel to the Auburn hobo jungle.

In 1940 the time went rapidly between summer jobs, repairing torn clothing, and three expeditions of my own planning to the North Cascades. Although these accomplished what we felt were some of the better new climbs in the range, the editor of *The Mountaineer* annual crammed them under a minor heading of "other first ascents." The same issue carried a major article on Tenpeak Mountain and also a four-page account of the ascent of Snowpatch Spire by non-local climbers. Our firsts of the north and south peaks of Gunsight (Blue) were dismissed in one 29-word sentence. The following year a new editor allowed me an article on "Twin Spires" and my brother one on "Climbs on the East Face of Shuksan."

On many of these trips I studied old techniques and tried new ones. While practicing roped skiing among the crevasses of the Nisqually Glacier on Mt. Rainier my brother and I innovated the idea of pre-tying three prusik slings on the climbing rope, a safety procedure we had never heard about previously. I found mechanical climbing sufficiently obvious in theory and just as enterprising in the use of common sense. We practiced the

8

"hip-piton" belay—a new technique in dynamic belaying, at least in the Northwest—on both rock and snow. Seeing a body-sling method of rappelling in a German magazine, we adopted it for descents.

Because of its accessibility, I spent a good deal of time in the Snoqualmie area working out techniques, signals, and double-rope methods for direct aid. At one session we skied to the base of the south face of Lundin and practiced on the steep wall above, with a consoling feeling that if one fell he would likely land on the snow beneath. Until this time we had carried pitons in our pockets—a method we now found had disadvantages. With a limited style and size of iron available, we sawed many standard sizes off, heated and thinned out others. After several such practice trips, often before I had even unpacked at home, someone like Will Thompson phoned to suggest "a trip to Mt. Constance tomorrow," or some other peak, much to the disappointment of my mother.

When it was not possible to get to the mountains to climb or practice, I played football or ran cross-country at night to stay in condition. I found that even climbing over the tops of pay toilets provided good exercise. In 1941 an evening job at National Biscuit Co. loading trucks kept me well-fed, though I thoroughly tired of cookies and eclairs. Because they were disappearing from the market due to the rubber shortage, I bought a few pairs of tennis shoes; I used them not only for rock work in the mountains but for such gymnastics as climbing on Monitor Rock, Glacier Boulder (a fine 20-foot erratic in north Seattle that should have been retained for practice), and campus buildings at night. This latter activity results in a special appreciation of the outer details of edifices. No doubt the fascination did not lie wholly in the climbing, but also in the charm and adventure of outwitting authority at night. As one writer pointed out, "it has long been known certain colleges have produced for a handful of opportunists facilities for a special kind of extra-mural activity. These little-publicized evening

Author exercising on Monitor Rock, later re-named Schurman Rock after its builder, Clark Schurman.

On the summit of the Middle Peak of Olympus, looking at West Peak.

Author, in center, on the Blue Glacier of Mt. Olympus. Note typical Boy Scout alpine garb of the period: short pants, pajama bottoms, alpenstock, and drinking cup attached to belt.

classes, far from leading to a degree, have sometimes had an exactly opposite effect."

In the fall of 1941, when the urge to climb had temporarily left most of my friends, Tom Campbell, Walt Varney, Helmy, and I did a new route on the west face of Guye Peak. This turned out to be one of our better episodes of that era. While Tom and Walt were merrily singing censorable tunes, at the same time reassuring me the belay was "bombproof," Helmy was standing on a pedestal to give me foot support while I groped for handholds in an overhanging crack.

I noted that Walt had a good deal of confidence and natural ability and learned quickly; I thought this was unusual "considering his age of 34." The next weekend the two of us did some face problems at the base of Chair Peak; on the trail back we encountered a group of girls, but their leader frowned on their joining us for some unplanned bouldering.

As late as November that year Walt, Louis Graham, and I made the first ascent of the Leaning Tower of Mt. Garfield. Despite the lateness of season the friction slabs and heather patches were quite dry. In a race against darkness to reach the road, we vaulted over logs and scrambled down rocks, ending a very busy 11-hour round trip.

In the winter we studied avalanches in Lunn's and Seligman's books and on spring climbs tested 5-foot skis. In a final pre-war expedition to the British Columbia Coast Range, during which my brother and I made the second ascent of Mt. Waddington via the difficult south face, these short skis proved invaluable for the extensive glacier travel and camp-packing. Our success on Waddington was certainly due in part to thorough conditioning and extensive tests of equipment and technique.

For me, the appeal of climbing came from a complex of motives, ranging from a longing to escape from the artificial civilized order and its social and political controls to a need for self-rejuvenation and a desire to restore my sense of proportion. I could see everywhere there was a penalty for too much comfort. An adventurous goal helps one discover those essential human qualities—curiosity, patience, fear, alertness, willpower, and bodily energy. I found climbing gave a unique sense of control over one's destiny. The exaltation one can get in the presence of mountains can be a memorable lesson in humility and an aid to self-realization. Even the freedom from constraint of fear in an uncertain adventure can give a greater appreciation of scenic glories. In action an imaginative climber can find a source of unified sensibility that gives the sport its emotional force and validity. This release has been recently expressed in another way by a leading British climber, Christian Bonington, who wrote: "The more popular the sport becomes, the better. Climbing is a wonderful release from the whole mass of tensions of urban life. For a brief weekend you can escape from all your everyday worries and cares into the absolute concentration that climbing demands."

2

From Dome to Goode

Glaciers held on mountain shoulders,
O'er a slope of granite clean.
Hurl thy flood through foam-washed boulders;
Nestle then in depths of green.

Lyman Lake, Edmond S. Meany

After a year of school routine the freedom of the mountains always called me strongly. In June of 1940 Bob Craig, Will Thompson, and I joined a party climbing Glacier Peak, then struck off east into the wilds beyond the Suiattle River, planning to reach Stehekin a week later.

One of the most impressive summits in this labyrinth of lateral ridges and deep U-shaped valleys is Dome Peak, with its massive Chickamin Glacier, one of the largest in the Cascades. The sustaining ridges on the green forest fringe are an eden of flowers and light grass. Often the rock basins are a clean-swept, cream-colored granite, holding meadowed oases and little lakes in shadowed troughs. The highest trees are sparse and worn. The geometry of the earth's crust is bold and naked.

Not until 1936 was Dome climbed, and then not by one but by two separate parties, each reaching a separate summit, each certain of the first ascent. Both these ascents (of the Northeast

Some of the most difficult climbing in the North Cascades is below the alpine zone. Here, with the South Fork of Agnes Creek roaring in June meltwater, Leif Patterson of the author's party is using pitons to make a careful crossing. Photo by Doug Leen.

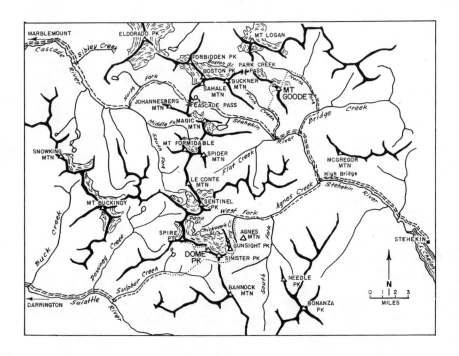

Peak by G. Freed and E. Larson; of the Southwest Peak by F. Farr, D. Blair, and N. Grigg) were admirable explorations of a mountain then so embraced in wilderness.

The uncertainties of Dome Peak aroused our curiosity, as did tales of nearby unclimbed summits. One of our stimulations was a description by a leading Mazama climber, who in 1926 observed the spectacular view toward the head of Lake Chelan from the summit of Liberty Cap, next to Buck Creek Pass: "Off to the north an even more fantastic picture was presented. Scores of peaks soared in vast array, blackly silhouetted against the darkening sky. There were flat-topped mountains with minarets on the corners; smooth, round domes; monsters whose domes had been scooped into great basins by the glaciers bursting down their sides; aiguilles, gendarmes, cones, and pyramids."

Driving along the glacial waters of the Suiattle, below the prodigal splendor of the forested valley walls, we had that feeling of expectancy familiar to every mountaineer when approaching high peaks unknown to him. In the mid-distance the valley sides swept up, green at first, then blue, breaking on high crags where the harsh details of rock were softened by distance. Silver-edged ridges etched their outline against the intensely-blue sky. We drove on to the mouth of Sulphur Creek, where a little hillock of ancient moraine would have been a perfect site for a Rhine castle.

On June 19 we left the Suiattle road, beginning our adventure. The first shock came when we discovered the trail was in mediocre condition, and that a 60-pound pack really weighs 60 pounds. The path wound among the trees of a dank, dark western hemlock forest sodden with lichen and moss. In the dark aisles between pillared trees was a murky world of humus, twigs, and fir needles, damp with moisture and protected by a mulch of decayed vegetation—a scene of pure enchantment, the tangled landscape of some fantastic dream. Thickets of poison-spined devil's club grew in moist bottoms, and vines on drier hillsides. Salmonberry, vine maple, willow, yew, elder, dogwood, and huckleberry formed a dense undergrowth. These, together with fallen trunks, made travel tedious. Yet all these troubles were reasons we were drawn here. The formidable protection of these peaks made them all the more attractive.

Unloading our packs for a rest we gazed at the chaos of savage summits and the few hovering clouds. Above, the vast belt of rainy green merged into white snowfields. A colorful crest of jagged rock rimmed the horizon to the south; directly opposite was Dome Peak, undisputed climax of the region, expressing in all its ridges and walls the intricate interplay of granite and glacier.

These would not be the lovely peaks they are without their mantling snow and ice, and the action of glaciers past and present. The supreme carving was done during the Pleistocene;

the retreating ice has exposed canyon bottoms and rock waste is strewn along the valleys. Fluctuations in climate have brought back icefields of intermediate size during more recent cold periods, and high up remnant glaciers are still quarrying away, plucking at the rock crests, which by now have been sculptured into noble spires throughout the connecting ridges of Dome, Sinister, Gunsight, Spire, and Agnes.

Reality came back when I caught my shin on a snag. We had come to the end of useful trail, estimated at 11 miles from the road, within range of a spur leading to the southwest slope of Dome. It appeared our best hope of escaping the bottomland tangle was to ford Sulphur Creek, then immediately climb a rocky gully to timberline. We took turns straddling a frail tree that spanned the torrent, getting wet to the waist. Then, as we climbed, the green valley fell away, shrinking below. Glacier Peak in its shining whiteness began to grow behind the unseen valley of the Suiattle, becoming incredibly tall against the sky.

Glacier Peak, etched into the sky eastward from Puget Sound, is unchallenged for majesty and size by any of its neighbors. Naturally, climbers at the turn of the century became interested, but always made the approach from the Chiwawa River or from Lake Chelan. Professor W. D. Lyman, the historian from Whitman College, was one of the first explorers to penetrate the mountains between Lake Chelan and Glacier Peak, during his travels about 1900. He described the peak as "ten thousand feet high, and bearing upon its broad shoulders miles and miles of rivers of ice, the most beautiful and significant of all the poems of nature." In his *The Columbia River* he wrote "The entire Chelan region is perfectly gridironed with canyons. There is no question that within this vast cordon of mountains there are more glaciers than in all the rest of the United States combined." One of his most acute descriptions concerns the view from the lake toward Railroad Creek, with "castellated peaks of granite, ribbed and capped with snow, with hues of gray and black, and red and yellow." His name is remembered by the lovely Lyman Lake, near the head of that important entryway into the heartland of these mountains.

The afternoon was warm but not enervating; the air had that fresh stimulating quality that often makes mountain travel so delightful. At about 6000 feet we rested in a field of lush heather and flowers. A table-like parkland spread across a high basin beneath Sinister Peak. In this fairyland of gardens the white bells of heather grew in profusion among clumps of valerian and luxuriant avalanche lilies. Groups of feathery mountain hemlock, dark alpine fir, and scattered pines met at the climatic boundary of alpine west and east.

Will spoke first: "We should climb to the last clump of fir to camp." It proved to be a good spot, with enough squaw wood for fire. In our loneliness that night we talked about climbing plans as we huddled around the crackling fire, the sparks flitting up into the star-jeweled night. Spire Point, a pretty rock peak hidden from our view by a rampart of Dome's west ridge, and first climbed by Dave Lind, Phil Dickert, and George MacGowan 2 years earlier, was agreed upon as our first objective. Spire was also climbed in 1938 by the four intrepid members of the Ptarmigan Climbing Club (Bill Cox, Calder Bressler, Ray Clough, Tom Myers) who traversed the Cascade Crest from Sulphur Creek to Cascade Pass—a route now known as the "Ptarmigan Traverse." In their epic effort, they also scaled Dome, Sentinel, Old Guard, LeConte, Formidable, Spider, Magic, Johannesberg, Sahale, Boston, and Buckner. Six of these were first ascents, and twice they conquered three peaks in one day!

Morning brought delicious cool air, the tonic of high places. The sun shone from a moistureless sky; only on Dome was there an auriole of harmless cloud. We hiked across snow fingers to a glacier pass between Spire and Dome. Winter still reigned on the north faces. On our left Spire, Formidable, and Spider flung skyward in arrogant ferocity. To the right, beyond the valley of Agnes Creek, rose gentler summits, almost bare of snow on the slopes we saw, and lacking the drama of their western neighbors.

Reaching Spire's eastern base we voted for an adventuresome new route that nearly circled the peak. First we crossed a steep knife-edged ridge to a parallel ridge on the west side of the peak via an exciting finger traverse. A final 100-foot wall provided tough climbing on a traverse, followed by a cheval to the summit. Will led this with a piton belay.

From the top of Spire we looked down into the closely-woven fabric of the west-side forests, sinking into deep valleys. Beyond the hazy outlines of Puget Sound, the dim Olympics formed the horizon. I could at this moment agree with Bruno's idea of the boundlessness of space and time. Certainly the serene mountain sunshine evoked a mood of unquestioning adoration.

We walked briskly across the snows of the Dana Glacier toward the Northeast Peak of Dome, now known to be the highest of the two summits. Looking up to the ridge separating us from the Chickamin Glacier, we saw a ribbon of reflected light edging the crest, mirroring the unseen snow of the invisible slope—a phenomenon noted by many early climbers in the Alps, including Ruskin.

The last step to the top was a huge rock, set there as if by a playful giant. We looked out upon a vast panorama of sparkling peaks, from Eldorado in the north to the shining volcano of Glacier. "There are moments when the mountains seem to welcome us as if we were long-expected guests," writes Arnold Lunn. "There are moments when they seem hostile and menacing, and there are moments when the mountains seem aware of our presence, but wholly engrossed in their own high business of communion with the unseen Powers that called them into being." So it was on this grand day, when the peaks neither welcomed nor repelled us, but seemed preoccupied with some ancient rite, in which our part was too insignificant to be worthy of note.

We had an excellent view of Sentinel Peak and the jungled valley of the West Fork of Agnes Creek. In a 3-day struggle with its brush and cliffs in 1935 the Portland party of W. Ronald Frazier, Dennison Lawrence, and Dan O'Brien made the first climb of Sentinel. On the descent Lawrence slipped, to be saved only by a diving tackle by O'Brien just as he was coming to a waterfall drop. After a bivouac by a fire, help from forest rangers was obtained, since he had injured a leg. The country was so rough that 2 days were needed to take him to a point where horses could take over.

On June 26 we packed across steep heather and snow slopes to the pass between Gunsight and Agnes Peaks, one of these heather slopes proving so precipitous we had to rope up. Here we frightened a chirping ptarmigan, which like the chameleon depends on disguises rather than speed to avoid enemies, turning an almost invisible white in winter, and in summer speckled to harmonize with its rocky habitat.

A cluster of whitebark pine, the gnarled and twisted timberline tree spread wide to combat wind (and with close-grained resinous wood excellent for fire) marked the entry to the pass. The meadow setting included clumps of delicate, fern-like larch. The needles, which cluster on little knobs along the branches, now were in their soft summer green; in autumn they turn to yellow pastels and in winter fall off, leaving a spidery bareness.

There is rightly some confusion about Gunsight Peak, our next climbing objective, perhaps because the current Forest Service map had placed "Blue Mountain" east of Dome, very nearby, and "Blue Glacier" on the opposite side of an entirely different peak 2 miles away. The Sentinel party christened this granitic formation "Gunsight," a well-chosen name because of the deep notch between the central and north summits. However, Lloyd Anderson, Lyman Boyer, and Agnes Dickert, who made the first ascent of the central summit in 1938, questioned the propriety of the name and allowed the colloquialism "Blue" to find its way into print. An effort is now being made to eliminate the mundane and reinstate "Gunsight." The steep snow summit adjacent to Dome on the east they called "Sinister," which remains accepted by climbers, regardless of what any map says.

Since the main or central peak had been climbed, our primary interest lay in the south and north peaks. We first examined the slabby north ridge of the north peak, finding it not to our liking because of unanchored snow patches. We retraced our steps. Will wanted to pursue geologic studies, so he dropped out while Bob and I contoured around to the snowy slopes of the Chickamin Glacier, planning to climb the south peak yet that day.

We kicked steps up a steep snow finger that led to a rock gully between the central and south summits. Here, a 100-foot near-vertical wall gave us a chance to practice acrobatics. Once beyond this, the summit was a certainty. In a half-hour we stood there, shouting at Will, far below, then built a rock cairn to register the first ascent.

Each memory has its own peculiar charm, whether it be the wild music of a storm or the glories of a sunny alpine day. At one time the climber can be dominated by the tingling horrors of cliff and tempest; on another he notices none of these, but revels in the vaporous softness of a valley and is lulled by the delicate tints of opal. This had been a day of participation and reflection, as well as one of delightful accomplishment. Now the shallow waves of retreating color on the west slopes became fainter as the sun sank. The crest of a peak to the north hemmed in the last rays beyond our sight; then came a cold inrush of semi-darkness.

A sharp frost during the night gave the morning snow a good crust for climbing. From the glacier the west face of Gunsight springs up sheer to three distinct summits divided by rocky cols, each at the head of a shallow rock couloir. The climb to the northern col is straightforward; from here we retraced the original route to the central peak. Returning to the col after

The northeast face and east buttress of Mt. Goode, above the North Fork of Bridge Creek. Dome Peak and the Chickamin Glacier are in center-left background, just right and below the distinctive volcano of Glacier Peak. The deep trench beyond Goode carries the Stehekin River and tributaries. Aerial photo by Austin Post, U.S. Geological Survey.

lunch we followed a rock band left across a sheer drop to the summit superstructure of the north peak. Here vertically-cleft blocks, almost welded together, suggested a weird archaic battlement. To our amazement, we found we could almost encircle the upper part of the peak on this spectacular band, like a promenade. There was no logic to the jumble of cracks and towers, and only by luck did we find the correct chimney to the true summit. But 130 feet up a question of further advance had to be asked, since the space between two towers widened beyond arm span. Will tried it first, stemming with arms and legs outstretched against the smooth rock until he trembled under the strain. Finally he shouted he had touched the top. We belayed him back; then Bob and I, in turn, repeated his maneuver. I had carried a stone in my pocket to place on the topmost block, but the promenade band was the highest place we could build a true cairn.

Soon we surrendered ourselves to gravity, rappelling to the glacier. In the morning we spotted goats high on the rocky slopes of Agnes Peak. Protected by game laws as they were in 1940, they seemed abundant in this portion of the Cascades.

Of the descent down Icy Creek I remember little, and that I would gladly forget. Muscling our way through a thicket maze, we fervently wished for a conflagration that would consume all alpine brush. Fenced in by cliffs we clambered down a bejungled gully to the flat bush at the edge of the West Fork of Agnes Creek. After a good wetting from the ford, we walked along meadows below the portal to the ice-hung valley. Once on the main trail to High Bridge the temperature rose and dust from our steps swirled in the air.

We must have seemed like pirates to a motorist on the Stehekin road, but he stopped to give us a ride to Golden West Lodge at the upper end of Lake Chelan. Soon the cottonwoods and rushing river gave way to a wide opening, and we saw the lake with its inimitable blue. Chelan is a pleasing lake; the shores satisfy my ideas of loveliness and even the little towns at the south end have not yet been spoiled by the industrial revolution. And its solitudes are yet virtually unspoiled by travel agents.

Several Stehekin tourists interrupted our reverie with questions about the torn clothes we were more or less wearing. Tales of the Agnes brush fight evoked an invitation to lunch, and more tales. This was one time virtually all our exaggerations were true.

Stehekin, the Indian word for "rough water," is an excellent base for climbing holidays away from the multitude. The approach from the mountain passes, as we came, is the most interesting, but not the most popular. The boat runs the 48 miles up-lake daily from the town of Chelan, an outgrowth of steamer service which began when the *Belle of Chelan* was built in 1889. It and the early *Stehekin* carried many miners, most of whom hiked 30 miles by trail to Horseshoe Basin. M. E. Field, who operated a hotel at Stehekin for many years, packed a mill site over Park Creek Pass into the head of Thunder Creek. In this rugged mining work, fall snowstorms often trapped miners and killed horses. Field's Hotel and the one built by Moore on his homestead near the head of the lake in the late 1880s were the principal bases for these miners.

In 1879, when the Alps were already heavily fortified, a military post was built at Chelan ("deep water") to guarantee the safety of white settlers. A few early parties reached the head of the lake by overland travel across the mountains and canyons from the Methow, not often without misfortune. The first settlers at the head of the lake, Henry Dumpke and William Sanders in 1886, were forced to fashion a rude canoe from a cedar log to return down-lake. The stream at the scene of their efforts is now called Canoe Creek.

Jack Ashby, pilot of the *Speedway* when we were at Stehekin dock, said a Mrs. Pilz lived at Canoe Creek all alone with her dog. "She's about 65. It's a mail stop; if she doesn't come down to meet the boat we go up to see what's wrong with her."

The lake, lying in a canyon of granitic and gneissoid rocks to a depth of 300 feet below sealevel, occupies a pre-glacial stream valley. The ancient Chelan Glacier, its source at the Cascade Crest, achieved a length of over 90 miles. The lake is often compared to Lake Lucerne in the Alps, but the pine forests and brown craggy hillsides have more in common with the Sierra Nevada. As the boat churns along the lake, the winding channel gives sudden disclosures of snowy peaks like Boston, Buckner, and craggy Goode. Creased and furrowed faces of the mountains rise abruptly from the water's edge. Fruit orchards and summer homes have intruded along the lower portions of the lake, and the voyage up-lake is interrupted by stops at various cabins and lodges. Unlike hotels in the Alps where innkeepers reply with unrivalled composure that it is proper to overcharge those who can afford it, in my experience most of the managers here are happy to actively bring a greater enjoyment of the wilderness to the vacationist.

Bob left us to take the boat to Chelan, but Will and I, still apostles of the wild, bought a few staples at the Stehekin store and thumbed a ride back up the river road. The driver, who looked all of 70, appeared frail for the old puffing car he was trying to keep under control on the twisting road. The ride ended at what was once (1904) an inn, near Bridge Creek; then we hiked the remaining miles of road to Park Creek. I had hoped we would be able to climb 9300-foot Mt. Goode, third-highest nonvolcanic peak in the state, but Will was determined to continue over Cascade Pass, which we did. Although we reached the road where it ended near Sibley Creek, we found no cars and continued hiking nearly to Marblemount before catching a ride. Hitchhiking then continued to Seattle.

In the mid-1930s Goode was a magnet for many of the more-accomplished climbers. Herman Ulrichs examined its defenses in 1934. He found that on the south side cliffy slopes led toward a summit ridge, but from there a subsidiary peak blocked the route. On the west face a large couloir seemed to offer a route into the heart of the peak, but ended directly beneath the summit under a wall he considered impossible, though he felt he was within 150 feet of the top. The other faces presented equally-forbidding situations, and his coarse flattery of the peak's invincibility gave it quite a reputation. In 1935 Joe Leuthold and Everett Darr of Portland tried a route above the couloir just south of the summit, but were halted by a smooth section of slabby rock above a chockstone in a chimney. Darr, the motivating force behind several attempts, wrote in *Mazama*, "Men that build a cairn on Goode will have earned a summit that has few peers among our American mountains."

In 1936 a Seattle group composed of Wolf Bauer, Joe Halwax, Jack Hossack, Phil Dickert, and George MacGowan attacked Goode, and in their account gave a vivid picture of the problems. "The rear wall of the chimney sloped back at an angle of 50–75 degrees, and was covered with ice and snow. Wolf drove some pitons. With some difficulty he stemmed up between the walls, here about 5 feet apart, crossed and scrambled to a ledge above, where he drove a piton to belay the remainder of the party." A flip of the rope then caught a projection and with prusik knots Wolf worked up and made a finger traverse to the ridge. The first man to arrive at the summit, a prankster, built a hasty cairn and announced the Mazama party had already been there. "We all stood around the cairn consoling each other until the deception became apparent, and the clouds of gloom rolled away."

It is curious but understandable that all these parties missed the two easier routes used on subsequent ascents; it was natural they should follow the gully, but faced with the steep chimney it seems strange a simpler way behind the gendarme on the ridge was not found until years later. Though the peak is no longer considered truly difficult, the ascent was a fine achievement at the time.

In recent years more difficult routes have been done and the major faces have been climbed. Five of us spent the Fourth of

July weekend of 1953 reaching the summit by the north face of the north peak. Don (Claunch) Gordon and I climbed the west spire of Goode in 1953 and in 1954 John Parrott and I went up the long, icy northeast face from the valley of the North Fork of Bridge Creek. Darr had said of the north side "The great Goode Glacier has scooped out a vast cirque with a vertical drop from the summit of close to 4000 feet, making this side practically if not absolutely impossible."

Wonderful as this last climb was, the tense moments came from water: first, the raging torrent of Grizzly Creek which we had to cross, roped, in the black of night; later, the whitecaps of Lake Chelan. John and I had motored and sailed up in my 18-foot catamaran on a calm day. But on the return a down-lake wind several times nearly pitched us on a forward roll. We ran before the wind much of the way on the jib only, and still made 40 miles in less than 4 hours.

In 1966 Tom Stewart and I returned to Stehekin by passenger boat, and aided by a fortunate series of hitched rides made another traverse of the mountain in just 2 days, climbing the magnificent east buttress, again from the brushy depths of Bridge Creek's North Fork. These trips fairly well completed the preliminary exploration of Goode.

Just as rugged, but not as glaciered, is the region between Agnes Creek and Lake Chelan. The highest peak—and the highest non-volcanic summit in the state—is 9511-foot Bonanza, a peak which has been aptly described as a "huge granitic spider" because of its complex flaring ridges and fringing summits, and was finally climbed in 1937 by Joe Leuthold, Barrie James, and **Curtis Ijames.** This Mazama ascent is accepted as valid, but since the climb really is not difficult at all, their story has interesting aspects. "Piton cracks were hard to locate," they wrote of the last 1000 feet, which took them 8½ hours. Previous to this, there had been several futile attempts: in 1935 Leuthold and Everett Darr attempted the southwestern cliffs, reaching the fourth-highest point on the mountain; the next year it would seem only pure chance held off a successful ascent when Darr and Ida Zacher came within 300 feet of the summit on the Holden Lake face; then a party attempted the north face, but only reached Point Two, finding themselves cut off from the highest point. Bonanza was originally named "North Star Mountain" by early miners and the 8300-foot mountain to the southwest was known as "Bonanza"—the one the U.S.G.S. climbed. During mapping the names became confused. Though two early Mountaineer summer outings passed through this general area, they did little real exploration.

3

The Forgotten Peak

The first party to climb Eldorado, in 1933, much admired the view of the North Cascades. They wrote "especially prominent was a high unnamed peak, heavily glaciated, directly to the east. It appeared to equal the height of Eldorado." "Forgotten," as some climbers of the time called it, has three cirques and three ridges, and from almost any view faintly resembles the Weisshorn. Perhaps it was the walls of steely-gray rock, or perhaps it was the remoteness in the wilderness, that kept climbers away until April 1940, when I accepted an invitation from Lloyd Anderson and Dwight Watson to explore the peak.

We drove to Marblemount. I love the Skagit valley above Rockport. Nowhere are the glacier-scarred ridges of the Eldorado country seen to greater advantage. On one side of the road are stumplands and second-growth fir; on the river side are fertile acres intensively farmed in checkered rows. One drives past vegetable patches, poultry ranches, dairy farms, and logging operations. The lower valley has of necessity completed the transition from logging to agriculture. Sedro, meaning cedar, for the old stands of red cedar, came to be Sedro Woolley, the head of Skagit navigation and a town made prosperous by gold-rush traffic of the 1880s and 90s. At Concrete, where limestone buckets on huge overhead conveyors emerge from a quarry, a powder-gray dust covers houses and foliage for miles

Cirques, waterfalls, and green hells of the rarely-visited headwaters of the West Fork of Thunder Creek, between Forbidden and Eldorado Peaks. Aerial photo by Austin Post, U.S. Geological Survey.

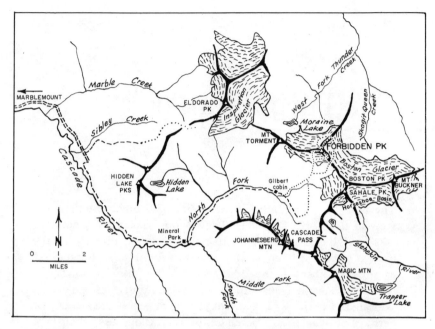

around. Now a bridge crosses the Skagit here, but we used to look for the ferry—a barge with a trolley on an aerial cable, and equipped with rudders that pointed the craft into the current so the flow provided the motive power; the 1928 Mountaineer outing used the ferry to get back to civilization after crossing Cascade Pass. At Marblemount, then no more than a trading post left over from mining and homesteading days, we stopped for a snack at a weatherbeaten frame building, leaning a bit, and timbered with a false front that gave little dignity. Before the first wagon road was completed to Marblemount, Indians were hired to pole dugout canoes with food stores from Hamilton.

Just who made the first traverse of Cascade Pass is uncertain. Most likely it was Indians trading between the Okanogan and Skagit, as we are led to believe by a reading of Alexander Ross' *The Fur Hunters of the Far West*. It has generally been supposed that Ross made the first non-Indian crossing of the

North Cascades in 1811, but an examination of his writings does not give convincing proof of his travel route and whether he used Cascade Pass or some other (such as, perhaps, Ross Pass between Agnes and Sulphur Creeks).

Ross, a Scot, was a member of John Jacob Astor's Pacific Fur Company and established a trading post at the mouth of the Okanogan River. Desiring to carry out a project of discovery, he allowed 2 months to penetrate across the land from "Oakinacken due west to the Pacific on foot." Since no other men were available, he set out with three Indians, heading northwest from the lower Methow River. There is no mention of Lake Chelan, but on the sixth day he reached a height of land on which the east side was abrupt and steep, and here found water running in the opposite direction. He continued west, but stopped while still in the mountains and went back the way he came. His manuscript, first published in 1855, is often vague and earthy and shows he was a man more active than scholarly. It is evident his interest in topography was slight and he contributed little to the knowledge of the country compared to the wealth of details brought back by Lewis and Clark. Captain Vancouver, among others, had little faith in the veracity of Indians and tended not to depend on their information. Ross, on the other hand, relied primarily on his Indian guide for data on where he was on this trek. Exact determination of his route must be left for some future historian.

Another group thought they were the pioneers, in 1877; Charles von Pressentin, the first white settler in the upper Skagit, John Rowley, and two others traveled to Lake Chelan via Thunder Creek, then returned by way of Cascade Pass. In August 1882 Lt. Henry H. Pierce led the 21st Infantry Army Expedition from Fort Colville to Puget Sound, seeking to establish a route for military use in case of Indian uprising. Though not the first crossing of Cascade Pass, this must have been the first of such magnitude, and probably the first with pack animals—some of which were gotten over the pass, though some were lost. Pierce's chronicle is the earliest carefully-written description of the region, and quite accurately describes avalanche tracks and the forests along the Cascade River. The party came from Lake Chelan (reached by crossing the main divide from the Twisp River) up the Stehekin River, which Pierce called "Pierce River" as far as Bridge Creek and "Symon's Fork" above. Here he tells how "the pack train toiled and floundered through almost impenetrable underbrush and swampy areas." Tradition says one soldier who made the journey later came back and located the "Soldier Boy" claim west of Cascade Pass under Sahale Peak, one of the first mineral claims in the district.

Galena ledges were soon traced from Horseshoe Basin to the head of Bridge Creek. Discoveries at Doubtful Lake were made in 1886 by George and John Rouse. Three years later, with Gilbert Landre, they followed the "Boston" ledge which cleaves the summit of that peak, exposed by the glaciers of Horseshoe Basin and cropping on the west side of the Boston Glacier, where a "great body of galena" was exposed in a cliff. They located the Boston claim, digging tunnels there, and the "Chicago" on its western extension. The Pershall Mine was established below Doubtful Lake; a narrow-gauge track ran up to the lake from a water-powered mill to carry lumber for cabins and mine timbers; mill machinery and pipeline remnants may be seen today. In 1890 the Boston Mine had "hundreds of tons of silver-lead ore" piled up awaiting transport.

While the Soldier Boy group consisted of five claims near Cascade Pass, the "Johnsberg" group was four claims on a ledge running up to the summit from the south bank of the Cascade River, 3 miles from the pass. On the precipitous flanks of Johannesberg Mountain, tunnels were dug into the rock 1500 and 2000 feet above the valley floor. Another 800 feet higher, a tunnel showed "3 feet of solid galena." The cabins at "Gilbert" must have been the base for this daring operation. The Johnsberg Mine was active again in about 1948–51, and sporadically since, reached by a trail or a 1-mile cable.

Not until 1891 did prospectors penetrate north beyond Ripsaw Ridge and the Boston Glacier to the head of Thunder Creek; John Russner and two others made this dangerous exploit, finding "a greenish ore rich in silver" at the 7500-foot level. The next year saw a rush to the new strike and several tons of ore were shipped to the smelter from various Thunder Creek claims. The largest single investment in the district, on the north side of the Boston Glacier, was by the Skagit Queen Mining and Smelting Company, which put in an electric power plant. For some years 80 to 100 head of mules and packhorses plodded regularly from Marblemount up the Skagit, then to the head of Thunder Creek. A great deal of machinery was packed in, mostly to sit unused, accumulating rust.

Some maps still show the "Cascade Pass Wagon Road," which in fact never got anywhere near Cascade Pass, despite decades of agitation by promoters beginning in territorial days, and a $20,000 appropriation by the 1895 Legislature to build a road from Marblemount to the Methow. In the '30s, however, the long-projected "North Cross–State Highway" was definitely on the drawing-boards of politicians and hay-ranchers and engineers with more ambition than good sense, and planned to go over the pass. (The route was later shifted.)

On our 1940 trip we found this gravel road coming to an abrupt end just beyond Sibley Creek, 13.5 miles from Cascade Pass. From road-end the trail immediately dropped 500 feet to river level, then passed through trees pushing up for light from deep, flat alluvial soil. Mosses and decayed vegetation nourished a luxuriant tangle of maple, red alder, black cottonwood, skunk cabbage, Canada dogwood, trillium, brackens, and ferns, all moving in their own secret rhythms in a tenuous balance between life, collapse, and regeneration.

The sword fern, one of the most common of the fronds, grows from 6 inches wide to 3 feet long in this valley, rising in thick graceful clumps from a central root stalk, with lance-like dark leaves. Three-petaled trillium dots shady glens and the Indian Pipe lives on decayed wood; in swampy areas the broad green leaves of skunk cabbage dominate the herbage. Fortunately these west-side forests are entirely free from poisonous insects and snakes, and when thrashing around in untracked bush one must only beware of the barbs of devil's club (*echinopanox horridum*).

The trail followed the Cascade River through a great forest of fir and red cedar 5 miles to Mineral Park. Though we saw no traces, once there were stores, shops, and the camps of several hundred miners at this forest "Eldorado"—from whose hoped-for riches came the name of nearby Eldorado Peak.

Beyond here the trail entered the North Fork and climbed steeply in the narrowing forested valley, reaching Gilbert Cabin in another 5 miles. Much of the way was a short distance above the river's south side, giving us a clear vista of exposed granite slabs close to timberline near Hidden Lake Peak. Streams seemed to "cascade" into the valley everywhere; I especially admired the plunging waterfalls of Roush Creek and thought what a nightmare of a bush-fight it would be to climb the steep mountainside any place nearby. Higher, we could see the shiny lower portions of the Eldorado Glacier, outlined sharply in white against the sky.

Henry Gannett, chief geographer of the U.S. Geological Survey, explored the Stehekin and Cascade River valleys in 1905, and commented "This gorge of the North Fork of Cascade River, with its precipitous cliffs, its score of waterfalls, each as high and fine as Bridal Veil, will some day become the Yosemite of Washington."

The genesis of the valley revealed itself from an alder thicket beyond Gilbert Cabin. We saw the valley head at Cascade Pass and looked across the river to the mile-high walls of Johannesberg Mountain. Its cliffs began to cannonade early in the day, as if waking to shake off winter snowcover with a roar. The terrific impact of these slides and their accompanying wind was shown by a wide swath through old forest below the pass; huge logs were snapped like sticks and lay in wildest confusion. Up the valley immense depths of avalanche snow piled atop the thickets, and near the valley bottom trees had been blown uphill from avalanche blasts coming off Johannesberg. It is difficult to imagine the terror one of these great slides can cause until one sees the havoc in its wake.

Just above the thicket the pyramid of "Forgotten" peeped over a forested knoll. With the thunder of Boston Creek's waterfalls in our ears we climbed on spring snow steeply through thick forests, our boots high above the buried brush, to the apex of a timber cone. The snow-covered ridge of a moraine rose ahead, and beyond, swirling mists suggested a high summit. The peak's eventual designation came from this veil, for we agreed "Forbidden" would be a more appropriate name. We made camp at the highest trees and prepared a bough bed for sleeping on snow.

We awoke to find visibility zero. Had we not taken a compass reading the evening before, it would have been senseless even to leave camp. We ploughed upward in soft April snow, the last man constantly checking the compass. Then succeeded a period of sheer boredom; nothing seemed worthwhile except to commit some act of violence to break the monotony of ceaselessly treading an eternal path. It was a relief to find the rock walls of the peak, and we were surprised our aim had been so accurate. Visibility was still zero.

Forbidden has three pronounced ridges and an equal number of faces. From photographs we were agreed our first choice of route was the west ridge, which has a long, steep couloir leading logically to its crest. Once certain we had properly located the couloir in the mists, we entered, and found the snow much improved—hard enough for good stepkicking. Remaining roped, we climbed a narrow snow ridge out of the central chute. Our concentration was so intense we did not notice the mists disperse as we kicked a way upward. The peak now made noble amends for its scurvy treatment of us earlier; suddenly we could see the summit spire and the long north ridge dropping gracefully toward Skagit Queen Creek. The opposite slope dropped off in a fearfully steep abyss. About 4000 feet steeply below we could discern the outline of Moraine Lake, and above it, the vast expanse of the Inspiration Glacier leading toward

Eldorado. The sky, sun, and clouds were playing war games. The west ridge, steep and serrated, was fearfully festooned with great snow bosses that appeared ready to topple; over its right side we glimpsed the snowy gap of Cascade Pass, hung artfully between gaunt walls of Mixup Peak and the gentler slopes of Sahale Arm. It gave us a mystic feeling to be above the mists, in a world where black and white were the only colors.

We led in turn. The first level spot on the crest had been swept clear by wind, but the ensuing slope was still corniced from winter blizzards. The ridge rose in a series of scalloplike edges with both flanks appallingly steep. (Thinking back later, it reminded me of the wild ice ridge I once climbed to the summit of Mt. Deborah, in Alaska.) Now there was malice in the gusts of wind; soon it was evident our attempt had been pushed to the justifiable limit. We had to edge along sideways, and beneath the snow was rime ice. For a time we stood staring at the wintry ridge. We knew it was too early in the season; reluctantly we retreated.

———————

Once the North Cascades have caught the alpinist he is likely to return soon. Dwight was the first to ski Eldorado snows, and though he had since tracked many other remote slopes he was anxious to return. He said he would "call up Anderson" about the possibility of our reaching Eldorado by ski from Hidden Lake Peak. A tempting invitation, which I accepted with no misgivings—the trip would be excellent preparation for mountaineering later in the season and at the same time give a new view of Forbidden.

Skiers have been called by Arnold Lunn "masters of one of the loveliest movements known to man." This exacting mode of motion can also be a branch of exploration. Indeed, the essence of ski-touring is exploration, unlike the repetition that goes into memorizing a standard run. Many years ago A. W. Moore pointed out to the unbelieving world that mountains offer as much pleasure and give as much vigor in winter as summer. But when skiing became an accepted winter sport, the Austrian

The spectacular mountain climax between Thunder Creek and Cascade Pass. In the foreground, the Douglas Glacier of Mt. Logan. In upper middle, the Boston Glacier, topped by Boston Peak left of center and Forbidden Peak right of center. Aerial photo by Austin Post, U.S. Geological Survey.

Colonel Bilgeri was the first to insist skiing is a *snow* sport rather than a *winter* sport. Actually, springtime is more suitable for mountain skiing than alpine climbing.

The slow melting-away of the tenacious snow began early that year. As we labored up the Sibley Creek trail scanty bits of soil were emerging from whiteness. Soon we donned skis with climbers and ascended through timber. In gullies huge balls of snow piled deep between trees. Long-frozen streams were brawling fresh from snowbanks. Spring was rebelling against winter's despotism. We pitched a snow camp among open trees northwest of Hidden Lake Peak.

In the morning our camp was shadowed by a ridge. Above was a break in the rock ramparts. There was no evidence of trail or earth, just clean white snow, grainy and surface-frozen from the cold night.

One knows the mountains deeper and better by watching their changing mantle through the procession of seasons. Most beautiful of the many and varied forms of snow is the dry crystalline kind. In pockets we came across drifts of this fluff; crossing a little roll we saw the sublime crystals of surface hoar. The stability of one particularly-steep slope concerned us. We checked the strata by probing with the ice ax, and though there was some depth hoar, the surface seemed to be safely coalesced. From the 6700-foot pass at the head of Sibley Creek we saw the pyramid of Forbidden. No more splendid peak was visible. Our route lay down a gully, and then across a long snow face broken by several steep rocky ribs leading up to "Triad Peak." There was no wind at all and the sun baked us unmercifully. At last we came to an impasse where we would have to descend hundreds of feet to traverse to the Eldorado Glacier. The slope began to ball and slide. Then a hissing roar of rushing snow came too close for comfort. An incident to remember—and a time to be sensible.

Quivering skis touched high speeds on the sweeping run back down into Sibley Creek. It was exciting to flash past rocks and trees we had taken so long to pass on the ascent. Soon we were in forest where the snow became too patchy and needled for decent skiing. A drink of cold snow water tasted especially good.

On the Memorial Day weekend Anderson, Jim Crooks, Dave Lind, my brother Helmy and I hiked back to our April timberline camp below Forbidden. The second day cold winds and fog rolled across the moraine above. We started for the peak with the hope things would clear, but hours later, on the west ridge, new snow was in the air. There was none of that heartening talk one hears when the worst is surely over, but our cumulative enthusiasm pushed us on.

Dave and I led off, in nailed boots. The rock was wet from melting snow. In two leads we found a protecting ledge a few feet down the north side. On the crest just overhead the wind howled with unchecked fury. On the face beneath, little slides occasionally sent down a clatter of stones, reminding us of our high, exposed position. Much of the ridge was so narrow we had to pull hand-over-hand along the edge, feet scraping for support. A notch blocked the route, but we saw a bypass to the left by way of snow-filled cracks. Fortunately, the joint system in the gneiss tilted up on this side.

Light snow began to fall. Flakes drifted over the rim of the void. Far below and to the left, a brow of bending and frosted precipice was lit by a pale glare diffused through low clouds. Nearer, white flakes twirled and circled intimately; beyond was an immensity of gray haze. Into these depths everything seemed to be descending without resistance, from the long lines of the ice-fast crags to the rays of darkness and shifting eddies of snow. The ceaseless movement of the snow spread to the rock. A thunderous avalanche from Johannesberg provided a background symphony for the ballet of swirling flakes. If we achieve success against a storm it will proportionately increase our satisfaction; Lord Conway said, "No man can really know the High Alps who has not been out in a storm at some great elevation; the experience may not be physically pleasant, but it is morally stimulating in a high degree and aesthetically grand."

It was unwise to continue. We signalled the other rope to turn back, then followed them down to the top of the couloir. Our parkas were stiff and frozen from wet snow, our eyebrows half-frozen with sleet, and our fingers dangerously numb. We had to sustain our training almost unconsciously. There cannot be even a touch of the anarchist about the climbers on a rope; they must be a team. Each climber must not only carry on his own actions perfectly, but make them in harmony with the movements of his rope companions. We descended safely to camp, there to consider plans for tomorrow.

As a party we were adequately strong with five. The best number depends on many conditions which vary with the expedition in view; it should be a flexible rule, adapted to the trip. Mummery, in the golden beginnings of mountaineering, advocated a two-man rope on a slope with objective danger, or even to temporarily unrope, since it is then easier for individuals to escape falling ice or rock. Too, it is absurd to say that if the second fails to hold the leader, the third can be expected to absorb the shock of two falling. The truth is, if from a party of three the least-skilled climber is removed, the two remaining will be distinctly safer on steep slopes than more; but if either of the more competent men is removed, the remaining two will be less safe. The advantages of three or more are chiefly in accidents, porterage, crevasse rescues, and in very major climbs. Solo climbing does not develop the ideal mountaineer, and as a habit is open to far more serious objections—though nothing develops alpine faculties so rapidly and completely.

Intuition has a place in mountaineering. It symbolizes the cumulative effect of many experiences and instincts. Possibly we were impelled by just simple optimism, but we left camp next morning with considerable hope, despite a steady drizzle that turned to snow above 8000 feet. Forbidden was becoming synonymous in reputation with the worst of weather. We began to feel it was all a mistake, but with the energy of morning retraced our long route to the ridge "step" which had blocked us the previous day. Again the wind howled, dislodging stones and snow lumps. The cold was hardly bitter, but it was penetrating. The drifting snow clogged our glasses and filled many rock holds.

Every step had to be made deliberately under such conditions, and each man had to secure himself carefully at belay points. When climbing together we had to be prepared for emergency belays. With the sun blotted out we seemed to lose our sense of time. Every familiar landmark disappeared, and only now and then did the mist break to disclose some fantastic form on the ridge above.

On a warm summer day the climb would have been delightful. Others have found it so since. Certainly varying conditions mock rigid generalities. Later, in *The Mountaineer*, Lloyd Anderson wrote "The continuous physical effort involved, the mental and nervous strain of working on exposed surfaces, and the possibility that each of our belays was subject to a sudden test, conspired to make this a long-to-be-remembered climb."

The ridge widened to a 40-foot block formation, the flanking walls dropping sharply into mist. Dave donned tennis shoes and led up, while the rest of us huddled, anxiously watching his progress. Twice he placed a piton for safety, and then clambered delicately over the last slabby part of the wall.

"It looks better!" we heard him shout. The romance of anticipation for the first time created an illusion of happiness. An attitude of climbing for duty was replaced by earnest zeal. The conquest of the step was almost simultaneous with a break in the blur above. Hazy sunshine gave new fire to mind and muscle. It was a stroke of fortune. Conditions improved by the moment.

From the top of the step we lowered a belay rope to speed Helmy, Lloyd, and Jim. The climbing became continuously easier, and we reached the jumble of blocks at the first summit by 11 A.M. In minutes we scrambled to the true summit, 100 feet east. Forbidden was ours.

The weather now allowed a slight view, but most of the Skagit peaks were invisible. We did not linger, duly concerned as we were about the long descent. Each step had to be made deliberately, and each rappel set up with caution. The next day triumph gave us fleet legs, and by noon we reached the car.

Now that approaches have been cleared of mystery, the ascent of Forbidden is not thought difficult. With the extension of the "mine-to-market" road to within 2 miles of Cascade Pass, the peak is one of the more accessible high summits of the North Cascades. In 1949 Harry King and George Bell of the Harvard Mountaineering Club did the north side of the east ridge, now generally judged the easiest way to the summit. Then came the time for more exacting new routes. Pete Schoening and Bill Fix climbed the west side of the slabby south face, using about 20 pitons and considerable nerve. Several years later Don Wilde, Jack Schwabland, and I completed the long, corniced north ridge; this knifed arete, almost a half-mile in length, is one of the majestic spots in our North Cascades. More recently, in 1958, four of us followed the entire crest of the craggy, narrow east ridge; in 1959 Ed Cooper and I climbed the mountain's longest wall, the sweeping northwest face. But alpinists are far from done with this splendid peak; its faces and ridges retain challenges for many generations ahead.

4

Leaps of the Kangaroo

Years have passed since my brother Helmy, Walt Varney, and I drove the dusty road along the Twisp River in 1942. We were out to make the first exploratory climbs of Kangaroo Ridge, with its pinkish granite monoliths, for a week's tune-up before a projected expedition to Mt. Waddington in British Columbia. The war postponed many plans after that summer; we had no notion then how little of the Cascades we would see the next few years.

Our first encounter with Kangaroo Ridge went back to the previous fall, when a group of us hiked from the end of the road to within sight of the monoliths. We thrilled to the delicate combination of mountain massiveness and delicately-carved spires. Below the rose-colored peaks were gentle meadowed basins where deer trails ran between the pines. All along the route we saw hoofmarks of foraging cattle, and occasionally we heard the clang of cowbells from roaming stock. Poor weather thwarted our climbing plans, though Walt and Jim Crooks decided to continue hiking northward to get a view of the Washington Pass region. Late that night, back at road's end, they woke the rest of us with an exciting story about a moonlight climb of Liberty Bell. We were eaten up with envy until we realized it was a *moonshine* climb; the rain hadn't let up for a minute. The trip, however, was not a complete loss: we discov-

The Temple. This bulky citadel of firm granite has yielded many routes since the author's first ascent in 1942. Photo by Tom Miller.

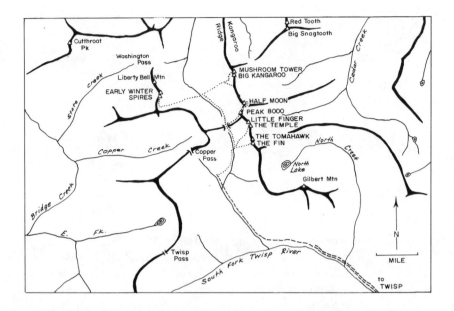

ered the climbing potential of Kangaroo Ridge, and on the return drive not only gathered a good supply of cherries from local orchards but made the first climbing visit to Castle Rock in Tumwater Canyon.

On our new trip rain again met us as Walt's Model-A Ford carried us toward Stevens Pass on June 14. Our spirits were further depressed at a coffee shop by a solitary traveler registering discontent at the intolerable weather across the divide. The Cascade Crest impedes air flow, but in this case rain had continued east. As a farmer he also objected to the political and economic pressure that had forced country residents to accept Daylight Saving Time. A poll in the backlands would have recorded an 80 per cent vote against such tinkering with "God's time"; the rurals nourished dark suspicions that urbanites were using the war as an excuse.

The wise Cascade climber is peripatetic, and goes east of the divide when windward slopes are awash with rain and fog. The sun did as we wished and hoped when it broke through the ceiling near Leavenworth. This valley of the east slope, with its semi-parched vegetation, has a climate much like the Maritime Alps, perfect for fruit-ranching; in the spring the highway to Wenatchee runs through a foam of white blooms. The pines and softly-sculptured hills recall the mountains above San Bernardino, and the fresh dry tang of the air is much like that of the California foothills.

Under the glare of the sun, the cliffs of the Columbia River were in pastel desert hues—muted reds, gray greens, soft tans. Once beyond Lake Chelan the valley is fringed with rolling sagebrush country. In 20 miles the turbulent Methow River enters at a little clump of cottonwoods, in early trading and mining days a river-steamer stop known as Ive's Landing. East of the Columbia, cliffs rise high to stark lava plateaus, but gentle hills and stands of pine and larch soon become the Methow mood. ("Methow" is an adaptation of the name of an Indian tribe that lived between Chelan and the Okanogan. The Wilkes Expedition of 1841 called it "Barrier River," but George Gibbs attached the label that stuck.)

As we drove north along the winding river the surrounding mountains took on a bright, sharp, clean-swept appearance. The fertile bottomlands make some of the world's lushest apple orchards, but up the Twisp River, a tributary of the Methow, the valleys become secluded and deep. Though prospectors have prowled here for years, to citified man the main quality is loneliness. Now and then one passes an abandoned sluicing trough. Here and there are remnants of deserted cabins. In August 1882 Lt. H. H. Pierce's Army expedition, when crossing from Fort Colville to Puget Sound, went up the Twisp River and over the divide—probably by way of the south fork of War Creek—to Lake Chelan. Near the divide, which they estimated at about 6000 feet, their course ran "between lofty mountains . . . some crowned by forbidding crags of granite rising to 3000 feet above the stream." They were looking north, perhaps toward the Kangaroo–Silver Star region. In 1883 Lt. George Backus followed the Twisp River to Copper Pass in one of several efforts to cross the range to the Skagit. Eventually he found the old Indian trail over Mebee Pass to be his best route. Captain George B. McClellan explored the lower Twisp for railroad-building potential, but stopped when he saw the valley was unsuitable. The Twisp Pass region is rich in copper signs, and in 1892–4 the upper Methow had considerable mining excitement. In 1899 the townsite of Twisp was platted.

At a grassy flat Walt halted the car, saying "Let's not stampede the sheep." We waited while several hundred woolies ambled up the road. Each spring they climb from lowlands to the bland ridges fringing the Methow and its many branches, wandering there until fall frosts force them down. Only the east side of the Cascades has good pastoral lands, and nomadism and transhumance are practiced here as in the Alps.

We parked the car at the end of the Twisp River road, marked "Gilbert" on the map, not far from the old Crescent Mine. (In 1892 many claims were staked around Gilbert's Camp on North Creek, then reached by the "State Trail" from Twisp.) We made up our 60-pound packs on a canvas spread between the trees, then began the simple 6-mile walk to basecamp. Leaving the Copper Pass trail, we followed the stock and game paths into the peaceful basin beneath Kangaroo Ridge. The stream we followed divided the slopes of grass, larch, and pine. Not the faintest breeze ruffled the vegetation, and the only sound, almost imperceptible, was that of the stream. The scene typified the Eastern Cascades: a tranquil valley, nestling dark spruce and pine forests, light browns, and a specter of peaks. Finally, brilliant blue sky with clouds poised above, speckling the valley with shadows.

A larch clump against a boulder seemed to offer a protected campsite in threatening weather. There was a wind and the temperature read 34°. To counteract the evening chill we built a large fire from the ample supply of dead ground wood. Beneath a starry sky, Walt began: "Long ago in the days of the Blue Ox there must have been a legendary Blue Kangaroo. This fabulous animal could bounce over a mountain. Some old prospector probably had his imagination affected by spring one balmy morning as he looked at a long ridge of granite towers, and visualizing the course Blue Kangaroo might have taken through the air on a series of running bounces, named it Kangaroo Ridge. Spring must have affected the jumper also, for these jumps are most erratic. Some are low, some are high, a few are true ellipses as a dignified jump should be, but in the lopsided ellipses Blue Kangaroo must have been bucking a headwind. And the most tremendous jump of all is flat on top, as though the critter had gained some 800 feet of vertical lift when a tail wind hit him, followed by a downdraft."

A lurid sunset presaged a good morrow. At 5 in the morning a peak far to the west was already pink with dawn. We found the grass and ground frozen stiff as a board, with powder drifted in patches in the meadow. We breakfasted leisurely, since this was to be a day of preliminary exploration. Walt felt indifferent, so Helmy and I climbed open slopes to a barren snow ridge at 7000 feet, and from there went on to the two southerly summits of the ridge—"Fin" and "Tomahawk." Because of the powder and verglas we kept on nailed boots. We then became concerned about forces aloft; opulent clouds were scattered like glowing embers along the main crest. Hearing a yodel we looked out to see a figure wildly speeding down a snow gully. Walt liked solo explorations; he was a former star miler and had hiked much in the Sierra Nevada.

Rather than risk poor weather on a steep wall, we turned to a reconnaissance of a bulky mass of pink granite shaped like the Great White Throne in Utah. To us it was "The Temple," and a fascination, dominating our view of Kangaroo Ridge. I had considered an ascent from this, the south side, but after further evaluation of the peak's defenses decided on a line of fracture cracks on the northwest side. It would be a steep route, about 75°, and require some 600 feet of rock work. In camp Walt had tea ready. "What's the matter, boys?" he said. "It doesn't look like it should take over 2 hours." He watched with a careful eye to enjoy the effect.

Half Moon, bold and austere atop Kangaroo Ridge. The steep south face, seen here from The Temple, was climbed by the author on a bright October day. Photo by Tom Miller.

During the evening we improved our shelter. The fire smoke curled up lazily 15 feet and vanished in a swirl of white blotches. To the west a bad storm raged, and its strongest bursts penetrated east. That night a bitter northwest wind blew over the high places with powder-snow flurries.

Morning dawned with some promise, but fresh snow covered meadow and rock. Why not leave Temple alone for a day? We agreed it would be wiser to attempt a climb in the central part of the ridge. At 10 A.M. we stood atop an 8000-foot point and paused to survey the possibilities. Our gaze quickly focused to the north: a short distance away rose a peaked granite dome that looked as if a knife had cut half of it away. Walt had seen it the previous day and had spoken of it as "Half Moon" so often we adopted the name. It appeared to stand on end—high, thin, and much like an upright wide-open book, but with a spine curved like a crescent.

Reaching the peak was a problem, but we had luck. Thin ridges along a jagged divide wove in and out among little rocky parapets. These we followed in a descending line. Consolidated snow on the edges was no guarantee of security, for the snow was not anchored firmly to the slabs. At one questionable point, logic suggested a route along a wall overlooking a branch of Cedar Creek. "Come along," shouted Helmy some minutes later, and we followed to find an easy traverse would bring us to the rock wall of Half Moon, perhaps 500 feet beneath the summit.

The ascent was a pleasant "Class 4 tour"—belayed rock climbing in tennis shoes. The first hundred feet had a smooth section of boiler plate with a finger crack up the center, straining fingertips and knuckles. Though this was the most strenuous pitch it was also the most assuring, due to a wide ledge at its base. More intricate was a stretch of broken rock near the summit, split vertically by a deep, hidden chimney. In turn we struggled breathlessly to its top. The virgin summit was only one long slab away.

Loose rocks enabled us to build a tall stone cairn; despite

storms and snows it was still standing in its entirety 15 years later. We left a tin with our names enclosed, then rested an hour. We pondered the existence of the flat, rootless lichens which cling to barren rock, partnerships of a fungus and an alga, the fungus producing acids that disintegrate the rock and thus supply minerals to the alga, the alga supplying organic materials to the fungus.

On the return to camp we reviewed The Temple, and in so doing scaled its smaller offspring, "Little Finger." The evening canopy of clouds showed a broad band of light purple penetrating several ranges back. Helmy suggested we try the big climb tomorrow. Walt decided he would watch. That night we had a roaring bonfire and a feast.

At the foot of Temple's west face is a table-sized flat rock suitable for storing boots—a timely reminder to don lighter equipment; nothing above looked so convenient. The first 120 feet of gymnastics were not sensational. I placed a piton 50 feet up. The handholds were good, and there was a remnant of exfoliation slab against which one could press feet. "Darned rock," I cursed, as I pulled out the two pitons I placed at the end of the lead to fix a solid anchor. They drove with a dull thud, splitting the crack wide open at the last moment. I searched more than 10 minutes. Why couldn't there be a good crack? It was technically unsafe, but we had to do it. After belaying Helmy I continued, the thought of piton protection uppermost in my mind. A 10-foot overhang blocked the route. There was only a single satisfactory hold and getting on it, while being pushed outward at the same time—well, balance was critical.

Once I was up 12 feet we were obliged to complete the climb; soon I was committed to frictioning for balance while hammering in a desperately-needed piton. It rang loud and with a high-pitched "ping." Helmy commented favorably, after watching anxiously. It was a place for solid anchorage. After slipping back a few times I made a vigorous push and with difficulty reached a fingertip hold on a crack to the left, then inched up a vertical wall to the rope's end. During this procedure I placed three pitons for safety. Looking overhead, *back* over it seemed, I saw a chimney. The lower part was branched like an overturned "Y," a side-chimney on the left affording an entrance to the main crack. This is the key, I thought. From our reconnaissance I recalled the general angle lessened above the chimney. Deciding I wanted Helmy's opinion on which line of holds to attempt, I brought him up on a hip-piton belay. He pounded out the pitons. I would need them above.

The first 20 feet, with an obstructing overhang, seemed nearly hopeless. Climbing a few feet I pounded in a good piton, threaded the rope through a carabiner, then looked up. My hands found a few side-clings. I had to climb fast or not at all. Fingers ached as I struggled. At the last moment a wondrous handhold permitted me to rise on a power pull and I was temporarily safe on good toe-footing. Placing another piton I climbed 15 feet toward the right-hand chimney, but stopped when I had doubts about an overhanging chockstone. Backing down to the piton, I decided to try the other route first. Luckily several chiseled holds made an awkward crossing possible. Twice when I then wormed my way up a chimney sufficient holds appeared, and finally a petite platform. The wall now dropped away steeply below.

With a piton anchor my wedged body afforded an adequate belay. Helmy grunted on the difficulties, suggesting I should have used direct aid. "Worse than anything on the South Tower," he remarked, referring to a first ascent he had made in the Bugaboos the previous summer. He took the lead to the chimney's top, then announced "The route looks better." The wind, only a zephyr until now, blew around the corner. We donned parkas and climbed on.

The finish had an appalling look, but gave distinct hope. In two short leads we arrived at a large low-angle slab Walt had called the "dance floor." We regained the chimney, now sloping at 60°, and by laybacks forced our way up a narrow section to a small patch of snow. Across a few easy rocks was the broad summit.

It was a joy just to be there in the sunshine, seeing and identifying peaks jutting far to the west and north. Citadels of glowing cavernous clouds billowed in the distance, white spinnakers above a sea of blue. I particularly remember the solitude and the utter quiet, disturbed only by an occasional burst of wind. We were kings atop a temple of nature.

Such meditations had to be broken—there was the descent to consider. We rappelled via the north face, a route we soon judged much easier than ours, but just now dangerously covered with verglas and loose snow.

The smell of burning pine at campfire that night gave us a spirit of communication such as comes only in the wild. Pride soon returns when perils are past.

On June 18, as a drizzle of fine powder fell, we moved camp across the divide to the head of Early Winters Creek. We did this in a divided fashion, Helmy and Walt taking the bulk of the camp over in one load, while I hiked back to the road at a 5-mile-per-hour clip for more food. At the car I finished a pot of cherries we had acquired near Wenatchee. At the end of this day we were in position to attempt the highest towers on Kangaroo Ridge.

Harmony is not nature's theme here, for the towers are not neatly arranged or formed in sequence of height. The ridge's top point, a triangular needle-block, crowned a reddish wall frowning from a great cliff to the east. We named it "Big Kangaroo."

From the west a 3000-foot snow-and-scree scramble led to the base of the summit block. The wind faded in and out with thwarted rage. A gray curtain of cloud hid ghostly turrets. Such occasions always found Helmy at his best. "Keep your hands on the crack!" he shouted, as I followed the rope on a horizontal traverse to the summit block. My gloved fingers found little comfort or security. Feet and hands grew numb, losing their delicate touch. With the drift of new snow in the air, it was no day to climb in tennis shoes.

Great excitement has a therapeutic effect. Lethargy can be quickly broken by an escape from destruction. Here it was the storm getting us drunk to forget failure. Though we turned back to escape, the misery was vitalizing. It was good to again see slabs bending over toward the green valley far below, and to feel the comfortable response of firm granite to an anxious grip. A glint of sun highlighted a break in the clouds, showing the fresh trickle of snow on the walls. We left quickly in the fastest glissade I have ever had, shooting down a continuous gully to the creek.

At dusk, the good symbol of frost was forming. True to our forecast, arrows of light radiated behind Kangaroo Ridge in early morning. By the time we reached the summit block the sun had cleared away the last vestige of ice. The final lead was delicate, for it was necessary to rely on tiny pressure holds, plus rock discolorations. Near the top I found a thin granite edge, grasped it for chinning exercise, and swung my right leg over the corner. At the tip there was just room for a squirrel to turn around.

The next highest summit on the ridge is a 300-foot monolith, several hundred yards north. Though it appeared a good climb for a helicopter, we had a full afternoon for human examination. "Mushroom Tower" had a route to the crowning overhang, we discovered. But what then? The suspense remained through our lunch of chocolate, cheese, and bread. Then we roped up. It was time to end speculation.

Two leads later Walt was negotiating some dangerous-looking rock far overhead. "There's a fat ledge up here!" he shouted. "Let's all sit on it." So he belayed us up. The ledge didn't prove all that roomy, but continued out under the overhang of the "mushroom" some 20 feet. Obviously it was the only place to begin, but there was a 12-foot overhang, absolutely flawless. We thought of the ledge on the Grépon sardonically known as the "Route aux Bicyclettes." A shoulder stand would have to be the prime mover in launching an attack.

The combined vote elected me to try first. It looked hopeless, even from the top of Helmy's shoulders. With one eye on Walt's belay, I put both tennis shoes on Helmy's head. Reaching up, I tried for hand traction, but I was too low, and my fingertips slid off lichen at each straining effort. There were no cracks in sight, and no usable holds. Helmy complained his head hurt, and with a supreme effort lifted my feet to his outstretched palms. I had no time to think of the 700 feet below. The voices below urged me to hurry: I had no time or energy to reply, every second spent was a second's expended energy. With all the push and hand-traction I could muster I placed down-pressure on the slab above the overhang. My feet and knees still dangled uselessly beneath. In a frantic effort I managed to straighten out my elbows and scrape my feet for support. It was the point of no return; it was either up or fall. Additional strength sometimes comes in such moments. One of my shoes stuck to something. I was suddenly able to palm farther up. I kept moving and breathlessly arrived at a handhold. In a lightning-fast action I moved my hand up, found a better hold, and got a foot atop the former hand spot. Soon I was able to set a fixed rope, to end our Kangaroo leaps. The last jump was almost one too many for us.

5

In the Heart of the Skagit

The virtuous find delight in mountains, the wise in rivers.

Confucius

The North Cascades give an impression of greater height and magnitude than other ranges of the United States. Glaciers armor the peaks, slabby precipices wall the valleys, and impetuous torrents rush down canyons. The maze between Glacier Peak and Canada is so complex the eye tires trying to untangle the ridges, decipher the drainage outine. The early geologist, I. C. Russell, noted that the sameness of peak elevations adds to the complex appearance of the North Cascades. "Instead of being a sharp-crested uplift, they consist in reality of a broad, deeply stream-cut plateau," he wrote. One party called the region "A wild waste of tumultuous mountains." Herman Ulrichs correctly stated that "for 20 miles or so between the Suiattle and Cascade Pass the range could only be crossed by difficult mountaineering."

Professor W. D. Lyman mentioned that an early miner, describing his view from one of the loftiest peaks (perhaps Sahale), had counted 200 distinct "snow mountains." It is not surprising that now more than 700 living glaciers have been identified between Snoqualmie Pass and the Canadian border. Harvey Manning aptly points out in *The Wild Cascades:* "What

The McMillan Spires, their north faces high above McMillan Cirque, stand as monuments to the ceaseless conflict between earth-shaping forces. Jack Mountain in background, beyond the Skagit River. Photo by Ed Cooper.

61

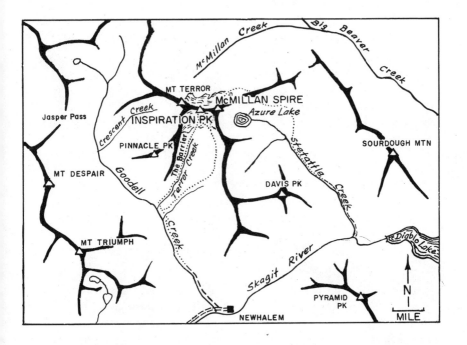

distinguishes the North Cascades is that though the ancient glaciers have mostly melted away . . . many are currently thriving; some are advancing." Its distinction of ice, he points out, "is not so much its relative plenty as its context of meadows, streams, and forests—a context not common anywhere in the world." Truly, it is rare. Professor Peter Misch has stated that in his experience no other American ranges, and few in the world, are so geologically complex. This is due partly to the close proximity of the peaks, a fact recognized by members of the Sentinel Peak first-ascent party, who wrote that the "peaks range regularly between 8000 and 9000 feet, and are as thick as bees in a hive."

Climbers whose names have become legendary prepared the way for the feats of their successors. Blanks on the map attracted men like Ulrichs, who at one time or other during his career of 21 first ascents and many other climbs touched most of the secluded valleys. He aspired to Cutthroat Peak and Mt.

Goode, but both eluded him. In 1934 he was stopped less than 100 feet from the summit of Cutthroat. "The other sides of this precipitous pinnacle," he wrote, "show no obvious route." A bright early success was that of the 1936 challengers of Goode, a group including some of the ablest mountaineers of the day. The Sierra Club party finally victorious on Cutthroat in 1937 admitted that "peaks of the Cascades are much more difficult than those of the Sierra due to the tremendous topographical relief and problems of climbing and accessibility."

From the climbing standpoint, the real credit for exploring the region from the Skagit to the Methow must go to Ulrichs, who made such first ascents as Maude, Fernow, Azurite, and Silver Star. Ulrichs ranks high among the pioneers of western mountains not because of climbing abilities, but because of a vigorous pursuit of unexplored problems. Many more severe climbs than his have now been made, but his spirit and courage have not been surpassed. In penetrating unknown valleys he spent a rounded life of adventure within a framework of achievable ambition, and his lively pen-pictures were a major factor in heralding the North Cascades as a future alpine playground.

The upper valleys of the three forks of the Cascade River symbolize this majestic region. One can look through a forest of profuse undergrowth and dense woods of large red cedars, hemlocks, and Douglas fir, often 250 feet high, and see heights of dazzling beauty. Especially magnificent are the waterfalls flowing from snowfields, leaping from cliffs and shooting through the sunlight, reflecting and refracting its rays. Trails are banked with berries, elk-horn moss, the glossy leaves of flower vines, and the small creeping raspberry vines running close to the ground, with their tiny clusters of bright red fruit-like beads peeping from beneath leaves. Mellow green shades are diffused in luxuriance and impenetrability. Huge fallen trees decay slowly and often support several generations of young trees on their prostrate sides. In days of bad weather these forests become somber with the dark gloom of clouds shedding themselves on the treetops. The Skagit-Chelan area is actually much more mysterious and secluded than the Olympic

Mountains, often called the "last wilderness." Two Mountaineer explorers, Art Winder and Norval Grigg, climbing on the crest south of Cascade Pass in 1934, praised the country they found. They wrote, "the surface has just been scratched. There are hundreds of peaks still waiting that have never felt the mark of nailed boots, and there are any number of glaciers and hidden valleys that have never been seen. Here are mountains for Mountaineers."

Perhaps the most frequently-climbed peak in this wilderness, and now an easy day from the road, is Sahale, "the great spirit," rising above Cascade Pass with a mixture of flowered slopes, snow, and an appetizer of rock. On top is a plaque incorrectly inscribed "Boston Peak" by surveyors; the true Boston is the steeper reddish peak just north.

On the first Mazama climb of Sahale, in July 1899, W. G. Steel described the startling view from the top: "Minarets along the crest beyond seemed even sharper than from the valley, whereas rough and broken glaciers glittered in the bright sunlight as jewels in a sea of snow."

Coming up the Stehekin valley, early explorers glorified the relatively-accessible Horseshoe Basin, curving to the east of Sahale. Professor W. D. Lyman described it as "a scene which surpasses anything the writer has ever witnessed, in a course of extensive mountaineering. A scene which is the crowning work of this whole gallery of wonders, which not Yellowstone nor Yosemite can surpass.

"The outmost northern rim of the whole basin is a semi-circular escarpment surrounded by minarets of granite, stained to a deep red by iron deposits, rising perpendicularly, to a height of from 1000 to 3000 above the inclosed amphitheatre, two miles across, which is known as the upper basin. . . . a great glacier, whose dazzling white surface, covered with green crevasses, contrasts wonderfully with the towering spires of red behind. In front the basin breaks off in a semi-circular descent, circling opposite to the red towers on the north, over whose perpendicular front, of apparently 2000 feet, the waters of the glacier pour in twenty-one waterfalls and cataracts."

Now the major summits have all been scaled and only pinnacles are left unclimbed. But until the last few years most peaks were very infrequently visited after the initial ascent, left years at a time to their solitudes of mist. Even yet few climbers know such beauty spots as the green lake on the north side of Sentinel Peak or the hanging meadows above the Middle Cascade Glacier. The most luxuriant floral growths of the area are on the south side of the Triplets, above the seldom-visited Middle Fork of the Cascade River—acres of avalanche lilies, lupine, and heather bloom. Between the rocks grow saxifrage and amid the crags is a sprinkling of juniper and black hemlock.

Remote terrain always seems the most perilous, and uncertainties of the Skagit area delayed alpine exploration. Aside from a few sporadic bursts upward, the pioneers were content to gaze from below, to marvel and worship but not to climb. The Indians felt even less at home among the peaks, perhaps because of the exceptionally-rich mountain mythology they developed. When boulders rumbled on the beds of fast-moving stream currents, when the storm clouds gathered over mountains and their forces shrieked with reckless fury, when lightning snakes darted among the peaks, is it any wonder the Indians felt this was a spectacle of war between the ranges?

Indians from the Fraser River tribes trapped, hunted, and gathered berries as far south on the Skagit as the Diablo area, long before the appearance of the white man. The Indians of the upper Skagit left no permanent villages there, or along the Sauk or Suiattle, but they used the land for hunting, fishing, and drying and curing food. It is known they hunted goat on Glacier Peak, Bacon Peak, and Mt. Baker, sometimes using a moccasin and a snowshoe with bear claws attached in front. Long before contact with the white man they used a stick to aid balance when walking on snow. By the mid 1880s the route from Fort Hope to the Skagit was well-trod by Hudson's Bay and other fur trappers, who improved the Indian trail, the Skagit canyon to the west being too difficult to negotiate. John Rowley is credited with making the initial gold find at Ruby Creek, a branch of the Skagit, after fighting his way through the canyon in 1872. A legendary character, John McMillan, came to the area about 1874 and lived under Jack Mountain, from where he trapped the upper Skagit; later he had a homestead near Big Beaver Creek. McMillan Creek now bears his name; Jack Mountain was named for "Jack" Rowley.

With the discovery of gold in 1879 on Slate Creek a true "gold rush" up the Skagit's canyon began. The area entered history in a big way—with a mob seeking gold along the lower river in canoes, scows, and skiffs. During this time the famous "Goat Trail" was built by prospectors, who were required to work on it a specified number of days; years later it was improved and maintained by the Forest Service. (The old Skagit River canyon, which had vertical and overhanging walls 150 feet high, is now completely drowned.) But the difficulties of this route inspired efforts to reach the Ruby Creek gold mines from the Mt. Baker area; deep snows on the passes stopped a trail venture in 1880. At the height of the rush, Ruby Creek had many camps—3000 to 5000 miners poured into the area. Those who came from Puget Sound went up the Skagit by steamer, then traveled by canoe 40 miles and finally by pack trail to Ruby Creek. They also came over passes to Slate Creek from the Methow, from Stehekin to Cascade Pass, and into Thunder Creek via Park Creek Pass or Thunder Pass (North Fork Bridge Creek). Coincidentally they explored up the Suiattle, Sauk, Stillaguamish, and Skykomish.

In the early '90s these Skagit pony trails were made good enough for heavy packing. Miners then took the railroad to Hamilton, the wagon road to Marblemount, and continued by trail to Cascade Pass or Ruby Creek. Later, light-draft steamers ran up the Skagit as far as "Portage," 8 miles above Marblemount.

Barron, a town on Slate Creek named for Alex Barron, had a population of 2000 at one time, with a wagon road built over

The Southern Pickets, rising from McMillan Cirque. From left to right: McMillan Spires, Inspiration, Ape, Degenhardt, Terror, and the Crescent Creek Spires. Beyond are Mt. Triumph to left and Mt. Despair in center. The snowy peak above Despair is Bacon Peak. Aerial photo by Austin Post, U.S. Geological Survey.

Harts Pass about 1902 by a Colonel Hart to connect with the one up the Methow from Ive's Landing.

Many North Cascades names smack of the prospector—Azurite, Ruby, Eldorado, Bonanza, Gold Bar—though in fact the rocks of the range proved to be no treasure house. One cannot help be amazed by the number of mines and prospect holes in precipitous places. On the walls of Johannesberg Mountain are several excavations that require nerve to reach. High-elevation operations in Boston Basin, Horseshoe Basin, Thunder Creek, and the Red Mountain Mines near the Canadian border represent a large investment in money and back-breaking work. The largest producing mine in the state and one of the very few successful developments was that of the Howe Sound Company at Holden, near the upper end of Lake Chelan, an all-year mine and community, surrounded by great peaks, which operated from 1937 to 1957. (J. H. Holden, in July 1896, found a great deposit of gold-bearing copper ore running through Railroad Creek mountains, and here located the Holden Mine.)

No other mining district of the Cascades matched the feverish activity and notoriety of Monte Cristo, however. Prospectors exploring up Silver Creek from the Skykomish in 1889 learned the mountains over the divide north were stained with red streaks of oxidized iron. Convinced a broad silvery-glistening streak was galena, Joseph Pearsall exclaimed, "It is rich as Monte Cristo!" Soon prospectors discovered Barlow Pass, the natural gateway from the west. Rockefeller interests pushed a narrow-gauge railway from tidewater to Monte Cristo at a cost of over $2 million, and by 1896 the "Eldorado" amid the peaks, with its saloons, gambling halls, and brothels supported a population of nearly 1000, ruled by M. T. J. Cummins, the "Count of Monte Cristo." While several million dollars in gold and silver were shipped to the Everett smelter, far more was spent in development, gambling, and stock promotion, much to the grief of investors. The creaking of buckets on overhead cables eventually halted; now a small wooden bridge over the bouldery Sauk leads to a nestle of buildings, rusty boilers, broken wheels and cogs, skeletons idle more than a half-century; the old town is now a tourist resort. High on the cliffs of Wilmon Peaks one still finds mine tunnels and a spectacular overhead cable.

By 1910 the mining fever waned; towns like Barron became "ghosts" overnight. The Skagit mines failed because the cost of hauling equipment in and ore out proved prohibitive; few of the seekers realized their dreams—some proceeded on to Fort Hope; others to the Klondike. The 1901 Boundary Survey party reported they found the Skagit trail from Ruby Creek to Fort Hope abandoned.

Then other resources were noted. Timber interests built an empire; in 1888 Lyman became an important logging town. In 1905 the Portland Cement Company mill was built at the town of Baker, which changed its name to Concrete; under an injunction to cease air pollution, the mill and quarry seem now about to shut down, and there is talk of returning to the old name of Baker. In 1907 engineers invaded the mountains, seeking the wealth of water power; two decades later Rockport was developed as a Seattle City Light operations center.

On the way up the 126-mile-long Skagit River, the natural gateway to the North Cascades, gentle forest-clad undulations lead the eye to the backdrop of colossal peaks. Mt. Triumph, the prominent rock peak north of the main valley, attracted Lloyd Anderson and his party in 1938, after opening of the auto road to Newhalem—previously reached by trail or railroad. Three of us retraced the Triumph route in 1939 and climbed the more remote Mt. Despair as well. Beyond Newhalem the road, river, and Gorge Dam's lake are boxed in by narrow canyon walls; frail scaffolding of the old Goat Trail can still be seen on the furrowed, cliffy mountainside.

Newhalem came into existence in 1919, when Seattle began constructing its system of hydroelectric dams; the Skagit is now ponded all the way to the Canadian boundary by Gorge, Diablo, and Ross Dams. From 1927 to 1954 access to Diablo Dam was by a "Toonerville Trolley" (electrified); now one travels with ease and speed—but much less charm—along a highway scheduled to cross the Cascades via Rainy and Washington Passes. A boat trip across Diablo Lake passes enchanted little basins surrounded by slabs of rock and clumps of fir. I remember the transient temper of the water, with its deep blue when the north wind bent the trees. We once arrived at the lake with hopes of catching a construction boat for a free ride to Ross Dam.

"These hikers are getting smart," the skipper said. "We used to charge money and bring up hundreds of tourists. Now we try to keep them out but you mountain goats find out about the work boat and show up all the time." At the other end, an hour later, we met a half-dozen women in skirts, who in order to qualify as hikers were carrying small rucksacks.

When Diablo Dam was completed in 1930 the newly-created lake enabled barges to ferry equipment and material for the difficult construction of Ross Dam, begun 7 years later. The dam and reservoir-filling was completed in two separate steps, finished in 1949. Meanwhile the timber was cut from the Skagit valley, above Ross Dam, and removed to the north through the Silver-Skagit road.

Little is known about early visitors to the startling summits above Diablo Lake. In 1931 William Degenhardt and H. V. Strandberg explored the alpine horizon to its south, traversing the main system of the Névé Glacier and climbing Snowfield, Colonial, and Pyramid Peaks. The even more inaccessible region to the south of Snowfield, along the sides and head of McAllister Creek, was not climbed in until years later, when parties began to work their way north from Eldorado. From the Snowfield region Degenhardt and Strandberg fixed their eyes on a group of amazing jagged peaks to the north—the Picket Range—which they had glimpsed from below when passing by the mouth of Goodell Creek on the Skagit. They could scarcely wait for the next summer to come to grips with these peaks.

In August 1950 I flew across the Skagit wilderness on a trip to

Canada. The summer had been dry, and many forest lands were closed to travel. Smoke pillars from numerous fires were building a dull, hazy overcast; some of the parched lands suggested a dead earth.

Flying through the Skagit valley I stared at the incredible Picket Range, the most concentrated mass of steep-walled peaks in the Cascades. It was one of the few areas Ulrichs did not visit, but he warned "on the other unclimbed peaks, pitons, judging by appearance, will be handy, if not absolutely necessary." The Picket Range evoked a metaphor in a recent *National Geographic Magazine* article which commented: "Sharp as a cougar's fangs, the Picket Range spikes a summer sky in the wilderness empire of the North Cascades." The name, however, derives from Captain George E. Pickett of the U.S. Army, who was in charge of Fort Bellingham in 1856 and later gained fame in the Civil War. H. V. Strandberg in the 1932 *The Mountaineer* commented that "viewed from the west the Picket Range appears as a vertical wall surmounted by innumerable high pinnacles, any one of which would afford rock climbing calling for the best of skill and technique . . . at the head of Terror Creek are several imposing rock peaks which form the Terror–McMillan Creek divide. These peaks seem to have only two dimensions, width and height. These would offer most difficult climbing, in fact, we might, without much danger of contradiction, say that these peaks are impossible to climb." He concluded this startling announcement with the suggestion that "a 7-day trip up Terror Creek would be extremely interesting and might settle the question."

When Strandberg and Degenhardt explored the region they entered by the dense valley of Goodell Creek. Not least of their problems was finding the right peaks. Though Terror's group stands out unmistakably from Newhalem, its base is almost lost among a vast jungle of forest, cliffs, and lesser summits. The party spent a long day searching out a route from the creek to the upper brush slopes, then camped beneath Pinnacle Peak. Climbing along "The Barrier" between Terror and Crescent Creeks, they could look directly west into Crescent Creek basin, a huge stadium of weathered granite, one endless rockery of alpine flowers. Pinnacle and West Peaks guard the ends, and "a long ridge in the shape of a horseshoe connects these peaks. The ridge is nearly 3 miles long, and it consists of one sharp pinnacle after another rising from 100 to 500 feet above the general level of the ridge and from 500 to 2000 feet above glaciers and snow at their base. They increase in height progressively to the east, the highest being the true summit of Mt. Terror (8360)."

On this first exploration they climbed Peak 8200 (now called Mt. Degenhardt), then descended the rock and glacier to the head of Terror Creek in an all-night ordeal; traversing east they peered down at Azure Lake, "most beautiful, very deep, and surrounded by perpendicular cliffs." They did not come to grips with Terror until the following summer, when they returned with a companion, James Martin. They then found a problem above a notch in its main ridge, but once above that, completed the climb without incident. They also climbed Pinnacle Peak, West Peak, and one of the twin needles in the center of the Crescent Creek basin, but abandoned thoughts of climbing the "impossible" summits at the head of Terror Creek or traversing the northern ramparts of the range to Whatcom Pass. They saw no signs of any previous human visit, and Gaspar Petta, the trapper who had a cabin on Goodell Creek, said he was certain nobody had preceded them into this alpine region.

Superlatives have a fascination for comrades in adventure, so after our 1940 expedition to the Northern Pickets Helmy and I were anxious to grapple with these summits of splendor. Reaching Newhalem proved as difficult as making the climbs. We hitchhiked from Seattle and after sleeping in the forest when left off by the last motorist driving home, we waited all the next day for a ride. It finally came at 5 o'clock, provided by a nervous, cumbersome woman whose auto antics were almost too much for us—especially with the white water of the Skagit close by the narrow road.

If the mountain traveler can stand a combination of inspiration and frustration, the horizon north of Newhalem is provocative. Jagged peaks glittered in the sun that afternoon, beckoning conquerors. Yet one look at the green hell of mountainside made us fume at the approach obstacles. Darkness caught us after we had done perhaps 3 miles; we made a camp of spartan simplicity, sleeping on the trail itself. It is said wandering bears detour around such "camps"; we certainly hoped so. Fortunately we were only annoyed—considerably—by the lowly mosquito. Through black forest came the faint hiss of Goodell Creek.

A half-hour of morning hiking brought us to a windfall obliterating the crude trail, and after some searching we concluded here was the spot our predecessors had forded the stream. In our judgment, any possible trail on the opposite bank was not worth a double wetting. The point settled, we continued along the eastern bank. By perhaps 10 o'clock we heard the rushing sound of a large tributary. A study of the map, with checks of hilly landmarks, made us certain this was Terror Creek. We easily crossed the torrent on a fallen tree, then followed game trails up its rough, wooded left bank to an open brush basin at about 3000 feet, amid thick alder clumps and footings of innumerable cliffs. We pushed upward through the jungle. When not forcing a way for ourselves and our heavy packs through festoons of alder, we were taunted by jabs of devil's club or the prickly needles of Englemann spruce. I cannot recall a more tiring and unpleasant climb to timberline than along the waterfalls of Terror Creek.

Finally we emerged onto talus avenues through the alder. These led us up to a series of steep moraine ridgelets covered by brilliant flowers and heather. Above, little streamlets flowed down ice-polished granite slabs. Higher, atop the crevassed glacier, rose a row of fantastically-serrated granite peaks, all slanting to the right as if pushed by a giant's hand. The one above camp was Strandberg's "impossible." We dubbed it "Inspiration" and laid immediate plans for an attempt. First things first, though: behind a clump of noble firs we saw colorings of blueberries; we ate hundreds that afternoon. Huckleberry brush

The Southern Pickets from Elephant Butte show a strong unity created by consistency of crest line and individual peak similarities. Photo by Harold Deery.

growing below timberline can be quite an impediment to travel, but the upland blueberries make a delightful walking carpet.

Indian paintbrush flamed these steep, miniature meadows. Lupine beamed in blue-and-white masses in sunlit spaces between spruces. There were clumps of giant hellebore, with heavy parallel-veined leaves and a tall stem bearing drooping panicles of greenish flowers. Thriving in less hospitable spots amid rocks were the five-petaled saxifrages. Hummingbirds flitted through paintbrush, fireweed, tiger lilies, and columbine. Occasionally we heard the curiously-ventriloquial call notes of the "coney" or rock rabbit, a witty little grayish-brown creature with large rounded ears but no tail. (Fortunately they are not as ravenous as their relative, the "snafflehound," that frequents the Bugaboos in Canada.)

From our camp, the morning sun illuminated every rocky tooth. We hurried breakfast and began climbing toward McMillan Spire, the double-pointed peak at the eastern end of the row. Dawn burnt on distant snows, and the sun lept upward, igniting peak after peak of the hidden ranges west to the foothills. We could agree with Smythe that the "distant view of snow must ever remain the greatest of all views." But the loveliness of snow is for meditation; we were hurrying to reach an unknown summit.

Before 6 we were already climbing crusted névé. A gust of autumn air, the vindictive shot of retreating shadows, quickened our gratitude for the sun. As painters learned centuries ago, beauty is at its best in the cool fragrant hour following dawn.

An hour's steady climbing on the glacier led to a couloir leading toward the col between McMillan and Inspiration Peaks. The sun had risen above the rock ramparts, bringing a flood of color and warmth.

Inspiration, to our left and now almost overhead like a skyscraper, looked unclimbable. But the eye could never tire of its superb lines. It seemed easy to believe the peak was in some sense a creation of man's adoration. We scrambled up McMillan's slopes—which always proved easier than they appeared. From the summit our eyes looked sharply down into the hanging glaciers of McMillan Creek. Below us, and on across to Terror, were crumpling sections of very steep glaciers, poised far above the green, brushy valley. Directly across the 5000-foot depths rose the Northern Pickets. Only the abruptness of the facing walls allowed us to grasp even partially the vastness of the intervening empty space.

In mid-morning we descended from the summit and crossed a broken stretch of glacier beneath the imposing south face of Inspiration. Helmy, whose skillful manipulation amid the crevasses saved us much time, was chopping a passage of steps. As I looked up in slanting sunshine, the cliff seemed to hang completely over our heads. Certainly the west ridge was our best chance, for it fell back enough to justify some optimism. But there was a stern 700-foot wall between the glacier and its flat crest, west of the peak. After this pause, really a ritual of superstition, we hacked our way around numerous seracs and crossed delicate snow bridges to a ledge at the foot of the peak. Here a chimney series offered steep but broken rock to the ridge crest. We left our ice axes and boots, and in tennis shoes started up the couloir system, which was complicated by several abrupt walls. We moved deftly up steep buttresses along the main chimney, climbing quickly even though roped; we had teamed together so much that time could be saved from merely knowing each other's habits.

As we rose, the bladelike west edge of the summit obelisk— which we estimated to be some 500 feet tall—loomed close overhead. One little spot was made dangerous by loose rock that had eroded the standing room next to a chockstone. We climbed this in turn, then clambered up a sanded granite slab. It was dangerous, but not really difficult.

What lay above? The west edge seemed to bulge with a gray overhang not over 100 feet away. A sloping slab led upward, and it appeared we might creep on all fours to the base of the upthrust wall. High above, the sharp summit showed above the soaring granite edge. A person can get dizzy bending his neck that way; we dropped our eyes, determined to study this problem out carefully.

Adjoining the south face was a vertical seam of the same shade as the sounder rock above the overhang. We had ignored this corner because of its great exposure above the glacier, but on further examination realized it was our best opportunity.

In 20 minutes the proposal showed hope; certainly it now appeared better than the rotten overhangs on our left. I led a steep section of the solid seam, a vertical corner just wide enough to permit an avenue to the broader face above. The holds were small, but sufficient. We kept alert to every move, belaying and climbing tensely, for this was the crux. If we were stopped here the climb would certainly fail.

I anchored above and shouted "belay on!" Using carefully-planned belays and balance climbing we continued three more leads. Then, to our surprise, the angle suddenly retreated; we had been too intent on immediate problems to realize how near the summit we had come. We felt the radiance that comes with success. The very top was only minutes away.

Judgments formed on a first ascent are notoriously untrustworthy, and the proprietary interest one takes in a mountain with which one has struggled colors the valuation of everything connected with it, but this "impossible" climb did seem spectacular—not on a par with the Southeast Peak of Twin Spires, but certainly more strenuous than Forbidden. Much that is worthwhile in life was packed into the short span of that afternoon. I remember our climb of Inspiration as if it were yesterday: a serene, silent peak, beautiful in sunlight, the perfect summit of dreams.

Arrows of light began to radiate toward Terror from an invisible focus behind the Pickets, and the late-day lighting did wonders for the snowfields. It also pointed out the need for haste. While dropping quickly down the west edge on several long rappels, we gained a special appreciation of the grandeur of the peaks: when ascending one tends to underestimate the steepness of a wall, the mind being occupied with technical details of the craft; on the way down one feels the full exposure and magnitude of the mountain.

By the time we descended the crevassed glacier and found a better route to camp through its pitfalls, the atmosphere bathing the Skagit peaks had lost transparency and changed to a gloomy blur. Night changed the appearance of the peaks we had left behind; they were felt even if not seen. It had been a day marked by the magic bond of cooperation which had given us a thin line of consistent success all through that summer.

But now it was the beginning of September, often a time of premature winter in the Cascades. Opening the tent flap in the morning, Helmy peered sulkily at the outdoors. There had been no light to waken us, and our suspicions were correct. The overhead canopy presaged a blow, evidence confirmed by two layers and scud lenticular clouds. Later in the day mists dropped over the craggy peaks. Then came a gray veil of rain, obliterating the landscape as we went to sleep. Why did it have to fall on us after such perfect weather and with several days' food left?

We could only part with regret. Elsewhere, perhaps in the Sierra, the sun was shining bright, but we faced a miserable prospect. Wet from a torrential night with wind and rain driving furiously at our thin white tent, we now had to wade soaked vegetation.

The tumbling struggle down steep thicket-land was pure misery. Even the "open spots" turned into traps disguised by devil's club and similar entanglements. Mossy rocks and logs were so slick we often had to avoid them or else cross them hanging onto anything we could grip. Once down Terror Creek we plodded and crashed through the flatter woods of Goodell Creek, gaining a soaked, powerful, unstoppable sensation. Wet clothes and gear made us feel heavier; the brush challenged us to a duel which we accepted with bulldozer force. At times we picked up traces of the trail. It mattered little, but I believe Helmy first found the path by falling headlong down a bank of huckleberry onto the abrupt surprise of a horizontal surface. In another hour of hiking our valiant, short, but highly-successful adventure was another memory. All, that is, except for the hitchhike home.

The Southern Pickets have beckoned me twice more, though not until memories of our original experience with the approach had somewhat dimmed. In mid-October of 1958, Dave Collins, Ed Cooper, and I camped overnight at the eastern side of the head of Terror Creek. Instead of coming up the cliffs and brush of the creek valley itself, we climbed a timbered sub-ridge directly east from Goodell Creek not far from where Terror Creek branches off; once at timberline we made a long traverse across basins, heading north.

The weather was perfect—a true Indian Summer—with no fresh snow at all on the rocks as we climbed Inspiration Peak via a new route, the direct eastern corner. The rock was generally excellent granite, often formed in gigantic blocks. Several of the pitches were quite difficult free climbing; piton protection was good, and I was thankful for that, for exposure above the glaciers and walls falling to McMillan Creek was tremendous. It was a spectacular new way up the peak; we returned by the same route, with numerous rappels to the glacier.

Another memorable trip was in midsummer of 1963 with Jerry Fuller. Our plan was somewhat unusual: we would make a circling traverse of the range, coming up Stetattle Creek, traversing around to McMillan Creek drainage, and then, by climbing over McMillan Spire, return by way of the old Terror Creek route to Newhalem. To do this efficiently, we took food for just 4 days, a minimum of technical equipment, and carried down jackets instead of sleeping bags. Fortunately the weather was perfect, enabling us to complete our scheme without delays.

The trail vanished in the brush of Stetattle Creek, and we were a full day hauling out of the deep valley to heathered meadows far above Azure Lake, where we built a fire to warm our bivouac. Climbing snowfields, we crossed the divide to the north, finding it necessary to glissade and descend snow for well over 1000 feet to get below blue ice and crevasses that fringed McMillan Spire's huge black walls. Traversing west and weaving in and out of crevasses we came under the great north face, at least 2500 feet below the summit. Several steep and fairly difficult snow couloirs and ice patches led us to the main rock wall. Climbing in a direct line to the top took some 22 pitches and all the rest of the day. Somehow we managed to get down into Terror Creek that evening, spending over 2 hours in inky blackness crawling and falling through alder-covered boulders to reach the bank of the creek where it broke out of the worst portion of the jungle.

6

Twin Spires

The story of Twin Spires dates back to 1940, when four of us stood atop Ruth Mountain one bright April morning, there to seek an untracked ski run. In the shimmering whiteness of the jagged North Cascade landscape two dark rock peaks stood defiantly isolated; from that moment the spires had a fascination all their own for me, and I memorized their sharp outlines.

The same year Will Thompson and Calder Bressler made the long trek to these peaks in the heart of the Chilliwack region. Thompson called them "Twin Needles" when he suggested I try to climb them. He told of being stopped by a "ridge of gendarmes" and a deep chasm. "Five hundred feet above, almost straight up, rose the summit," he said. They called off the climb in late afternoon on viewing tottering slabs of gneiss balanced on a knife-edged ridge.

I sat down on my skis and ruminated. What was the force that impelled me? Something complex and indefinable, the attraction of uncertainty. Perhaps the answer lay in the bending valley of the Chilliwack with snow-covered forests and the distant glimmer of high snowfields. Wayne Swift and I unfolded a map. It appeared seamed with inaccuracies. One obvious error was in assigning much too low an elevation to Redoubt; the position of Twin Spires was not even marked.

The creased and furrowed faces of Twin Spires, the Northwest Peak on the left, the Southeast Peak and Ridge of Gendarmes on the right, from headwaters of Redoubt Creek. Photo by Dan Davis.

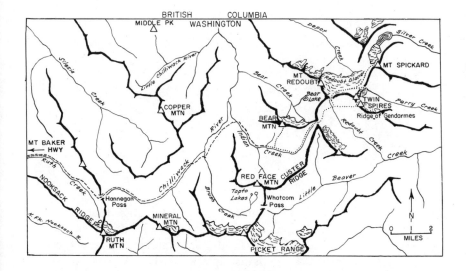

In the direction of Shuksan the atmosphere was hazy; farther
west a cauldron of seething mists kept evaporating, and in a
grandeur of sudden revelation the shining peak of Baker thrust
itself through.

Before skiing down, I looked once more at the phantom spires.
They seemed a climber's dream, waiting to be made real, to be
conquered. J. W. A. Hickson says "mountaineering is a concentrated form of exploration, in which the tedium of delay is cut
out and dramatic intensity thereby heightened." Mummery describes the true climber as one who delights in the "fun and
jollity" of new ascents. "There is for every man a type of
climbing," says Geoffrey Winthrop Young. The spirit that ani-
mates some men to solve a new ascent is akin to that which
challenges others to solve mathematical or philosophical problems. While a difficult climb may call forth all the latent powers
of man, the greatest reward may not be the conquest of the
peak, but the conquest of fear and the discovery of security.
"The true mountaineer," Frank Smythe says in *An Alpine Journey,* "does not attempt . . . the summit . . . to achieve a
record. He does not expect his motives to be understood by the
crude materialists of the world."

1941 brought an end to the pre-World War II era of Cascades climbing. Thoughts gravitated to Europe, where there now was little mountaineering for sport. It was thus with somewhat a somber feeling that Helmy, Louis Graham, and I set out for Hannegan Pass and the hinterland on June 15. At the Ruth Creek road we left a 6-day food cache hidden in a tree for a trip to follow, to the east face of Shuksan and Nooksack Tower. In addition we left a cache at road's end. We carried dehydrated and light food for 12 days and planned to walk 23 miles to the meadows at the head of Redoubt Creek.

The first day we hiked down Chilliwack Creek on a ·good trail familiar from our trip into the Picket Range the previous summer. But on the second day, some distance up Indian Creek, all but the merest vestige of a path disappeared, and to avoid brush we took to the rockslides. Beneath Bear Mountain we followed grassy salmonberry patches along the stream. The music of the water was muted by the forest of silver fir, and the stream itself was liberally obstructed with dams built by beaver, the engineers of the animal world. Evidence here indicated presence of the wolverine, whose cunning amazes those who have witnessed its clever robberies of traps and caches, and of coyote, timber wolf, and cougar.

In the forest of Indian Creek we noted the abundance of the pale blue Mountain Bluebird, which uses flycatcher methods of securing insects, the Western Winter Wren, who revels in the shadows of the forest floor, and the woodpeckers who noisily hunt larvae with their sharp beak and tongue.

The view typified the Cascades: a stream rushing between dark firs; higher, a specter of snowy peaks, a brilliant blue sky with clouds poised above, casting scattered shadows.

Toward the end of the valley we climbed through a basin of scrub evergreens, rocks, and finally heather to a 6500-foot pass overlooking Bear Creek. Flanking us were the precipitous northern walls of Bear Mountain and across the valley rose the massive form of Redoubt. Our route lay eastward across an intervening ridge.

Soon we would see the Twin Spires close at hand. What would they look like? Toting our heavy packs up to the crest of the last divide, our minds were full of conjured-up mental pictures of the peaks, and bursting with curiosity as to how these visions would compare with reality.

The impact of the first view surpassed our maximum expectations. We dropped our packs and stared: across the basin of Redoubt Creek, barely 2 miles away, the two giant black pyramids rose into a bank of storm clouds. Flanking abutments gave them a cliffy, aloof structure. It was readily apparent why Thompson had such admiration for the peaks. Beneath them I could see a sharp valley, splaying out with precipices and waterfalls to the forest level. But the upper basin where we planned to camp was a band of welcome tranquility, impressive yet benign. Today, though, it looked bleak, for a watery sun bleered through a smudge of dampness. The spectral peaks were tangled in mists. Even as we glissaded down to the basin a drizzle began, followed by an onslaught of rain before we could pitch our tent. Lighting the fire was an unpleasant chore but once the alpine wood caught flame it burned through the night. Bombarded by rain, acrid smoke stinging our eyes, cooking dinner was miserable. In the icy rain blasts, my red flannel shirt dyed my skin and underwear red. Finally I took off soaked clothes and crawled into the sleeping bag.

A bag is a dull place to spend a day. With the weather continuing socked in, we passed the time taping tent drips and trying to keep dry. My diary states "whenever the rain halted we would rush to the fire with our bags and wet clothes in an attempt to get them fairly dry before more rain fell." While I was cooking dinner outside, my shirt became so soaked I had to wring out a stream of the surplus water. When we closed the tent for the night, rain turned to wet snow. Our happiness came from adapting ourselves to the environment. Most extremists are essentially unhappy persons; they are symptoms of a world that has become socially and mechanically too complex to serve as an easy environment. Amid a welter of conflicting philosophies, I have always tended to one principle: to get the most from life, man must sample its contrasts. So with our trip. Activity is heightened by following a period of anticipation and contemplation.

The next noon, however, brought a lull. Helmy and I, mostly for exercise after some 40 hours of inactivity, climbed snowfields to the 7400-foot col between the spires. Just beyond the great west face of the Northwest Spire was a small glacier, crackless except for a few tension rifts, enclosed by flanking walls of the two spires in its steep drop to headwaters of Perry Creek. Verglassed cliffs of the lower Northwest Spire offered little hope from this side; distant views had suggested the Redoubt Glacier, at the head of Depot Creek, as the most likely route. On the right we peered through the sinister mist which wound like a serpent around the higher Southeast Spire. The white-glazed summit, 1000 feet above, looked terrifying; shortly clouds closed off all but a bulge of iced rock rising into nothingness.

From previous vantages and on the advice of Thompson and Bressler, it seemed the key to the upper walls of the Southeast Spire was the long Ridge of Gendarmes curving from the west. To further our knowledge of the peak we decided to climb this ridge, but soon the dropping temperature signalled the snowflakes to come from a surge of black cloud. The spirit might still battle with the storm, but honor was satisfied and we chose to halt before being caught by the tumult. A bewildering succession of swiftly-changing effects was created by the war of storm and sunshine. The distances of sky lost their transparency in a blur of indefinite gloom, the only surviving hint of color being a rosy glint on a snowfield miles away. There was no limit to the variety of this wintry landscape or to the variety of its shifting shadow colors. At one moment the sharp movements of wind opened a passage for the sun to restore the third dimension, resolving the fusion of plane surfaces into separate and successive ridges; at the next the intricate labyrinth of interlocking ridges hung suspended above the mists, flat and dimensionless as if etched on board. Although the issue was never in doubt, weak light filtered feebly through clouds. But it was mixed with loose snow, migrating in little whirlwinds. Then the strengthening wind lost its indecision and gave an impetus to volleying puffs of snow across the rock ribs. Footholds were made precarious by the mask of fresh snow. It was time to return to camp.

With a hollow rumble of thunder, black clouds were illuminated by fountains of lightning leaping through the night sky. We awoke pessimistic, but morning brought an abatement. By noon we mustered desire to scout the Northwest Spire, and struck off via a steep gully to the Redoubt Glacier. From the divide we could see the sheer west face of the peak; certainly the route must be elsewhere. Running north to Glacier Peak (now Mt. Spickard) was a connecting ridge, well above glacier level. "If we can get on that ridge, the summit should be possible," Helmy commented. I agreed; that seemed the spire's most vulnerable section. Back at camp that evening the mountains were warming in the first high-country sunshine of the trip. A rooty scent was rising from the drying earth and the fresh snow was melting away from high rocks of the spires.

Noting our descent and the lull in the storm, Louis had packed up camp; acting on an earlier decision we moved about a mile closer to the peaks. A quaint little spruce grove atop a cliff offered a pretty campsite. A swift brook ran within 20 feet of the tent, then dashed off in a series of miniature waterfalls.

Sunset tinted the scattering clouds; rays of light lingered on the snow-plastered spires. Louis had a recurrence of a back ailment, so it was decided Helmy and I would set out for the Northwest Spire if the weather held. It did; we awoke at 4 to find icy cold. We were still in shadow, but it was apparent this was to be a beautiful day. In a shivering half-hour we breakfasted and packed our rucksacks, then repeated our route to the glacier. In brilliant sunshine, full of optimism, we traversed névé 1½ miles to the base of the north ridge.

The climb to the ridge at 7600 feet was treacherous. Above a steep snowfinger came iced rocks covered with a veneer of verglas atop which fresh snow was sometimes caked. We used ax picks, as well as boot nails, to full advantage. Once on the ridge fresh snow covered a ribbon of old snow along the crest. By kicking well or chopping with the adze we moved safely up, roped together. Less than 200 feet from the peak several abbreviated gendarmes blocked the narrow ridge. Behind them the crest merged into the 100-foot face of the summit superstructure. A factor in our success would be routefinding; as Young has written, "But whatever we may be as climbers no one of us is a born mountaineer; mountaineering in its wider aspects can be only learned by experiment." By careful study we found the correct ledges to bypass obstructions, and started up in tennis shoes. Helmy led beautifully. Eighty feet of it was near-vertical, and exposed over Perry Creek. He climbed a bulge, skirted a snow patch, and was on the summit at 8:30. The sun was still well in the east.

Our rejoicing at the quick success was rapidly cooled by examination of the Southeast Spire, perhaps 100 feet higher than our standpoint and rising a half-mile away in splendid isolation. It looked grim, especially from this foreshortened view. Most impressive were the ice-thatched northern wall facing us and the great precipice falling east into Perry Creek. A tracery of fresh snow aided in developing a general plan. Even with this help we saw no semblance of a route except from the saw-toothed Ridge of Gendarmes. The Gendarmes' last mile, leading in from the southwest, was a series of teeth; the last one overhung the deep, narrow gap. We ruled out as hopeless a direct approach to the gap between the gendarmes and the peak by way of the 1000-foot cliff falling into Perry Creek beneath; it was vertical, rotten, and plastered in the lower portions by amazingly-steep sheets of glare ice. The gap would lead to the most difficult summit we had ever attempted—perhaps, we thought, the most difficult principal peak in the Northwest. Could we traverse the awesome black walls of the peak from the Ridge of Gendarmes to reach its upper northwest face, where the route seemed to begin?

We turned eyes eastward where the two Hozomeen Peaks stood

out amid a choppy sea of mountains, many unnamed. Nearer were Glacier (Spickard) and Redoubt, both only a shade under 9000 feet.

Glacier looked close and easy, a good objective for the remainder of the day. As my diary states, "We did it in 2½ hours for the hell of it." Wooden poles on the summit gave evidence of an early survey party.

As an interesting early mountaineering note, Glacier Peak (Spickard) was used as a boundary triangulation station in 1904, the survey party reporting the "peak is pyramidal in shape, is surrounded by glaciers and is difficult and dangerous to climb." Thomas Riggs and a survey party climbed it in 1905 to find evidence of the previous ascent. North, toward the border, is amazing Glacier Lake, whose waters fall into Silver Creek and the Skagit River. Riggs' description is a classic: "a lake of indigo, over a mile long, its lower end confined by a narrow ridge of rock . . . where the outflow dashed through a crevice only a few feet wide and fell almost sheer for several hundred feet." The glacier at its upper end broke off from a perpendicular wall "covering the surface of the water with innumerable miniature icebergs." It is a scene of desolation more fitting Alaska or Greenland than the relatively-temperate Cascades.

While looking at the blue of Chilliwack Lake, Helmy interrupted my geographic scanning with the shout, "Goats!" They moved as white specks on a talus slope in a basin to the east.

Our thoughts ran back to the problems of the higher spire. We had ropes, pitons, and determination. In Europe many climbers never bother with mountaineering as a craft, but take its pleasures and leave the responsibilities to guides or to chance. Guides in the Alps have done much to safeguard inexperienced climbers, whose aim is often just to reach the summit, and learn as little as possible on the way. Here we were our own guides, had to select our own equipment, cut our own steps, make our own belays, and place our own pitons.

Returning from the two ascents Helmy and I felt in better condition for the Southeast Spire. Weather had stabilized and the afternoon's warmth had removed fresh snow from the gaunt walls. After dinner we packed rucksacks for June 22.

At the first glimmering of dawn we left the tent, Louis saying he would come up to the col to watch. We roped at a thread of icy snow between buttresses, then crossed a crevasse and booted steps up a frozen slope. The biting wind on this north exposure had kept much of the fresh snow from evaporating. Climbing was precarious. We nicked many steps with the ax pick. Finally a long, rotten gully narrowed to a climax at an overhanging chockstone. We knocked enough rime off the bad rock to get at solid holds. Once past this crucial point we climbed to a notch next to some miniature pinnacles. The huge western wall of the spire rose in front of us, gray perpendicular cliffs defending the summit, at least 500 feet above.

"What a place!" I shouted as we reached sunlight for the first time that day. My first feeling was one of distress, like being stranded. Beneath us rotten rock curved off so steeply we could not see its base. Four more wild-looking gendarmes separated us from the last gap. Our desire to continue overcame apprehensions. It seemed we were crouching in the shadow of the spire's walls, fragile trespassers among the monstrous walls of nature.

Helmy climbed high on an adjacent pinnacle and was soon out of sight behind a corner. Eventually he yelled something I couldn't understand and pulled in the rope; deciding he wanted me to climb up, I did. At the corner I peered along a horribly-exposed wall and saw him perched on a small ledge with a rock-anchored belay. Reaching his position demanded a delicate traverse on steep, loose rock. Then came three more ropelengths of the same. Crossing a series of rotten gullies and maneuvering along miniature ledges brought us to the last gendarme—broad and steep on our side, but (as we later saw) merely a gigantic flake only a few feet thick, with a careening tip overhanging the gap to the spire's main wall. The gap itself was an ill-defined jumble of sharp notches and half-pinnacles. (Rock in this area has been termed generally as highly-quartzose gneiss, showing irregular wavy laminations, with some outlying slaty rocks.)

Unable to find a solid anchor for a spare rope to descend on, we retraced part of our delicate route, then climbed down steep and dangerous loose-rock gullies on the south side of the crest. From a point lower than the gap we traversed a loose little band circumventing two nasty-looking teeth to reach a cannonhole beneath a bridge of chockstones connecting the perpendicular face of the spire with a pinnacle. With only the two of us, we had been moving quite fast; at just 8 o'clock we peered down the stupendous north face.

It was no place for the timid. In the shaded and cold profile to the right, perhaps 200 feet away, was a broad ledge that seemed to be the only part of the face offering an exit to the wall above. Everything inbetween appeared especially hostile. Looking down the face, all we could see were rotten chimneys and tiny snowpatches, all dropping off as the face grew convex. We surveyed the problem and decided to make a descent on the north face, then cross toward the big ledge on broken rock.

First we belayed each other down loose snow in a 65° gully. We sank to our knees! Anchorage was bad for the low man, but after 100 feet we had made a precarious traverse over a hanging snowpatch. In about 50 feet I was able to pass the rope behind a projection which acted as a belay. The next lead was steeper and slipperier; I placed two pitons in this stretch; we left them in for the return traverse. The sloping ledge gave temporary security, a good place to change to tennis shoes. We cached axes, boots, and spare clothing, then exchanged a few shouts with Louis, who had arrived at the col, far below. We could easily hear him. His comment was that our position looked "terrific." He reminded us to "take it easy—you've got a hell of a drop below." He confirmed our thoughts that we should climb directly up, then bear slightly right.

We alternated the first three leads, which were steep but sufficiently broken to permit nice balance climbing. Then the way steepened to a concave face with an upper overhang. I climbed left, but was soon without holds to progress, so came back to the belay. We searched for a better way, and in desperation decided to try the rounded face to the west, some 150 feet to the right of the overhang. The profile looked bad, but appeared to be our only hope.

Helmy brought me up from a piton belay, then I worked up to some fragile rock. Entirely through my own fault I came to trouble. My hands were reaching up back over my head and the holds could not be trusted. I began pulling myself up a series of small overhangs, using cracks for foot support. I managed to place a protection piton while suspended from fingertips of my left hand, then pulled up to the next hold by frantic chinning. One foot found a small resting place, and I looked up. It was only 20 feet to where the route beveled back, but a row of picket-like gray flakes barred the way. They overhung and appeared rotten. I had no option but to try a near-impossible return. Just above the piton I couldn't find the foothold for my right shoe, and during intricate groping nearly lost my finger holds. In an exhausting moment of seeking any desperate hope I found another handhold. Temporarily safe, I unhooked from the piton, removed it, and climbed down the remainder of the pitch. With the end not in sight my morale was almost shattered. I rested in a gloomy mood after reaching the security of the belay spot.

We thought about the alternative: a traverse right to the face in profile. Helmy was sure this was the area that showed a lacing of fresh snow after the storms; after the last experience I wasn't so certain. We criss-crossed leads. From 60 feet above I heard him shout, "We must climb directly up now!" When I reached the belay, the great gap between the two spires was directly below. One bit of encouragement: leveling across, we were getting a sight near the upper rock of the Northwest Spire.

We came to a blank 80-foot wall. I remember it as a very shallow trough, almost vertical, but with a few little cracks and knubby holds. It was the secret to success, we felt, if it could be climbed. I led off, placing two pitons at alternative positions some distance up the lead. At one point I did some difficult mantling with nothing for the feet—the kind of place where one moves fast or not at all. Fortunately I felt light, agile, and strong. A block enabled me to give Helmy a direct belay through a crack. Now we were above the convex overhang, but still some distance west of a gully we had to reach. A peek around the corner was relieving: we could reach a promising gully via some ledges and blocks.

The gully rose steeply to an 80° shallow trough in the last 70 feet; then the angle appeared to lessen, for we could see blue sky above. Helmy passed a tiny snowpatch and anchored himself partway up the gully. I led the remainder of the pitch, pounding in three ringing pitons for safety. Possibly this was the most difficult section of the climb, but the rock was so sound it felt safe. I was pleased to find a solid belay anchor, just over the worst part, and twirled my red mountain cap in the air. Helmy realized I was certain of better things. He climbed up well, taking out the pitons.

Some looser material above was mixed with a bit of unmelted snow, but little matter; the summit was just beyond a final jagged crest to the right which—though exposed—we traversed as an anticlimax. Our pocket watch read noon when we stood on the highest rock, where we built a cairn. While admiring peaks of the Chilliwack and Pickets we noted a few puffs from the west, a possible change in the weather. We could not see down the south or east faces, but they seemed long, rotten, and steep. Will Thompson's comment that the spire "stands right in the middle of the valley, with no approach but the 'Ridge of Gendarmes'" seemed especially appropriate from here. After a quick lunch we headed down.

Long rappels, using both the spare rope and the climbing rope, took us to the big ledge in good fashion, avoiding much troublesome terrain of the ascent. From here we made the wet, unpleasant traverse and ascent to the snow-choked gully. Needing a belay spot, I crossed and clambered onto a boulder—one we had used on the ascent.

Suddenly everything began to move, lurching outward. I felt my feet being moved outward. Instinct told me the entire block was toppling; I flung myself into the steep gully, landing on all fours and clutching at the slope with my ax. Simultaneously the piano-sized rock bounded off the cliff, sounding like an exploding shell, struck lower rocks, was silent a few seconds, then burst into further crashes. I was still terrified when the clamor subsided, and no doubt it unnerved Helmy, who watched the episode from his belay perch. If the rope had not been taut, the block could readily have struck it and pulled me off. Or, I could have lost my balance after the rope had been cut or mashed. In years of mountaineering this was perhaps my narrowest escape. We had used the same block earlier in the day: this points to a rare danger in climbing and suggests one must constantly suspect the unusual.

Trembling, we clambered singly to the notch above, belaying the best we could. The spire had been a grim adversary, the most difficult climb we had ever done.

Louis was relieved to see us scrambling off the lower rocks, having heard our shouts amid the cannonading of the tumbling block.

After a final night in the pretty basin of Redoubt Creek, we began the long pack-out, voting for Bear over Redoubt as our final climb. Clouds hid the peaks as we rambled down forests and the faint trail of Indian Creek, until it became lost in a series of windfalls. Louis had lost his shirt on the trip in; miraculously we found it in the midst of a trackless forest.

On the climb of Bear we found interesting foot and arm-jam cracks on good, grainy granite. Reaching a platform between the box-shaped summit tower and a sharp summit to the right, we decided to have some fun on a new route. Starting from the gap, we climbed up a very steep face which featured two unusual V-shaped chimneys, one above the other. On the right was a knifed rib that overhung the north face, where we watched a rock drop unhindered until it disappeared from view. The climb was strenuous, and had its interesting moments changing belays at a tiny platform between the two cracks. Eventually we finished by climbing left up some hard but solid rock.

I remember reaching the end of the Ruth Creek road in the intense afternoon heat, shaggy with perspiration, then going up into the forest to locate our cache.

7

Shuksan: Showpiece of the North Cascades

Shuksan, as seen from Mt. Baker Lodge, is one of the most celebrated tourist attractions in the state of Washington. To the Neuk-sack Indians, who lived off fish and game in nearby valleys, Shuksan meant "steep and rugged." Though this is true enough, it was also one of the earliest of the high Cascades to be climbed. A half-century has passed since that summer afternoon in 1906 when W. M. Price and Asahel Curtis stood on the 9127-foot summit. Though the ascent was accomplished with little of the boasting that followed the first climbs of Mt. St. Helens and Mt. Hood, local enthusiasts stoutly claimed it was the most difficult peak in the entire range. Other enthusiasts, such as C. E. Rusk, insisted that Joe Morovits climbed Shuksan in 1897. There is skepticism about this claim, but it should be pointed out he certainly had the opportunity during his many years of residence at Baker Lake, and he carried out many feats requiring remarkable endurance. However, if Morovits did climb the summit pyramid he left no cairn there, nor any written records. In 1927 C. A. "Happy" Fisher pioneered what is now the popular—and much-climbed—route up the peak, via Lake Ann, the rock chimneys that bear his name, Winnie's Slide, and the ice tongues of either Hell's Highway or the Hour Glass to the Sulphide Glacier ice plateau and the summit pyramid.

Climbers approaching Nooksack Tower. The standard route, pioneered by the author in 1946, follows the central ice gully and then the black rock face of the highest crag. Photo by Dee Molenaar.

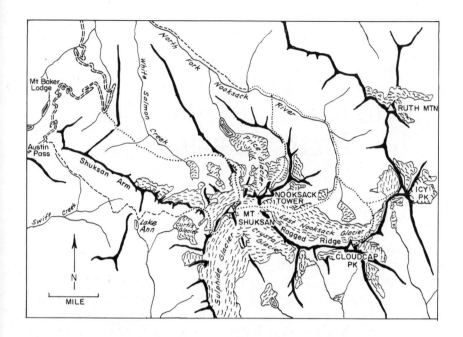

From the road to the lodge one can see spectacular cliffs of the Hanging Glacier cascade broken ice down savage rock barriers. The western exposure of Shuksan, as viewed from the direction of Table Mountain, is a familiar sight to tourists who continue beyond the lodge. From Austin Pass the jumbled humps of Shuksan Arm rise as a western shoulder to the peak itself.

But Shuksan has an intimate side never seen by tourists or even by the casual climber: the great eastern cirques, where two great glaciers topple in shining ruins from the summit ice tables. At the head of the North Fork of the Nooksack River are cliffs threaded with waterfalls from glaciers above the enclosing rock slabs, which sweep around in a lofty semicircle to culminate in a jagged turret of the summit.

A sentence in the 1916 issue of *The Mountaineer* fortified the persisting belief that Shuksan was impregnable from the north and east. "No approach to the mountain seems possible on this side," it said. The slender sheer pinnacle girt with swirling clouds "seemed invulnerable" to the Mountaineers who explored the Ruth Creek area to see this belvedere at its best. They commented about a great glacier in the center of the east face "made up of myriads of shapeless ice masses clinging in unaccountable fashion to a thin rock bed."

Ruth Mountain is a simple peak and its upper slopes offer fine spring skiing. But most of all it is a splendid viewpoint. I remember standing by my skis on the summit one April morning and marveling at Shuksan's brilliantly-colored walls—black, rusty, and gray—and its silvery snows against an intense blue sky. Above the East Nooksack Glacier was a grooved face of rock smattered with a tracery of ice and capped with a frail wedge of towers. Down its massive bulk ran ice flutings of the sort so common in the Himalaya, vertical grooves in white ice formed by constant downrush of avalanches which carve out parallel channels separated by thin edges of ice. This striking effect was also apparent on the northeast, the Price Glacier Cirque where Nooksack Tower pierced the void like a spear. What climbing problems!—the peaks along the crenelated wall at the head of the cirque; the Nooksack Glaciers; the thrusting pillar of Nooksack Tower; the rough northeast ice cascade. I was sorry to don skis for the run down, but regrets were tempered by the knowledge I would return.

Nooksack Cirque is more difficult of approach than the 7 map miles from the road (at the time of my first visit) suggest. Tall forests flourish (or did then) along the overgrown trail cut years ago. Then the climber must work his way up 3 miles of gravelly creek bed, constantly fording the icy river, before reaching the recessional moraine at the cirque wall. Now a spur logging road near deserted Camp Shuksan leads to the trail. Driving past the collection of eight crumbling cabins it is difficult to believe that in 1897 they were headquarters for a mining settlement of over 1500 persons.

These remnants of the "North Fork Gold Rush" have a fascinating, little-known history. Henry Custer, topographer for the U.S. Boundary Survey in 1857–8, was the first white man to visit the upper North Fork, and during his mapping ascended Ruth Creek to Hannegan Pass. By 1892 the "State Trail" had been constructed from Glacier Creek to the 20 Mile Post on Ruth Creek. The question of who made early ridge explorations after Custer is interesting. The effort to find a new way to the Ruby Creek mines by avoiding the Skagit Canyon was one reason for the promotion of the Mt. Baker mining district and indirectly led to exploration of the Shuksan area. It is known that in 1891 a man named "Packer" made a reconnaissance of a proposed toll-road route east from the Nooksack, but it is not certain how far he went. For this purpose Banning Austin and R. M. Lyle explored Austin Pass and ventured to the head of the North Fork of the Nooksack, where they were shut in by "impassable cliffs." In 1893 they ventured over Whatcom Pass and descended into the valley of the Little Beaver, and likely explored Chilliwack Pass as well. In 1896 pack trains were taken over Hannegan Pass but it is uncertain how much farther they went. The difficulties of this route and the eventual waning of the prospecting frenzy quelled further serious efforts toward a toll road.

In 1896 Hamilton C. Wells located the "Silver Tip" claim on Ruth Creek, adopting the name from an oversized grizzly who lived nearby, dubbed "Old Hannegan" by the prospectors. Within a year there was a local gold rush: Hill City (Shuksan) had a frantic settlement, mostly tented, of 1500; Wilson's Townsite was at the junction of Ruth Creek and the North Fork; Gold City was at Mile Post 18, near the present end of the Ruth Creek road. Jack Post marked out many a prospectors' trail and eventually discovered the "Lone Jack" ledge near Twin Lakes. Leaving the State Trail at the 19 Mile Post, prospectors forged a route over Mamie Pass to the Silesia Creek watershed and Lone Jack Mine—a much-used route during the summers of 1897–9. The goats along the cliffy valley of Ruth Creek furnished abundant meat for the miners.

On Memorial Day of 1941 Lyman Boyer, Jim Crooks, Helmy, and I waded braids of the green Nooksack toward its glacial origin. The size of the main torrent suggested heavy, melting snows. Thrashing hip-deep in icy rushing waters was a strenuous and dangerous job. Safely across the principal channel we sat and rested, listening to the loud chorus of spring streams newly liberated from the silence of winter snows.

In the lowlands nature has come to terms with man; the quiet, disciplined loveliness of spring in the country always seems unsatisfactory to those who remember the strong and turbulent contrasts of mountains in this season. And here the Nooksack valley was resplendent in depth of color, with rock peaks emerging from their white mantle and mountainsides scarred with the destructive blast of snow avalanches.

Chilled by a strong down-valley wind—a katabatic wind caused by slippage of the relatively-heavier and colder stratum of air along the walls of the upper valley—we continued along gravel bars to a campsite at the cirque headwall.

The East Nooksack Glacier is the finest Cascade example I have seen of a double cirque. The great semi-circle upper cirque curving from Cloudcap Peak to Nooksack Tower is a Valhalla of Ice; the lower cirque makes a tighter curve beneath incredibly-polished slabs, and contains a remnant ice mass, snow chutes chocked with avalanche debris, and the terminal portion of the glacier—usually cloaked with dirt and rock in late summer. The muddy torrent emerging from a mass of brown boulders is some distance from the white ice. Evidence of continued glacier recession is seen everywhere.

Any ascent from the floor of Nooksack Cirque is necessarily long, since the base height is just 3000 feet. Our first day we climbed Icy Peak for a full view of this titanic mountain fortress. On a rocky slope we saw and "captured" two kid goats; their parents showed their anger by rolling stones on us. On a snowfield we encountered pink patches of the microscopic *proctococcus nivalis*, which propagate in summer on lower glaciers and snowfields.

Despite very cloudy weather, next morning Lyman and Helmy set out to climb Shuksan via the East Nooksack Glacier. A 300-foot section of the ice chute, a narrow avenue feeding from the edge of the summit ice plateau, angled at about 50° above a large bergschrund. Helmy mentioned the "hissing of snow avalanches sent shivers down our spines." On the final pitch Lyman cut a hole through the cornice to pull himself over. "It was 3:15 P.M. when we stood on the plateau of the broad Crystal Glacier, 500 feet below the summit which was still ½ mile to the west. As we caught an occasional glance at the final peak which seemed so well within our grasp, a stiff and icy wind pierced our soaked clothing and added to our misery. We realized that to continue would have resulted in a forced bivouac on the snow and at the mercy of the weather. Since we were out to establish a new ice route and not just to climb Mt. Shuksan, we felt that we had succeeded in our undertaking. Even as it was, Lyman and I virtually had to run down the lengthy slopes below the chute to avoid being caught in the darkness." Though conditions forced a halt short of the summit, the great east face had been conquered.

Scarcely a month later Helmy and I revisited our camp in the savage cirque and made the first climb of 7300-foot Cloudcap Peak, the dominant summit at the south end of the valley. We awoke in the night to hear a dull roaring sound and above it a succession of sharper crashes. The moon transmuted to purest silver the snow torrent and the peaks. In the morning not even the sun could relieve the austerity of this place, which always seemed to hold an aura of hostility.

Subsequently, trips to the cirque were often discussed, but not until 1945 did we actually set out for there again, with plans for the first east-west traverse of Shuksan. Every climber feels his pulse quicken at the prospect of adventure when the car leaves for the hills, but on this particular escape to the mountains adventure almost ended when the State Patrol waved Jack Schwabland off the road. Jack, Bill Granston, and I were driving rather rapidly along U.S. 99 near Mt. Vernon in order to have

The northeast face of Mt. Shuksan, with the cascading Price Glacier and soaring Nooksack Tower. North Cascades ice here has carved what once were called "impossible" walls. Photo by Bill Long.

time for some sleep before the ascent. Jack politely explained all this, and we were allowed to proceed with only a stern warning.

But sleep was not to be. At 1:30 A.M. on September 9 we left the car by flashlight. Luckily the odd hours had little effect on our endurance; we crossed the Nooksack and climbed bushy rock gullies to the west. By dawn we reached an alpine ridge at 5000 feet just north of Nooksack Tower and southeast of Price Lake. Our objective, the splendid unclimbed Price Glacier on Shuksan's northeast wall, rose dimly out of shadows in the faint morning light, showing just a taint of fresh snow. Early light played havoc with the succession of ridges east which lit with a golden haze as the stars twinkled out. It would be a clear, bright day. Ruddy reflections cast by the first phase of sunrise greeted our eyes, with a long horizon of orange and yellow surf on the Chilliwack peaks.

The contrasts were striking. The mosaic of ice gullies on the stupendous walls above had depths of indigo-blue, and soon a blinding-white surface shone in the sun like a glowing curtain. In morning light the glacier variegated into every conceivable form of intricate grotto, with piles of ice masses, seracs, and crevasses. A series of natural steps in a ruinous staircase presented a fanciful picture. Long gashes cut these steps into cubes and towers, some of which were cracked off and tilted across chasms. Frail bridges provided another link in this exotic fairyland of ice architecture. Perhaps most wonderful of all was the serene quiet.

We quickly grew cold while admiring this vista during a fast breakfast snack. Now, in full daylight, a chilly zephyr greeted us—the breeze of the ice. I took the lead when we roped, and crossed a rock rib to the main glacier. Time passed quickly. Our irons bit with a crunch into the crusted fresh snow. Luckily we were in shadow; later the sun would make the surface dangerous. When we began to break through a layer of trap crust the gravity of the situation concerned us. Would it be justifiable to continue? The sun had had only one day to touch the face since the last storm. We agreed it should still be safe during morning.

At about 7000 feet we climbed through fractured ice benches in a pattern of zigzags. We were nearing the climax bergschrund at the glacier headwall. Several little ice pitches required finesse and difficult crampon work. Occasionally there was some step-cutting—an art requiring exact energy, not brute swinging of the ax. "To the lover of ice craft," says Frank Smythe, "there is something peculiarly satisfying in the hard clean stump of the ice ax pick meeting ice, and step cutting brings the same sort of satisfaction that the sculptor experiences when working with his chisel."

The next problem was how to get past the double bergschrund and its 55° glare-ice slope. It was already 10 o'clock; the sun's direct rays were rapidly softening the veneer of fresh snow. Jack belayed me to investigate the fringing rock wall—after I first tried, unsuccessfully, to cross the central schrund's wall. Climbing onto a narrow band of gneiss I anchored myself to a piton and belayed the others across. Fresh snow clung to the rock in patches 4 to 8 inches deep. Brushing it off the holds I continued on, edging along little sills above the ice, yet underneath the protecting overhang of rock. A few pitons gave much-needed security. In seven rope lengths we had worked up and left sufficiently to force an exit by means of the steep blue ice of the upper chute. I remember driving an ice piton or two . . . then, only a curious wind-eroded cavity had to be crossed and we were on the edge of the summit ice plateau. Shuksan's top, in a white mantle, was easily reached. The gullies of the summit pyramid were so full of loose snow we were able to glissade down the usual route to the Sulphide Glacier, and from there descend on tired legs to Lake Ann. Lack of sleep and a trying ascent had pretty well depleted our stamina; once on the trail we several times fell asleep while resting. And, after getting a ride down to the car at Ruth Creek, Jack dozed off at a sharp turn below the lodge and his 1937 Studebaker rolled over and pinned itself to a tree. After being pulled back on the road we pushed out the caved-in roof by the "back and heel" method.

The day after Helmy and I climbed Cloudcap Peak we discovered the way up the 2000-foot black walls of Nooksack Tower, which long had been the object of our ambitions. A warm day urged us into exploring possibilities of the long east ridge. But there were too many obstacles: a gap between rock and ice we had to stem for 300 feet; a row of serrated rock teeth separated by unsafe couloirs. From the edge of these we looked down on a more-likely route which begins with 1000 feet up a 50° ice couloir on the north face, then follows a steep seam of black rock with a network of tiny sloping ledges and a number of knobby outcrops. Looking down, it seemed fearfully steep, but less difficult than the exposed ridge we had covered. "Nothing but actual necessity will induce most men on a holiday to exercise or educate their observation," says Young. Nooksack Tower is one peak that required study. Defeat is both a humbling and corrective process—it compels one to examine the self and the problems of a challenge. Defeat is inevitable. Is not the great theme of Greek tragedy the inevitability of defeat and the triumph of surviving it?

For 5 years after that attempt I nursed vindictive thoughts, until July 1946. Meanwhile another party tried the tower and failed. I had known Clifford Schmidtke, a former Mountain Trooper, since my first skiing days, but not until our weekend on the tower did we climb together. He had taught rock technique to troops in the Appenines during much of the war, gaining respect of soldier and officer alike—in particular that of a certain British officer, who after watching him on a practice wall called the students to attention, telling them to "watch carefully now and see how this climb is done." With great gallantry he went 25 feet up Cliff's route, lost his balance, and toppled headlong into a gooseberry bush.

Rather than camp at timberline on the ridge by the Price Glacier we slept on the gravel bar of the Nooksack and got off to

108

an early start. Recent rain made the dirt gully to the ridge slippery footing, and we were glad of our ice axes. Soon the sun smiled kindly as we followed a game path along the ridge in radiant warmth. The tower threw a jagged etching on the white curtain of Shuksan's face; it somewhat resembled the Aiguille Noire de Peteret on Mont Blanc.

Once on the glacier we scanned the slope for a way to force the principal bergschrund beneath the steep ice couloir. With the aid of a few steps Schmidtke was soon around its right side and on the inexorable funnel above. "Come along," he called down some minutes later, and I climbed to his belay. It was my turn to lead, and I crawled up the slope, kicking small steps for 800 feet of elevation. Time passed quickly as we worked up alongside the rock; the crunch of iron on névé and the clattering of an occasional stonefall were the only sounds breaking the silence. The sun had begun to loosen surface rocks held onto the wall by a rime veneer. Once a small snow slide hissed by, but Cliff, who was in a position to see better, motioned me on. Kicking and cutting proved so tedious it seemed wiser to abandon the couloir in favor of a trough to the right. This led to the rock.

We were now high enough to become aware of our wonderfully-isolated position, away from the main wall of Shuksan. Standing on a small band of rock we changed to tennis shoes, leaving ice axes, boots, and crampons securely braced against a pile of rocks. Above, rock slabs towered skyward. I watched my belay carefully, paying out rope as Schmidtke went 90 feet above, and waited. He braced himself, put on a good standing hip belay, then motioned me up. I took the lead, following a line of least resistance up a rounded arete of steepening rock. Several leads later Cliff was slowly climbing a shallow trough, throwing numerous spurious handholds into space behind him, and soon I heard the clinking sound of piton-hammering. In time rope ran out again and I was pleased to hear a happy shout to get ready.

It was the only piton we used on the 1200 feet of rock, but

belayed climbing was prudent everywhere except on the last 50 feet. The view from the summit was genuinely awesome, for we could see all the wild precipices and tumbling glacier walls along the whole length of Shuksan.

Several hours later we were rappelling down sheet ice at the edge of the couloir, placing an occasional piton in rock to fix a safe anchor. Shadow was engulfing the glowing precipices above. Great peaks east took on a heliotrope shade in the afterglow. The setting sun had thrown a darkness on our dramatic slope. Verglas again was forming on the rock.

A group of neatly-dressed tourists were just being served supper in Mt. Baker Lodge when Bob Craig and I entered the informal dining room tired and hungry from 11 hours on Shuksan. Warm food! How tasty it looked! Several guests took a flattering interest in our disheveled attire and insisted we submit to conversation. Their suspicions that we were fresh from adventure were compounded by the fact we had not taken off our alpine hats.

"Were you up there?" a man at the end of the table asked, pointing toward Shuksan. "Righto," Bob dramatically informed him. "We just finished climbing the north buttress." As a few more startled people stopped eating to listen, I added that "Otto Trott and Andy Hennig climbed the glacier and ice wall directly facing you in 1939, but we decided to climb the skyline further over." "Why, this is quite historic," said one of the ladies. We were urged to sit down and tell of the ascent. At the time we believed our climb to be a new route. Not until many years later did we learn that Ben Thompson, with two friends, had climbed this buttress in the 1920s. Early climbing records were rather loosely maintained.

Mt. Baker Lodge is one of those friendly, irregular-shaped buildings which have grown from small beginnings, all the while haunted by fire and financial distress. A sloping ramp now leads to the reception desk, lounge, and the little taproom so popular in ski season. It has a typical western rustic atmosphere—and one wouldn't think of ordering wine with dinner. No fireplace or old paintings represent changes in successive strata of taste, but the lodge does have its tradition. The old lodge was built in 1926 during the period of popularization of skiing, when snowshoeing and tobogganing were losing their early appeal, and was associated with the new interest in mountaineering in the 1920s. The lodge and its vicinity were the location for such famous motion pictures as *The Call of the Wild* and *The Barrier*. To the movie-going public the scenery represented Alaska.

Skiing has been revolutionized since Clark Gable was there in 1934. In those days skiers dressed with woolen leg wraps and despised ski schools, but today both lessons and lifts are extremely popular. Certainly the chair lift to Panorama Dome is renewing the popularity of this fine ski region, which abounds with fine north slopes.

The tradition of the great European ski centers (with the exception of Sestrieres, where I skied a few years ago) matured slowly, in contrast to mountain resorts of the American west which were invented overnight. Three decades ago the road from old Camp Shuksan, site of a pioneer homestead and boom town, was a bumpy dirt cut through shading groves of cedars, hemlocks, and firs, but now it is a paved road busy in summer and winter. Even so, it is a slender thread through wilderness: walk away from it a few hundred yards; all is primeval, and one wonders how a road could be constructed through such a jungle.

—This amazement of the tourists at the Lodge, in September 1947, began on a warm evening when Bob and I bivouacked in a sleeping bag cover on the last bit of heather on White Salmon Ridge at the foot of the north buttress. Silence was total, broken only by the distant roar of a cascade from a hanging glacier. The night was tranquil and warm; neither of us had difficulty getting rest. It was a genial morning as we prepared to leave at 6. The weather had entirely recovered from a recent passion and lapsed into a doldrum of Indian Summer. Down the valley, in a stuffy atmosphere of tumbled blankets, drowsy folks would soon blink at sunlight filtering through windows, but we were already alert and eager for unfinished adventure: we felt the complacent satisfaction and smugness of early risers.

Rather than try to get up a face of smooth slabby rock we traversed left on an apron of ice to an exposed hanging glacier, then climbed it and an ensuing ice finger. Bob took the lead at a snow-choked schrund to eventually bring us out onto the ice buttress above the great rock barrier. I have accompanied Craig on numerous climbs, including some in Alaska, and this was one of the happiest partnerships in my experience. Endowed with physique and intrepid spirit, he has the restless force and fine attunement of nervous senses, the imagination and artistry, which are always a surer passport to mountaineering success than brute force.

About 9 we paused to glance back at the long ice slope we had just climbed. There were no marks where our crampons had just bitten into the hard slope; no handiwork of our human companionship had made an imprint on the route. Nature's intimacy was inviolate that day.

The slope was relentless, but we did not have to belay. Climbing in combination smoothly is not a simple art, but if done properly can save vast amounts of time. At about 8600 feet we crossed onto a salient of the Price Glacier; the snow was colder here and the ax point squeaked sharply when pushed into the névé. Quickly we crossed a small schrund and followed snow to the east face of the summit pyramid. Climbing in sneakers, we soon were on top. It was almost noon. Haze typical of fall began to saturate the mountain air.

8

Ten Days in the Pickets

Above the wilderness between the Skagit River and Mt. Baker rise the jagged, ice-carved peaks of the Picket Range, wearing such stirring names as Fury, Phantom, Terror, and Challenger. The jumble is roughly organized into the southern, or Terror, group, and the northern, or Fury, group—two fortresses ringed by cliffs and jungle. Each group stands at the head of an L-shaped northeast-facing cirque, with the chief summits strung along a continuous ridge. So difficult of access are these peaks that not even early-day prospectors, who went practically everyplace in the Cascades, explored their valleys and meadows. The only breaks in these immense fortifications are on the east, where raging Luna and McMillan Creeks cataract down from the two great cirques. But these valleys offer no easy avenues of entry, choked with brush as they are and devoid of any trail.

Helmy and I made our acquaintance with the northern group in 1940 during a 10-day trip from the Nooksack River to Diablo Dam. We hiked over Hannegan Pass, down the Chilliwack, and up and along Easy Ridge to the snows of Challenger—a route pioneered in 1936 by Phil Dickert, George MacGowan, and Jack Hossack in making the first ascent of Challenger. In 1938 Will Thompson and Bill Cox had ventured even farther when they battled through the difficult bush of Luna Creek to do the first

Mt. Challenger and the Challenger Glacier, the icy spectacle that anchors the north end of the Northern Pickets. Early explorer Henry Custer, likely the first white man to view this splendid scene, called the mountain "Wailagonahoist." Aerial photo by Austin Post, U.S. Geological Survey.

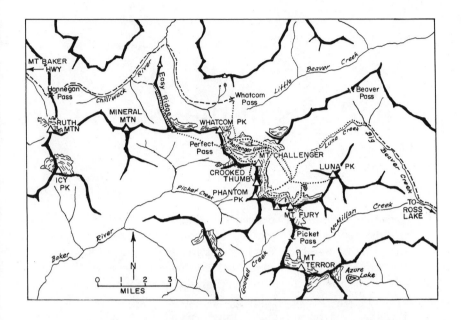

on Fury. Nowhere in the valley had they found any trace of predecessors. They also climbed Luna Peak, which they regarded as the highest point in the Pickets—but maps now show Fury's west peak to top them all by several feet.

Unable to find companions for this trip, Helmy and I had compunctions about its advisability; nevertheless, on July 7, with 65-pound packs, we started the 5-mile rocky trail to Hannegan Pass. Along the way a porcupine clawed up a tree to avoid us.

At twilight we made camp beside the Chilliwack, where a thin trickle of water edged a dispirited way through a bed of white boulders. The setting sun had thrown a shadow over camp, and our altitude was just sufficient to set a chill in the air. Evening deepened tones of the forest attic as we unpacked our impediments and prepared a quick meal of noodles, corned beef, and pudding. Once we heard a rustle nearby, and as Helmy shined the flashlight around, a deer caught in the beam stood surprised for a few seconds before diving into the shelter of the night. The continual gurgling of the stream faded with the coming of sleep; the last thing I remember is a surge of wind, a rustle of boughs overhead.

The morning sky was scattered with clouds. The forest was cold and breezy; deep valleys such as this have a trick of drawing the wind. But soon the mounting sun lighted the river and shot rays of warmth between the trees. Resuming our hike we came across an old cabin with large cedars growing out of it and two beaver traps hanging from the shakes. Prospectors and trappers around the turn of the century penetrated these valleys, and we wondered if the reason they left was the voracious mosquito population that kept us from stopping to rest.

(In 1893 the State Legislature provided $20,000 to build a road over Hannegan Pass and via Beaver and Ruby Creeks to the Columbia. Banning Austin and R. M. Lyle were engaged to make a preliminary survey as far as the Skagit River. They crossed Hannegan, descended an Indian trace down the Chilliwack 8 miles, then followed a faint trail which took them to Whatcom Pass, where they could look into Little Beaver Creek. From 1886 on, there was much talk of a toll road to connect with the Ruby Creek gold mines and those farther east, but the entire project later was abandoned because of the steep grades to Hannegan Pass. Originally, the Chilliwack Creek trail was made by Indian hunters, who went up the Chilliwack valley and on over to Little Beaver Creek; they had connecting routes with the Nooksack and Skagit. Hudson Bay trappers improved the old Indian trail on the Chilliwack, and in 1908 the Forest Service built a trail down it and on over to the Skagit via the Little Beaver.)

Worse was to come when we left the Chilliwack trail, forded the stream, and began to plod the switchbacking path up the steep slopes of Easy Ridge, suffering under hot sun and heavy packs. Thoughts ran to those famed porters, the Lurs of Baghdad.

Once on the ridge we quickly forgot the ills and tortures of the climb. The view was impressive. And though some theorists hold that thirst can be quenched by avoiding the thought of water, we rejected their arguments when we came upon delightful little ponds of clear water, set amid hollows in the heather that carpeted the melancholy alpine barrens with bright flowers. One can buy heather in the city for 50¢, described in nursery catalogs as "Scotch Heath having a rose-colored calyx with a whorl of green bracts at the base," but for full appreciation one must see the plants tumbling in rosy cascades over gray boulders, under a deep blue alpine sky, each rosette of blooms ready to root in any scrap of soil. We slept on the heather near ridge crest.

Next day we continued toward 6000-foot Perfect Pass and the Challenger Glacier, which rims the meadowed pass on its broad sweep toward Whatcom Peak; in the opposite direction the glacier flows along numerous spurs and points in a glittering display of shining ice toward the peak of Challenger. From Easy Ridge the many summits between Challenger and Fury almost fused, and we tried in vain to single out routes on individual peaks. As we hiked a long contour, always on the same inside boot-edges, these alluring summits slowly began to seem within reach. At one spot we had to descend hundreds of feet to cross a deep dike—really a canyon at this point—that called for moderate rock climbing, not quite so moderate with our heavy loads. Later, from a quick scramble up Whatcom Peak, we decided an ascent of Challenger would clear much of the mystery, as well as prepare us for really difficult climbing. Observations suggested the best time for an attack would be very early in the morning, so we made haste to prepare camp.

Snow reflects every quality of the atmosphere: it may be luminescent and charged with subtle colors, or lively like jewel drifts; or it can be dead and blank when shadowed by clouds. Too, the wind molds snow in many and varied forms. From Perfect Pass (a superbly-appropriate name) the moonlit snow seemed to radiate rather than reflect light, as if from some secret source. Beyond the glacier the Chilliwack peaks were faintly penciled by outlines of shadowy valleys. Unlike inhabited hills that sparkle with cheerful human constellations, here the darkness /was complete except for the lonely stars. As Arnold Lunn has written, "The night had broken the bridge of human associations which man laboriously builds between himself and the mountains—these shadowy masses, fading by slow graduations into the sharper darkness of the star-pointed night, had recovered their inhuman aloofness." The night was so entrancing we slept on heather rather than unroll the tent. At a time like this, valleys seem confining as a prison, but there is space and air in the immensity of the starry sky.

Perhaps it was the chilly breeze of the ice, but we automatically awakened with the dawn. In an hour we were climbing, roped, up a glacier trough in clean, white névé. When steeper slopes approached 45° we were consoled to see we could kick steps. A glacier hollow and then an ice hogback led to the base of the summit block. We changed to soft shoes and were soon on top of Challenger, apparently the third ascent. It was 8:40.

The sparkling morning did justice to the spiked array of surrounding mountains. We looked across the great cirque to Luna and Fury. In the serrate skyline nearer were several intriguing unnamed peaks, and we spotted what we thought was a summit Will Thompson had mentioned to us. "Crooked Thumb," as we dubbed it, did not look hospitable from our side. Since we knew from photographs the east wall was quite sheer, we decided to drop south and contour to the west face for an inspection of defenses.

An hour later we had descended a very icy snow couloir a bit west of Challenger's summit. Behind a mask of uncertainty Crooked Thumb concealed a face of naked danger. There were slabby rotten walls leading directly upward, and until we saw a snow finger cutting into the cliff, we had misgivings about where to tackle the ascent. Choosing this finger we found the surface so hard steps were needed. Chopping and kicking, we carefully worked our way to its head. Faced then with the necessity of climbing insecure rock, we changed to sneakers. The next 400 feet were an almost continual courtship with calamity; the outer substance of the rock often came loose. Finally a rock rib on the right offered egress to the crowned summit ridge, where the "thumb" dominated the sky. Stock in our venture soared.

We scrambled along the crest. On the left the walls seemed to hang directly over the Luna Creek cirque and ahead a thin edge flared directly onto the summit thumb. On the north a menacing overhang spoiled any route, but a line of fracture cracks to the left enabled us to scale the last pitch without pitons. Content on the summit, we built a cairn and left a register bottle with a paper recording our first ascent. We had a bird's-eye view of the Picket Range. Immediately south lay a crest of isolated spires, some of which we hoped to climb during the trip. Farther away rose the ice-plastered walls of Terror and its awesome neighbors. Besides studying peaks for routes and admiring their splendor we saw the advisability of moving camp to the base of Fury.

Two climbing arts were of much use on the descent: rappelling and glissading. While the average alpinist is competent at rope descents, few are adept at snow-sliding, and not many have ever recognized the technique must be learned. Certainly a thousand pleasures await the man who commands its deft use; Young writes that "Glissading is an art that rewards the skillful." High above Perfect Pass the glacier dipped 500 feet in two series of 45° profiles; in moments our curved tracks were all that remained to mark the excitement of the slide. Lower down we practiced slalom glissading. The sport lacks few of the thrills of its winter counterpart.

On July 11 we trudged east across the wide glacier to a pass on Challenger Arm overlooking the cirque of Luna Creek, and from there made a scrambling descent on slabs, heather patches, and snowfields. In several hours we reached the terminal moraine of the valley head. The glacier here was nearly level and entirely uncrevassed, though dotted with "glacier tables" (rock slabs left poised atop sheltered pedestals of snow when the surrounding area melts) and humped by morainal ridges. The poor footing

120

on loose gravelly slopes made the valley crossing seem very long indeed. We then had a tedious 1000-foot climb up sliding boulders to a little bench which held a rock-basin pond we called "Luna Lake."

A bit of grass amid the ice-polished slabs rimming the tarn was the ideal spot to pitch our tent. Immense cliffs soared thousands of feet above, fearfully steep and adorned with chaotic hanging glaciers. The icy armor of the eastern faces of Challenger, Crooked Thumb, and the peak we were to call "Phantom" present perhaps the most splendid wall in the Cascades. One large glacier topples in a shining ruin from a col next to Phantom, varies its pattern by fanning to a wide brim at the brink of rock slabs, only to commence again—fed by avalanche rubble—at the base of the headwall. In winter this secret valley must be even more magnificent.

Glaciers in the Pickets tend to have a hanging section above slab cliffs and a residual valley glacier below. Cirques such as this are evolved largely by the erosive action of ice masses embodying them, and not so much by avalanching and the shattering of rock by frost action. At the bergschrund or roture between the upper rock wall and the glacier the moving ice tears the frost-split fragments from the wall, undercutting it at the same time. This explains the typical steepness of rock walls just above the ice.

Close above camp lay an icefall clinging to a fringe of Fury. Occasionally there came the harsh roar of falling debris and the thunderous crash of an avalanche; as I looked quickly up, stones were flying down cold slopes.

Helmy cooked a tasty meal, but there was scarcely time to eat before dark. When we retired, a dark cloud let go a volley of raindrops. Sleep was impossible: the wild flapping of the tent shook us with each gust. Unexpectedly the moon rose, as if to signal an end of the ephemeral wrath of the elements. Then at last the wind quieted and the last thing I saw before closing my eyes was a bright star poised above Phantom.

Ice-polished slabs and cracked, hanging glaciers armor the walls of Luna Cirque. To the left, Crooked Thumb; to the right, Challenger. Aerial photo by Austin Post, U.S. Geological Survey.

After a leisurely breakfast we started up the gentle slopes east of the lakelet. To quote from my diary, "We climbed Luna Peak in the afternoon, mostly for the view. The climb is ridiculously easy from the lake. The weather, however, was seen to be changing, and we had doubts about tomorrow."

The prophecy was correct; on the tomorrow clouds and a drizzle fogged the peaks. Our schedule called for the ascent of Fury this day; luckily we had studied the route carefully, and therefore decided to attempt the climb unless a hard rain began. An early start brought us by about 8 A.M. to the abrupt rise of the heavily-crevassed, tumbling glacier on the gigantic north face. Little could be seen through the mist, but snow conditions were good. Danger from avalanches seemed small, providing we avoided traversing beneath seracs and the central rock face of the peak. For several hours we zigzagged up through the steep maze of holes. When Thompson and Cox preceded us, they kept to the moat between cliff and ice on this portion of the ascent.

We were crossing a particularly-steep glare-ice slope when suddenly the air was rent by that terrible cry, "ROCK!" The shout was mine, and thus not particularly alarming to *me*—not at first, anyway. But it was disconcerting to see a big rock missile bound toward us in long and strangely slow-motion ricochets. With no good chance to dodge, we watched the bomb glance off an ice block and skim over our rope. More falling rock hummed and whined to the right, off a black cliff. Stones leaped furiously through the air, gouging long scars on the snow. We thought that was a good place for them to leave scars. We kept a sharper eye out for rockfall after that, but no more came.

Meanwhile the desultory drizzle ended, and soon the mists vanished with magical speed. Far above, a frosty crest gleamed in sunlight as the cloud ceiling began to ravel into silvery threads. To the east was a great arch of blue sky, a clearing which began low on the horizon and continued north toward the upper Skagit valley.

We had just congratulated ourselves the worst was over when we saw the 800-foot ice couloir separating us from the ridge had a yawning bergschrund at its base. We found a route around the gap and pressed on. The snow was very hard, and my toes grew numb from kicking. Helmy took the lead for several hundred feet; then we alternated at leading and belaying. A huge cornice sat athwart the ridge. To pass it Helmy had to chop a small tunnel. Beyond, raising our eyes, we saw a snow ridge sweeping up in a perfect curve between vapors, sunlit against a pool of blue sky. Fury's 8288-foot east summit was close at hand.

On the south side of the peak we saw what seemed a better route (and some 20 years later was found to be so by the first party to climb it). In spring, when brush is covered with snow, one can find possible entry into the Pickets by way of McMillan Creek. In that season, though, avalanche danger is considerable; some of the great slides completely cross the upper valley. Not until the 1960s did a climbing party use this approach.

Back at the lake we were amazed to see Will Thompson, Ray Clough, and Calder Bressler! Thus far in North Cascades history, only one other party had ever visited this spot, and now here were *two* parties at the same time. (Any alarm at the population explosion was premature, however, because not until 1950 did the cirque see climbers again.) Will and his friends had followed our route over the Challenger Glacier and intended to climb Fury the following day.

With food supplies short, Helmy and I voted to limit our own climbing to one more peak, the box-shaped Phantom, which appeared to be the only significant unclimbed summit remaining in the group. Our distant studies indicated a route might be possible up the cascading glacier at the cirque right-angle. There seemed to be two crucial points: a wall of seracs hanging over the moraine at the top of the basal slabs, and a huge schrund splitting the entire upper glacier.

In the morning we descended to the valley moraine and left our

Mt. Fury and Luna Cirque, from Challenger Arm. The author and Dan Davis climbed the north face and steep ice arete leading to the east peak. Photo by Tom Miller.

packs cached on a prominent boulder. We eventually found a tricky way up the slab barrier, emerging at the lower edge of a wall of rotten ice and dirty rock debris. To avoid toppling ice fragments we hurried on, steering a course toward the glacier center.

Beyond an ice pinnacle we paused to watch threads of mist curl against the east glacier wall. The air was completely still, and hot, and stifling. We were stricken by glacier lassitude, our energy sapped by the steaming mist, by the suffocating heat of a savage sun. With an effort of will we forced ourselves onward.

Above the first icefall the glacier leveled a bit, but called for modification of usual climbing technique: so broken was the slope with interlacing crevasses and ice jumbles we had to change belays constantly, usually every 50 feet, to minimize the chance of swinging lengthwise into a hole.

Past this area we climbed faster and in about 2 hours reached the immense schrund at the glacier bottleneck. There were two choices: the wall on the left or the wall on the right. Both meant leaving the ice. A clatter of rocks down the steep glacier ended indecision. First we climbed under several bridges of ice frozen to the rock; we got wet crawling through a tunnel. A short pitch brought us to névé that seemed at least 60°; we left this as soon as possible for crystalline rock.

In due time we reached a little col and looked down on the head of a glacier facing west. No human had ever been here before. The sun was still steaming through a mist. The air was calm. All was quiet.

"Look up!" I heard Helmy shout. A snow patch—complete and entire—was sliding off a rock platform. Fortunately the thundering fall was far enough away to give us no great fright; but it was so close the impetuous power made us thoughtful.

Some years ago I stepped into a crevasse, unroped. When I crawled out and saw the beauty of the British Columbia Coast

Range I suddenly awakened to the magnificence of the world, of life. As mountaineers know, the dangers of their sport etch memories with a sharpness of detail unmatched on quieter levels of existence. Those who bivouac appreciate the night more than tourists; the loveliness is paid for partly in the currency of suffering. The mountaineer may not need the courage of a ski-racer, but he must have fortitude. His thrills are as much of the spirit as of physical sensation or erotic exercise. He strives continually for that which is not attainable, struggles against nature for nothing. In climbing he is revolting against fate, but he is finite and cannot escape. Man may be foolish, but in climbing he must learn to calculate the risks and calmly face them when the calculation goes wrong. Feats that depend more on luck than skill are pernicious, investing mountaineering with false virtues that tempt the ignorant to a ritual self-destruction. But those who abandon safety rules for heroics cannot always be cured by mere condemnation; many ascents which flirt with death are felt by those who do them to be challenges containing the most poignant fruits of life.

A large portion of the literature of mountaineering describes with gusto the risks taken; an equal amount of writing rebukes those who run the risks. Neither the preacher nor the sinner fully understands the other. The preachers need to realize there is no place, no activity, in the world free from danger and that part of the essence of mountaineering lies in deliberately "cultivating danger" and then avoiding it; to this end skill and keen faculties are acquired, pain and exhaustion endured. The sinner's lesson—often learned too late—is that most accidents arise from poor technique or recklessness. It is on record that men wearing patent leather shoes, silk socks, and light cutaway coats have accomplished the ascent of Mont Blanc, yet only extraordinary fortune saved them. Without adequate equipment and craft one is merely blundering into a chance melee with the elements; as Lord Schuster once wrote of the typical innocent, "He may, with the good luck which sometimes attends children, drunkards, and persons of weak intellect, escape the dangers without even knowing they were there."

127

The avalanche on Phantom warned of danger on the steep snow above, so we kept to rock ridges in our course to the squarish summit tower. Its climb was a matter of delicate tennis-shoe work, requiring nearly an hour. The highest point was just a sliver. Just beneath, in shadow, we rested from the climb and the sun's heat to enjoy lunch.

At 6 P.M. we picked up our packs in the cirque and by nightfall had hiked perhaps a mile through moraine scattered with patches of alder. We didn't really camp that night, just threw sleeping bags atop level stone beds. The morning was hot and smoky, a condition apparently to the liking of insects. These and the thickets of Luna Creek made that day a purgatory. In a particularly-tangled cottonwood grove we blessed the bears, whose fresh paths were a big help. Helmy—whose hunger surpassed his gratitude—had visions of cooking bear flesh in Assyrian fashion, cutting strips of meat and broiling them over an open fire, but I pictured meeting a mother bear with cubs.

After the worst imaginable struggle with flies, devil's club, willows, and alder on the bottom of the valley flood plain, exhausted by a 3-mile struggle against bush, logs, and marsh, we arrived at the Big Beaver trail about 1:30. Our only remaining food was oatmeal and orange concentrate. We ate the oatmeal dry, without sugar.

Fortified by little but zest for a full meal we trudged on to Ross Dam. At 10 in the evening we had covered 19 miles of trail. We had no argument about sleeping before continuing to Diablo.

We had been 10 days in or near the marvelous Pickets. Returning to Seattle required one final day of hitchhiking and standing at gas stations asking for rides. But barely was this adventure over when we were ready for a new one.

———

My only other visit to the Northern Pickets was in July 1963 when Dan Davis and I climbed the direct north face of Fury via the 3000-foot buttress of steep rock and knife-edged ice that leads to the top of the east peak. Camped on Challenger Arm, we reached the summit in 9 hours; descending via the easiest way, the col above Luna Lake, and across the bottom of the Luna Cirque, another 6 hours were required to get back to our tent.

9

The Battle for Hozomeen

*Far better it is to dare mighty things, to win glorious triumphs,
even though checkered with failure, than to take rank with
those poor spirits who neither enjoy much nor suffer much,
because they live in the gray twilight that knows not victory
nor defeat.*

Theodore Roosevelt

Of the many North Cascade summits that interested me before
the war, the south peak of Hozomeen ranked high. Various
interruptions delayed an attempt until October 1945, when
Wayne Swift and I vainly tried to reach the mountain from
Allison Pass on the Canadian side. The Hope-Princeton Highway was still some years in the future; we took an improved
wagon road that went up the Nicolum River, down the Sumallo,
then up the Skagit. This route followed the 1846 trail of Alexander C. Anderson—the first white man to penetrate the Hope
Mountains—and the Dewdney Hope Trail. (When gold was
discovered in the Similkameen in 1859 Governor Douglas in
Victoria commissioned Lieutenant Edgar Dewdney and the
Royal Engineers to build a good pack trail to replace the rugged
Brigade Trail of the fur traders. Where the Sumallo joins the
Skagit an old Indian trail led down to the mouth of Ruby Creek;
this route from the north became the best way to the Ruby
Creek mines. Indians, explorers, and early prospectors must
have seen the Hozomeen Peaks from the west as they traveled
along the Skagit.)

*South Peak of Hozomeen from Lightning Creek. First-ascent route
closely followed the right skyline. Photo by W. H. Mathews.*

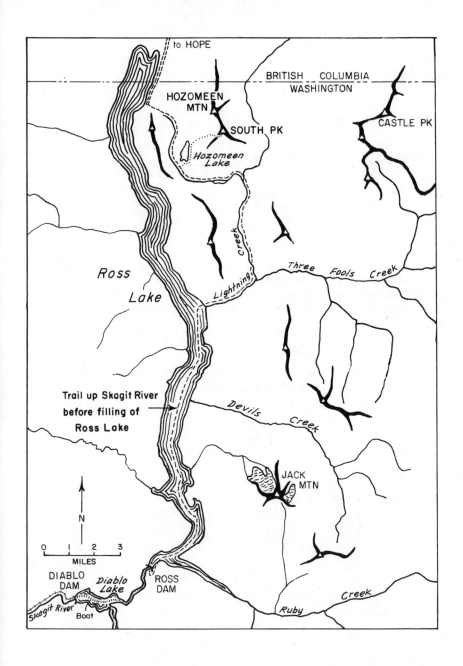

to HOPE

BRITISH COLUMBIA
WASHINGTON

HOZOMEEN
MTN

SOUTH PK

CASTLE PK

Hozomeen
Lake

Lightning Creek

Three Fools Creek

Ross
Lake

Trail up Skagit River
before filling of
Ross Lake

Devils Creek

JACK
MTN

N

0   1   2   3
MILES

DIABLO
DAM

Diablo
Lake

ROSS
DAM

Skagit River

Boat

Ruby Creek

Part of the early exploration of the North Cascades was done by trappers for the Hudson Bay Company, which in 1670 took possession by royal charter of the territory then called "Rupert's Land." The North West Company was formed in 1787 and these two were bitter rivals until they merged in 1821. Each company had scouts watching the movements of Indians, traders, and trappers but little history was recorded of individual travels.

Until 1849 Fort Langley was the lowest post of the Hudson Bay Company on what was then known as Frazer's River; in that year a new fort by the name of Hope was established at the mouth of the Coquihalla, a short distance below the head of navigation at Yale. Anderson, a scholarly officer of the company, was the prime instigator of overland exploration east and south of Hope when he began searching for road routes across the Cascades to the Thompson River country to avoid the deep canyon of the Fraser. With an Indian chief as guide, he went to the headwaters of the Similkameen by way of the "Simallaow." Anderson claimed the Indians said the river which is the Skagit was the same as the Noo-sakh, discharging near Bellingham Bay. This is borne out by a map of 1858 to the "Gold Region of Frazer's and Thompson's Rivers," which shows the Simallaow and Skhaist Rivers joining, then heading southwest to undetermined points.

Driving over rocky streams in water up to the floorboard of my old Ford sedan, and getting stalled in mud where corduroy logs gave way, made a fitting prelude to an ill-fated trip. From a high lodgepole pine-covered ridge we sighted the gaunt black Hozomeen Peaks, but the wind had changed abruptly, as it often does in late fall, and dark rain clouds raced in to obliterate the world and send us home.

Swift and I probably reached a point near the Skyline Trail (an old trail that climbs east out of the Skagit valley from Whitworth Ranch) at the head of Nepopekum Creek, where a geologist studying the region in 1923 wrote, "a striking view of both mountain and plateau is obtained . . . North stretches a uniform, almost monotonous expanse of the plateau country, cut by deep valleys and exhibiting a remarkable uniformity of skyline." Looking south from the same vicinity, H. Bauerman, geologist to the North American Boundary Commission from 1859–61, wrote of "two very remarkable peaks of black slate, which rise precipitately to a height of about 1800 feet above the watershed. They are called by the Indians 'Hozameen.' "

In glacial times the Skagit valley's trough carried an enormous stream of ice down toward Puget Sound, with one center of ice dispersal moving out from the Hozomeen Range and the extensive massif culminating in Castle Peak. Pre-glacial valley gradients were steeper and canyons deeper than those of ranges east. The pioneer geological report of Reginald A. Daly states "The erosive work, including the formation of cirques and the sharpening of ridges by head-wall recession, continued long after the maximum glaciation was passed. As a result the Hozomeen Range is one of the most rugged of those crossed by the Forty-ninth Parallel." Daly went on to say the "ridge culminating in the remarkable double summit of Mt. Hozomeen is wholly composed of pre-Cretaceous rocks" and when referring to the south peak spoke of the "nearly or quite inaccessible horn of Mt. Hozomeen."

Such early geologic reports described the valley of Silver (Silverhope) Creek and the Klesilkwa River as separating a portion of the Cascade system known as the "Skagit Range." "To the east of the Skagit lies the Hozomeen Range," separating its waters from the Similkameen. Here Bauerman wrote that the "south Similkameen originates in three small lakes fed by the melting of the snow on the Hozameen Mountains, at a height of nearly 5,000 feet." (These would be the Lightning Lakes.)

We knew little about Hozomeen except it was massive, rising 6000 feet from the low Skagit River, closely south of the Canadian border, to two separate rocky summits just topping 8000 feet. The north peak, highest by 60 feet, had been climbed in 1904 as a triangulation station for the International Boundary Survey, following the one easy route. In 1944 two Canadians traveling via Lightning (Quartet) Lakes made a perfunctory investigation and decided not to return. Reviewing climbing literature we found nothing more about the mountain.

Hozomeen restlessness found its next outlet in June 1946, when Mel Marcus, Herb Staley, and I set out on a 27-mile hike from Ross Dam. At this time Ross Lake was not fully flooded to its present height and 24-mile length. At Newhalem we disclosed our plans to the trainman, who with studied courtesy declared "You'll never make it." On the weary trail to Lightning Creek his name was often taken in vain, perhaps because we suspected he would be correct.

Lightning Creek was nearly the end of our trip. We thought we could cross with a long pole held upstream, a method not unlike that used for centuries in Indonesia and Central Asia. Because of his height Mel was elected to try first; when his pack began getting wet I suggested—in a shout over the river-roar—that he might carry it balanced on his head. He didn't think the joke was funny, and when the icy water proved unbearable gave up the attempt. Finally we searched out a broader portion of the stream, roped up, and forded.

Through clouds we saw the complicated mass of greenstone and cherty quartzite comprising the south peak, but along the trail to 2800-foot Willow Lake forests hid the mountain. The lake was a distressing place to camp, crummy with garbage littered around an old log cabin. Simultaneously with our arrival, Oregon jays clustered in the trees, knowing by seeming magic we had food for robbing. Deer mice rustled in the slum cabin all night; despite a rain we stayed outside.

The next morning we climbed to rocky ground above timberline. The weather was deteriorating and the view of the peak shook our hopes. Beyond the col between the south peak and a southwestern summit the ridge springs up in a series of sharp edges toward the final summit's edge, actually a rounded flattening that appears as a face problem rather than a ridge traverse. We could only gaze and wonder how long it would be before the peak was friendly. A blistering wind whipped around a corner and struck our faces with icy malice. Soon a rain squall followed. Each of us seemed anxious to win the race back to Ross Dam; actually we all ran along at about the same pace, but the "contest" lessened the monotony of the long hike.

The Memorial Day weekend of 1947 ended poorly, but began even worse. Our Hozomeen group was eating breakfast in the Fraser Valley town of Chilliwack when an exchange of amusing conversation between me and Chuck Welsh caused Jack Schwabland to blow coffee all over the counter waitress.

We drove on, following the new logging road that began west of Hope on the Fraser River and wound up Silverhope Creek and over the divide to the Klesilkwa and Skagit Rivers; this new approach enabled us to motor within several miles of the mountain's base, just beyond the border station, where timber had been cut away for flooding of the valley by Ross Dam. (In 1884 Bauerman wrote of this place, "The Skagit at the Boundary-line is a small stream, only 50 yards wide. The river flat is about 2 miles in width and is covered by a thick growth of timber, principally cedars of large size, with an undergrowth of willows.") But clouds had been coming in at two levels, a bad omen. From the trail up to Hozomeen Lake we looked back at the peak and saw only a mist. At the lake we chose a spruce nook for a campsite, then paddled about in a raft. I ran after a bear we heard thumping through the brush but he disappeared before I could get him to pose for a photo.

Several hours after the fire died I lay awake, listening to loons and owls, wondering whether we should extend ourselves on the mountain in weather so doubtful. Then it began to rain and I slept easy. The next day didn't really dawn at all, and an uneventful trail took us back to the road.

I was becoming obsessed with the notion that Hozomeen was the word for "bad luck" in some unknown tongue. But in 2 weeks I had organized another party—Chuck Welsh, Mel Marcus, Jerry O'Neil, Herb Staley, and Ken Prestrud. Perhaps I felt that with six we could somehow frighten the weather gods and overwhelm the peak.

We made the long drive by night, stopping for coffee at restaurants where we were not known. Under a starry sky we hiked to a lakeshore camp by flashlight. Catching only a few hours sleep, at dawn we rafted the lake and climbed a steep rock gulch through the great cliffy mountainside to timberline. Here we headed directly for the 6500-foot saddle southwest of the peak, and reached it by climbing a snow-filled gulch and a broken rock face. We ate a bite and changed to tennis shoes.

We all studied the curtain of precipices with mixed feeling. I later wrote in the *American Alpine Journal*, "Looking up, we could only see a steep area. The rotten face to its right was composed of a series of short overhangs and high-angle slabs, but it might be climbable." The face of the promontory, farther to the right, seemed uncompromisingly hostile: even to reach it would mean a dangerous traverse. From the top of a buttress we saw a solar halo forming to the west, with extensive darkness over the lowlands. Rain was probably already drenching the Olympics; again it seemed the mountains had ceased to be our friends. But the summit structure jutting beyond a foreground of treacherous pinnacles was still in sharp focus. We stared at the uncompromising final 300 feet—the only way we could see.

The first pinnacle blocked the ridge. Its direct climb would delay us by hours. Then there were more. So what else was possible? The rotten face to the west was entirely out of the question, but closer scrutiny down the steeply-pitched east face indicated some ledges running along. Welsh announced he had little desire to become involved in a storm in a place like this. The same mood of caution touched us all, but the prevailing impulse was to continue.

Roped in two teams of three, we descended 100 feet from the buttress, and saw a ledge below leading the route north. We passed a snowpatch and did a tiring "chinning" step, and then took the ledge for several hundred feet across dangerously-steep gullies and ribs. Finally we came to a corner and saw a way to the ridge beyond the pinnacles. We had bypassed them! "What a piece of luck," I thought. It had not been so bad after all.

We clambered rapidly together to the smooth crest, riveting our eyes on the wall above. The defenses could be mastered, though perhaps not easily—especially now, in our race against the weather. Efficiency was the motto. I wanted to throw a big rock off the west edge where the wall dropped sheer into a branch of Lightning Creek, but there was no time for foolishness.

We began the attack quickly, heading for broken spots between a series of short overhangs. Marcus, Prestrud, and I led off; following on the next rope were Welsh, Staley, and O'Neil. We kept both ropes close, the last man removing safety pitons. Two belay spots gave good protection, and from a dirty ledge we found some holds to climb a vertical pitch to the right of a prominent white overhang. The next lead was across a slab where tennis shoes proved their superiority to nailed boots. Soon we were at the base of the overhanging band, a structure that seemed to lead far off to the promontory to the east. Once climbed, the elusive summit would be ours, hopefully.

Prestrud anchored on a ledge and I groped around on rotten holds, setting several pitons. Not much security was available anywhere here; the holds were loose and the cracks poor for iron. Just beyond my outstretched fingertips there appeared to be a tiny pocket, and then some holds. We changed tactics: I belayed myself to the piton, held in by tension. Marcus with his 6 feet, 4 inches should be able to reach the holds, we felt. From a shoulder stand he did, and with a boost from my free hand his feet finally stuck on something. Shortly he reached a belay ledge. The rest was routine, with upper belays for everyone.

At 3:30 we all stood smiling on the summit. We ate a late lunch and built a cairn. Sullen snows of the Eldorado country burnt with a violent and angry red, in precarious splendor on the brink of impending calamity. The sky was yet blue up the Fraser, but cumulus pillars rose from valleys west; between them we saw the labyrinth of the Picket Range and solitary Jack Mountain, undisputed king of the Skagit. An embracing mist soon concealed all details of the horizon in purple haze.

Whenever the sky is colorful, beautiful, or interesting, the mountaineer becomes wary; we hurriedly began the descent. Two long rappels took us below the band; we then zigzagged to the arete. Across the scant ledges of the pinnacle we again felt the exposure. Before we could climb back to the buttress a bitter wind struck, bringing wet snow that sheeted our clothing and chilled our bones. Six soaked and shivering climbers, whipped by fierce wind, made the 200-foot rappel from the buttress crest. A pity it is that no camera was in place to capture that dismal scene.

We hurried, hoping to avoid a bleak bivouac. Clouds and rain merged with oncoming darkness. We reached our cache of boots and ice axes; then rushed down the wall of loose rocks and the snow gully. But we were caught at last, and stopped in a clump of evergreens, from where it seemed unwise to continue in the murk.

Combined efforts eventually produced fire, and white smoke wafted through the trees, curling below a sea of green tree tops. Rain pelted steadily. We tried snoozing against tree trunks but the hillside offered no satisfactory rest. Giving up on sleep, Welsh and I built a fire on a talus slope; the fire slid down the loose rocks and once more we cursed.

It was a long, long night. At first dawn we beat through soaked brush to the lake to dry out by a blazing fire and refresh ourselves with food; we then walked to the road. As we crossed Willow Pass in a jack-pine forest, a butterfly, the Greek symbol of immortality, fluttered away from our never-to-be-forgotten Hozomeen trail.

10

The Canyon of Granite

Driving over Stevens Pass one cannot help notice how sharply the Cascades separate two climatic zones. From misty, luxuriously-green hills and white-water streams pouring through dank, mossy canyons, in the space of a few miles the forests thin, the air clears, and rolling hills with their lighter-barked pines stand out against the blue sky.

It is apparent, too, that snow vanishes more rapidly on the drier east side, allowing an earlier spring. This is largely due to the downslope wind, the "chinook" (called "foehn" in the Alps), which literally eats snow. Many Northwest residents regard any warm rainy southwest wind as a chinook, but a true foehn requires ascent, cooling, and precipitation on the moist side of a range and a corresponding drying and warming action on the lee. This adiabatic cooling forces the bulk of the precipitation to fall on the west-side slopes, and often in winter destructive slides occur. In 1910 two great avalanches demolished a mail and passenger train stalled outside the snowshed west of Stevens Pass, killing 118 persons. On the east side, where there are dangerous gulches, the mountainsides have less snowcover and are generally safer.

About 30 miles east of the pass, between Tumwater Mountain and Icicle Ridge, flanked by sand hills forming a natural chan-

On the first ascent of the Spider's Web route on Midnight Rock, where autumn dyes the canyon slopes with red and gold. Photo by Bob Sprenger.

nel for air currents, the highway enters Tumwater ("rough water" in Chinook jargon) Canyon, a shadowed chasm carved by the Wenatchee River, its granitic flanks dotted with a sparse growth of pines. Autumn dyes the cliffy parapets with brilliant red and gold flames of vine maple. Spring brings to bloom clusters of rock lily. Spring, too, brings the Wenatchee to a boiling, roaring torrent—an unforgettable sight of devastating power—and bejewels the rocky walls with dozens of small streamlets. Drury Falls can be seen tumbling a thin spray hundreds of feet from a vertical canyon rim. Water is the theme of the Canyon and the land beyond; the precious fluid is piped and channeled to irrigation ditches near Leavenworth. Once a railroad construction camp, this town marks the beginning of the famous Wenatchee apple region, where nearly every square foot of tenable valley land is claimed by orchard.

The opportunity for adventure on rock is practically limitless in the profusion of granite cliffs within Tumwater Canyon and on the numerous formations of solid sandstone in valleys to the east. The mountainous background makes practice climbing more appealing than on outcrops in Puget Sound lowlands. In spring the region provides a fine training ground for summits still snowbound, and the generally sunny climate of the rain-shadow often provides an escape from dreary, west-side wet-ness. It is a natural place to learn the arts of rock climbing, to tune nerves and fingertips, to restore confidence, to re-educate the mind in how to concentrate and thus ignore the latent menace of the void. In these rock sanctuaries even the charm of natural beauty may be lost on the enterprising climber. As was said recently in a climbing journal, "If you have seen a group of these freaks eating cold spaghetti from a can, using pitons for spoons, because they are too lazy to build a fire and forgot to bring utensils, you will understand why the rock enthusiast is happiest when he can drive his car to the foot of the moun-tains."

While some mountaineers cannot comprehend the mania for bouldering and expertise on practice routes, many pure rock climbers cannot understand what they consider the tedium of

Under the first roof on the Spider's Web route on Midnight Rock, a spot requiring strenuous effort. Photo by Jim Stuart.

peakbagging and expeditioning. Fortunately for the sport in general, most individuals nowadays have a growing interest in all types of climbing.

In one of the least refreshing of the seemingly innumerable recent commentaries on climbing, a writer categorized climbers as "Peak Grabbers," "Stunt Climbers," "Record Breakers," "Scientists," "Camera Enthusiasts," "Explorers," and "Mountain Lovers."

At various times I perhaps have fallen into all these categories. After I had been climbing about 10 years I felt a definite need for special devotion to rock climbing for its own sake, the kind that could be done in the off-season and on weekends. I recalled that one day while returning from a rained-out September trip to Kangaroo Ridge, a group of us parked in Tumwater Canyon to take a close look at an imposing rock formation not far above. Because of the weather we climbed only a short distance, but the quality of the rock and the route possibilities made an indelible impression on me.

Possibly because 1948 was one of the wettest years in Northwest history, a number of us began to make regular weekend trips to "The Canyon," beginning in late winter. The rock formation I had previously visited quickly acquired the not-so-original name of "Castle Rock," and an abutting pillar somehow became "Jello Tower." By then several climbing parties had reached the tower's top, but none had completed a route up the main rock's final face. Jack Schwabland, Wes Grande, and I cautiously did this, bestowing the name "Midway." Though not really difficult, the exposed step-across from the top of Jello Tower has evoked care ever since that first climb, and has now become a classic move.

On subsequent weekends other appealing formations were named and climbed: a group of tilted sandstone fingers near the town of Cashmere that eventually became known as the "Peshastin Pinnacles"; rock splinters scattered across the landscape; and innumerable Canyon routes.

Noting that an apparent wall across the river from the road was really a separate tower, four of us set out for its conquest with a huge and varied arsenal of equipment, all designed in some manner to assure success. To this donnybrook Ralph Widrig even brought a powerful bow and arrow; if all else failed, we could reach the summit by archery. Our pessimism turned out to be wholly unwarranted, for one corner had excellent piton cracks and good holds to allow a short, steep climb. After this quick success on "Tumwater Tower" we scanned the Canyon slopes, almost in a fever, hoping to locate grander and more difficult towers.

On one greedy, ridiculous quest, two carloads of us raced up to what seemed a new, large tower hidden amid the trees on the far Canyon walls; "Moss Tower" proved so uninspiring I elected to remain on the ground. Much more worthwhile was a sandstone pinnacle rising amid the hills north of Leavenworth: "Chumstick Snag," discovered and climbed by Pete Schoening and Tom Miller, proved a tricky friction ascent and has become fairly popular, despite being "lost" for years, many parties being unable to find it.

With the availability of nylon rope and a wider variety of pitons, harder routes became safer; some that previously seemed hopeless were now attempted. Crack routes such as "Outer Space" on Snow Creek Wall and "Roller Coaster" on Midnight Rock became realistic ventures when Joe Hieb made some large angle pitons.

(Using 10 gauge hot-rolled plate, pitons up to 3 inches wide proved soft yet durable. At first our equipment included homemade contraction bolts, 3 inches long with two saw cuts intersecting at right angles, to fit a drilled ⅜-inch hole. Though this piece of iron could support 2000 pounds, about 30 minutes was required to drill a hole; we began to experiment with smaller commercial bolts and finally adopted ¼-inch and ³⁄₁₆-inch Rawl Drives for hard rock.)

Though longer and more difficult routes were pioneered on

*Exposed climbing above the second expanding flake on the Wall Street
route on Noontime Rock. Photo by Fred Beckey.*

Snow Creek Wall and Midnight Rock (the name commemorates John Rupley's "rescue" of me and a companion from a final pitch, well after dark in a rainstorm, with a flashlight and a "rope" of tied-up clothing), Castle Rock remained the mecca for weekend climbers. Free-climbing standards steadily improved, as on the now classic "Angel" crack and the continuously-difficult "Canary" and "Century" routes. There was an improvement in names, too, with such descriptive bestowals as "Cat Burglar" and "Rain Shadow." And there was an improvement in scenery, at least to the climber, when all the firs on "Logger's Ledge" mysteriously disappeared. As someone defensively pointed out, the trees lacked beauty and gave climbers claustrophobia.

Since elimination of these trees, Castle Rock has become a favorite stop for goosenecking highway tourists, the parked cars often creating a traffic hazard. During a day of fall color emblazonment, Pete Schoening, Wes Grande, and I were completing the first climb of the "Devil's Delight." A throng of motorists as well as some pipeline workers across the river were greatly interested in our proceedings. Drowsily awaiting a belay from above, I heard a yell from Pete. Alarmed, I queried "What's wrong?" Assured all was well, I took my turn at the pitch and was duly informed the shout was to warn some girls who had stepped into the bushes near the road, unaware we were directly above. I mused that perhaps I wouldn't have warned them.

For evening entertainment Tumwater Canyon lacks the civilized refinements of Yosemite Valley. Some nights we dropped in at barn dances in nearby towns, but restaurant-sitting in Leavenworth was our favorite pastime. While hardly a gourmet's paradise, the town is suitable for an overpriced meal and occasional sensations caused by torn climbing wear and uninhibited male conversation. More than one plump waitress has made a heroic effort to steer chatter into channels proper for those ordering meals. However, as often as not we were overshadowed by the locals. One evening an inebriated apple picker more than drowned us out with cackling interjections of "catsup please!" But instead of pouring the catsup on his hamburger steak, he drank directly from the bottle. The catsup gone, he glaze-eyed around the cafe, not sufficiently coordinated to find his fork with both hands.

Throughout the United States, when postwar climbers began to specialize in new solutions to the problems of mountaincraft, rock climbing became important in its own right, not just as a training exercise, but as a sport. Areas such as the Shawangunks in the East, Devil's Lake in the Midwest, El Dorado Canyon in the Rockies, and Tahquitz Rock in Southern California gained popularity. Yosemite Valley, the greatest of all, came of age with a sharp increase in the number and length of routes: Lost Arrow and Sentinel Rock were climbed, though not yet El Capitan. Young men whose experience was limited to adventures on academic precipices at colleges from Harvard to Stanford were encouraged by friends to try serious rock climbing (and at the same time encouraged by authorities to abandon the nocturnal exploits of tying flags to campus gargoyles and pitoning up the walls of a Physics Building). Many found rock climbing fitted their spirit and taste, their need for a new challenge in a civilized environment.

To be accepted as it now is in Europe, climbing must gain public recognition, an impossible goal so long as unsound ideas and misconceptions are engendered by inaccurate press coverage. A digression is necessary here to place both Cascade and American rock climbing in perspective with that of the Mother Alps.

Mountaineering is a western notion, the idea never occurring to the ancients of the East. Generally people of toil, except in Greece, had no time for sports. Few historians have done full justice to the role played by the English—who had to travel 500 miles to find high mountains—in developing sports "native" to Switzerland. The British also were pioneers of the esthetic revolution which found beauty in the Swiss mountains. Significantly, most of the early romantics were men of intellectual distinction who through their drawings and writings influenced the public to respect nature. It is interesting to note Shelley wrote of glacier pinnacles "covered with a network of frosted silver" and that the decade in which Darwin published *The Origin of the Species* also saw the beginnings of systematic mountaineering.

Climbing then had to achieve emancipation from science and reveal itself to the world as a pursuit worthwhile for its own sake. Even when the sport had become barely accepted in Europe, writers such as John Ruskin taunted that technical climbers regarded mountains as "greased poles," implying the gymnast is incapable of enjoying scenery.

In the Alps the monarchs were generally climbed first; the same was true of the Cascades. Later the more attractive satellites were approached. That great pioneer, Alfred Mummery, not only broke the absolute tradition of guided climbing, but did much to raise standards of the possible by scaling peaks in the Alps previously considered hopeless. Though there are still skeptics who do not believe in specialization, natural evolution has led to marked changes in climbing standards. Early alpinists, whose courage and stamina left little to be desired, would be amazed at the acrobatics and training necessary for today's more difficult routes.

The Bavarians introduced the wholesale use of iron, and on their local cliffs in the Kaisergebirge scarcely a potential handhold is not part of some recognized route. The piton, cornerstone of the new technique developed there and in the Dolomites, is not the stepladder pictured by early British imaginists—it doesn't make the climb easier but rather makes new demands on enterprise. (Once there was a clamor against crampons in the Western Alps and rubber shoes in England; in the same era ladders were carried around by such distinguished pioneers as De Saussure, Whymper, and Dent.)

Self-righteous conservatives have long fought the invasion of new equipment, claiming it debases the sport. Articles in the *Alpine Journal* once contained severe strictures on modern methods and the "Foolish ascent of the North Wall of the Grosse Zinne," a Dolomite climb requiring hundreds of pitons.

Chumstick Snag, a difficult and deceptive little sandstone pinnacle near Leavenworth. Photo by Fred Beckey.

One feels sympathetic to condemnations of a recklessness that sacrifices safety for self-assertion, competition, and personal achievement, but the writers making these condemnations unconsciously and falsely associated these goals with the piton and carabiner. Victorian critics failed to distinguish between the use of new tools for safety and the use of the same tools by men bent on suicide. When men impelled by heroic urges abandoned the laws of safety and climbed the big faces in poor weather, not only they, but their use of pitons—the greatest contribution to climbing since the rope—were treated with contempt. Even in such influential places as the *Alpine Journal* it was suggested that ascents by "mechanization" should not be recognized as first ascents. Frank Smythe, the famed English alpinist, was very concerned by advances of technology at the expense of the human spirit.

Annals of the more daring of the first "modern" climbs are filled with adventure, nationalism, and condemnation by traditionalists. The Schmid brothers' ascent of the North Face of the Matterhorn in 1931 was castigated by the influential R. L. G. Irving, who wrote that "spiritually the Germans have gone back to the pagan ideas that stand for the ideal of self-exaltation." It was easy to link resurgent nationalism with a sport cultivated by the Nazis, and link all piton climbing with nationalism. However, it is now recognized the Facists ruthlessly exploited alpinists for their own purposes; they attempted to make climbing an Olympic sport and to turn the Alps into a battlefield. Certainly gold medals and eulogies encouraged risks, but many of those who did severe ascents in those years were not climbing to the gallery but were seeking their personal spiritual goals.

The distrust of any wall climb as utter recklessness came into British writing as an infection from the Puritans, whose objectives and appetites for condemnation change through the ages. I cannot help think Puritans demand too much of human nature. They fail to realize that constant exposure to danger does not necessarily destroy the delicacy of sensibility to real danger.

151

The British tradition had no place for advertisement, but was characterized above all by an alliance between caution and robust adventure within recognized rules gradually formed as a result of hard-won experience. These general ethical guidelines have been accepted by most of the better mountaineers of all nations, and have certainly influenced Yosemite climbing, where the new ethic emphasizes "how" a climb is done. This influence, in turn, has had its effect throughout our nation—including the Cascades.

We are all to a greater or lesser extent creatures of fashion, many a direct result of profound changes occurring in the world. Today hiking and climbing have entered a new phase. Exclusive traditions, once cherished by a small cult, are disappearing before the onrush of ramblers of more casual spirit. Mass escape to the hills from debased civilization is a new expression of the pantheistic return to nature of Shelley and Rousseau. Men have not removed the romance from mountains by climbing them, and the use of technical equipment doesn't dull human perceptions. Mummery pointed out that the dramatic force of a splendid, bold, and appalling foreground increases the esthetic value of an ascent.

Little groups of climbers preparing for the high peaks by practicing arts of balance and strength in places such as Tumwater Canyon prove the exclusive and aristocratic traditions of oldtime mountaineering are disappearing and being modified by new generations whose pioneering instinct can find expression only in new terrain, really in the direct tradition of our alpine forefathers.

11

Cashmere Crags

The flatlander's notion of a mountain top is a sharp point with scarcely room for one person to stand. In fact, few such summits exist, because only hard rocks such as those of the Chamonix Aiguilles sufficiently survive the attacks of frost, sun, wind, and rain to exhibit really acute peaks. In the North Cascades are numerous areas of similar granitic rock, as well as others where gneiss predominates. None, however, is so extensive as the Mt. Stuart batholith with its baroque and rococo architecture of pinnacles, and its huge blocks broken off by frost action along joint planes.

Professor I. C. Russell, who explored the "Wenache Mountains" in 1898 and 1899, was likely the first person to describe this land of crags and lakes. Anyone who has seen the region will instantly recognize his picture: "In the eastern portion of the range a magnificent amphitheatre has been hollowed out, which discharges its waters northward into Icicle Creek. In the more elevated portions of this amphitheatre there is still a small glacier, below which, and at the bottom of a steep, bare slope of polished granite, there are two rock-basin lakes, known as the Twin Lakes. To the north of these, and beyond a great cathedral-like mass of clustering granite spires rising within the amphitheatre . . . there is a third and smaller rock-basin lake. . . . This Twin Lakes amphitheatre was the source of a large glacier at a former period . . . from 5 to 6 miles long."

Author (in middle) and party approaching Lighthouse Tower in the Cashmere Crags. Photo by Bob and Ira Spring.

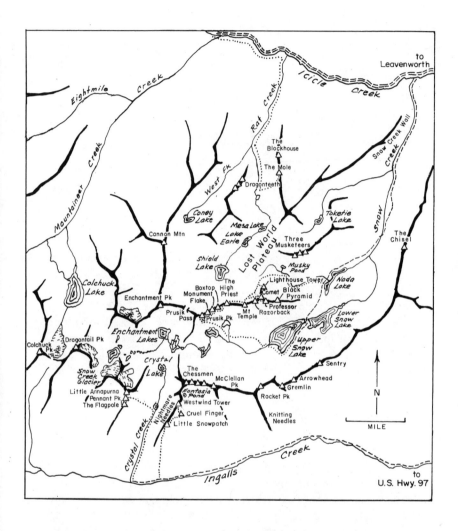

A casual glance from the valley of the Wenatchee River gives
no reason to suspect the unique alpine country of lakes, jagged
towers, and meadowed slopes dotted with larch. "I found 5 or 6
most beautiful small lakes grouped in a wonderful glacial valley
all ringed with alpine larch. From the highest lake over an entrancing fall tumbled the water it received from a small glacier.
It was an enchanting scene. I named the group 'Enchantment

Lakes,'" wrote A. H. Sylvester after one of his explorations for the Forest Service between 1908 and 1931.

The Mountaineers on their 1914 Summer Outing found the attractive parklike meadows of Ingalls Creek, bordering the granitic upland, but limited their investigations to the immediate vicinity of 9415-foot Stuart, which they climbed from the south side after questioning if the steeper north side was possible. Its first climb may have been in 1873 by Angus McPherson, who left a stick with his name on the summit. (An early miner told C. E. Rusk he found the stick there.) The periphery of the region attracted early commercial interest. Cle Elum and Roslyn sprang up in 1886 after the discovery of great coal deposits. Before that, in 1853, soldiers under Captain George B. McClellan found gold-bearing quartz veins and in 1879 a wagon road was built over Blewett Pass. Once 250 miners worked placer claims at Blewett; cabins, tunnels, and tailing dumps are still in evidence along Swauk Creek, and the remnants of an assastra, a crude ore-grinding apparatus.

In the center of the high country are Nada Lake and Snow Lakes, the latter messed up by the U.S. Bureau of Reclamation for the sake of an irrigation scheme. In 1946 Keith Rankin, Bill Herston, and Ken Prestrud made the first climb of the 8400-foot highest peak of Temple, a central spine of jagged granite west of Nada Lake. They reported the region full of unclimbed towers "that should delight the heart of a rock climber."

Intrigued by their report, on May 17 of 1947 Bill Dunaway, Mel Marcus, and I ignored the skepticism of the weather forecaster and drove over Stevens Pass. Skies were moist on the west side, but cleared beyond the pass. Fired with energy we set off in early afternoon, climbing the many switchbacks along Snow Creek. Between shadows of pines the sun was hot.

At Nada Lake we slept the light sleep of those who intend to arise early; I came sharp awake at one point when a furry beaver scurried over my sleeping bag. After breakfast we climbed alongside a waterfall to a hanging valley west, emerg-

Prusik Peak and Gnome Tarn, in the Enchantment Lakes area. The author made the first climb of the sheer south face, seen here. Photo by Robert E. Landsburg.

ing in a larger basin with crags close to the south. Most talus and heather slopes were already bare, and we only climbed on snow above the highest trees. It was hard to believe there could be so many summits; several of the seemingly hand-chiseled towers had the pure lines of Euclidean geometry. Writing later in *The Mountaineer*, Ralph Widrig described them as "tall menacing spires that streak skyward like Dantesque flames."

We had come to climb Temple's west peak (now called "The Hight Priest"), but all around lay virgin rock for many trips to come. The west peak stands on the main Temple ridge in military formation with other and more striking summits. We built a small cairn on top, then hurried off to repeat the ascent of the main peak. Clouds dissolved a little to reveal, just east, an expanding vista of cold gray spires touched by golden light; far away on the Columbia Plateau sun rays slanted through rain clouds to pick out gullies in the cliffs of ancient lava fringing the river.

North of the Temple ridge, where a rolling alpine upland called the "Lost World Plateau" drops toward Icicle Creek, we saw a beautiful dome of white rock. In an effort to reach it, next May Ralph Widrig, Wes Grande, and I clambered up Rat Creek's steep slopes of buckbrush and snowberry. On a snowfield near timberline we surprised a group of traversing coyotes; in scampering away they started a slide. We made camp beneath the dome, which—typical of our subsequent arbitrary nomenclature in the Crags—we called "The Mole." It was an alluring summit, with apparently difficult walls that fascinated us. Gazing up at the high south face Ralph thought he saw a possible line of attack—possible, but safely away from temptation. Toward the east we derived some encouragement from partly-broken rock, but granite facets appeared to bar the most likely route in two places. For a quarter-hour we indulged in the customary procrastinations of climbers, discussing possibilities, re-making rucksacks, and uncoiling rope.

After close inspection we decided against going near a large chockstone that hung in menacing fashion above the gully separating the peak from another wall. The face of The Mole was broken, but connections were lacking between many of the ledges and cracks. From the gully a thin crevice angled left on a slight overhang; we thought we could do it by layback technique, helped by some small protrusions of feldspar.

Dwarf pines can grow in the most incredible spots. Here one gave a convenient handhold, and in a few more moments another provided a belay anchor. The rock above was unusually sound, offering minute holds interspersed with narrow cracks and ledges. I placed a horizontal piton and continued up to the safety of a ledge, pulling myself over the edge and using it for a sitting belay. "Get ready to come up!" I yelled—and heard my words echo back at me from across the chasm.

On reassembling we had a short debate. A preface to the doubtful upper wall was a 100-foot, high-angle depression. From our cumulative enthusiasm came a group-built faith we could get up. Wes led the pitch expertly, placing two angle pitons for protection. Here the route was blocked by a large imbedded flake, split off about 6 feet from the main wall, and undetected from below because it fused with the face. We hoped to traverse across its top to a new line of cracks. Wes climbed a V-crack at the right edge of the flake, and then shouted down, rather disgruntled, that we would have to climb through a transverse tunnel. Ralph called back encouraging him to continue, saying he was beautifully qualified by his experience digging ditches. Ignoring the personal barb, Wes soon called "I'm through!"

The climber on granite is often fronted with the unexpected. Geoffrey Winthrop Young describes the Grepon traverse as a "delightful instance of unreasonable progress just made possible by a series of apparently gorgeous accidents." Here, we were surprised to discover a vertical hole leading up under a granite roof. Stemming in perfect safety, in no time at all we were on top of The Mole, where we found several clear pools of water in little bathtubs.

But now we paid attention to the obvious gathering of towering clouds. This was not a good place to be in a lightning storm. Even Ralph, generally stoic and sarcastic, cracked no jokes as we scrambled toward the first rappel.

One of the finest trips I have had in this region was on the Memorial Day weekend of 1948, with Ralph Widrig, Pete Schoening, and Art Holben. That spring is still remembered for violent floods. All over the Cascades roads were washed out, and getting by Tumwater Canyon required a detour. We parked at Icicle Island Cabins and slept comfortably on the resort's lawn; the informal charm of an English garden was absent but non-paying guests shouldn't complain. High waters had taken out the bridges on the rampaging Icicle. The only way across was a cable from which was suspended a small, one-man carrier.

Later, on the hot trail, we decided it was high time for this granite wonderland, so different from other sections of the Cascades, to have a general name. Ralph's suggestion, the "Cashmere Crags," won our approval, and has since gained wide acceptance—usually shortened to "the Crags."

Around the head of Upper Snow Lake were precipices and spires in forbidding array. At dusk the last cloud vanished, the last glow faded, and the sky lit up with stars; there was no breath of wind. But at dawn we awoke to find ourselves imprisoned in heavy masses of gray clouds which almost obscured the summits. With that perversity peculiar to the mountains, a local storm was in the brew. We were anxious, but experience told us the skies would clear again, for the Crags seem to get the best weather in the Cascades. After climbing snowfields to Enchantment Lakes our faith was confirmed as a warm sun suddenly broke through the rafters of cloud. In the other direction our eyes lifted to the impressive spires on the Temple ridge. Those at the west end looked most inviting, so we directed our legs that way. Ralph and Pete made off to a squared monolith we called "The Monument," while Art and I explored the feasibility of the last summit in the line. We climbed to the west ridge, decided there must be a better approach, and traversed to the basin under the sheer south face. Here we change into kletterschuhe and made ready for what promised to be an exciting first ascent.

For 180 feet the spectacular route led up cracks to the ridge; some of this involved direct aid with pitons. In a few awkward traverses and one short aid overhang we reached the base of the summit horn, here some 40 overhanging feet above. We appraised several possibilities, and finally decided the quickest way would be to lasso the horn from an adjacent block. Art climbed 20 feet, and with the spare ⅜-inch nylon began making looping throws. Eventually he succeeded. Now it was my turn: I tied three slings to the fixed rope with prusik knots and began to raise myself, lifting one sling at a time. Getting over the last few feet was the worst part, for my weight made the loop slip around the overhanging anchor block. "Prusik Peak," one of us volunteered. The name stuck.

While perched on the summit we caught sight of other strange activities. Our companions had climbed a 60-foot solitary crack on the four-sided shaft by means of horizontal and angle pitons. Then Pete traversed completely around the tower on a 6-inch ledge to receive a weighted line thrown over the top by Ralph. Blocked by flawless rock they adopted tactics similar to ours: a direct ascent on the rope over the summit. It was entertaining to watch their antics.

Across the basin of Enchantment Lakes was every color contrast the eye could wish for: the radiance of snow; the soft, shimmering emerald of lakes. On the western horizon lay the opalescent tint of low clouds, hiding the bulk of Stuart and its satellites. A congregation of blue-gray pyramids, an extension of the ridge of McClellan Peak, blocked the view into Ingalls Creek; later they were given names such as Arrowhead, Gremlin, and Rocket.

It was night when we reached the cable at Icicle Creek. To our dismay someone had anchored the carrier car to the far side.

The Flagpole, a slender sliver visited by more birds than climbers. Photo by Fred Beckey.

Author stemming an open chimney on Rocket Peak. Photo by Bob and Ira Spring.

Being the bravest, Pete volunteered to cross on a sling and carabiner. Pulling himself over was strenuous work—and below, the violent river rushed along in darkness.

The Crags welcomed us many times that summer of 1948; one of the most successful jaunts was to the spires on the east side of Temple. Pete, Ralph, and I left the sleeping campground on the Icicle while the morning star still disputed the dawn and dusk lingered under the pines. Morning flooded over the hills by the time we topped the first series of switchbacks. Familiar mountain scenes appear to recur; I never emerge from the forest at Nada Lake without a homecoming delight in the peaks above.

"Razorback," the first summit from Temple, proved an enjoyable roped climb offering samples of all varieties of Crag granite, from rotten to bombproof. With accelerating zest we turned to the next two summits, "Comet" and "Meteor." To reach the latter, which stood in the void like a spaceship, we had to slide singly down a slab: the landing ledge seemed to shrink to a mere wrinkle; the green basin below would be the next stop if anything went wrong. We left a rope for the return, since the possibility of sliding up the slabs seemed remote.

After a small but tasty lunch we clambered across steep broken rock to our principal goal for the day, a large isolated spire whose twisting shape somehow earned it the title of "The Professor." After glancing appreciatively at my belay Ralph climbed up a vertical crack into the slanting sunshine. All went well, but to mitigate exposure he placed two safety pitons. After a short arduous section, Ralph, who now seemed in top form, swept over the last barrier of an overhanging block, demonstrating delicacy and acute perception, an instinctive feeling for the task. During this interesting ascent I had little to do but follow the belayed rope.

When we returned to the basin beneath Temple, a few hours of daylight remained, and we felt an attractive pinnacle rising 100 feet above a spur ridge north of Temple—"Lighthouse Tower" —would be a fitting finale.

We first tried line-throwing tactics on the tapering cylindrical tower, but failing in this climbed to a hidden flake of exfoliation granite that led to a platform about 20 feet under the flawless top. From a tiny belay ledge, the flake crack above showed as a gray, offset line on a slightly-overhanging wall. While belaying Ralph, I pointed out a little traverse I had been loathe to undertake; it involved bringing the fingers down to knee-level. Ralph complained such a caper would throw him off balance, but with the correct combination freshly in mind he proceeded to where he could free one hand to pound a piton. Reaching left over to the crack he then could hammer an angle iron. Since the crack was impossible to climb without aid he placed a sling in a second carabiner, put his foot in the upper sling loop, rose up and inserted another piton. Though it slid down a bit, it wedged and held weight. Twenty feet up, the crack flared out too wide for angle pitons, but with a long reach he managed to hammer one above, where it narrowed again. Due for a rest, he came down on the rope. After I hoisted myself to his highest piton I struggled over the final bulge before the ledge, using some barely-adequate fingernail holds. Anchoring to a piton I threw a weighted line toward the summit. On the second try it went over. Pete and Ralph then traversed to the opposite side of the tower and pulled a spare rope across the top.

We had been too engaged with the route to notice the valley shadows. Nada Lake had taken on a desert air and the town of Leavenworth was only a faint mist of gray against the rolling hills. Far to the north a cloud floated on a hazy blueness. Through warm and drowsy air came music of an invisible torrent. "Up rope!" I heard a shout from below.

Soon Pete came up on prusik-knotted slings, continuing directly to the summit to lessen danger of the rope slipping on the rounded top; there was a momentary scare when the rope did slip a bit, but it was just a rope twist or elongation. In another 10 minutes he was a dark blur atop the peak.

166

Stumbling down rockslides to Nada Lake in the dark was no pleasure. Rather than walk all the way out the trail that night, we crept between two mattresses in the cabin and slept amid sounds of active mice.

Often on dreary days I wandered in spirit to these flowery meadows with clear-running streams and star-filled nights. But not until late September did a group of us find time for a full week in the Crags. Between the end of summer jobs and the start of Autumn Quarter at the University of Washington many climbers were available. Pete arranged for a pilot to fly from Kenmore Air Harbor on Lake Washington and drop supplies among the pines beneath Lighthouse Tower.

We were on the scene when the plane came over, ready to spot and retrieve the bundles—dufflebags containing food, ropes, and gear. But to our alarm, the small plane suddenly went out of control; a load had fallen against the right-hand stick of the dual controls. Flying slow and low, the pilot, helpless, crashed into boulders. Fortunately he escaped unhurt except for shock and bruises. All plans were abandoned, of course, until we could escort the pilot to the road and then bring in a party to carry out salvageable parts of the plane.

When at last we could think of climbing, the temperatures and the chill gray skies were those of winter. Pete and I started for "The Boxtop," the unclimbed prominent castle-shaped tower behind Temple's west peak; the remainder of our group elected to try other summits of the Temple ridge.

As expected, the route turned out complex and interesting, starting with the ascent of some fissures, a piton traverse, and a difficult pitch to a prominent ledge. Here a huge 40-foot overhang blocked progress, but surprisingly, a window extended beneath an arch through the entire west edge of the formation. Beyond the window we found a way on the north face to the last traverse, which led around to the south again. A final 50-foot crack became slick when clouds let loose a shower of

The spirit of the Cashmere Crags in the exploration era. Don Wilde, the author, and Pete Schoening, variously attired in war-surplus and other cheap equipment and clothing. Photo by Fred Beckey.

hail, then snow; had it not been for a few unique protuberances, or "chickenheads," decorating the sheer walls along the crack, we might have been defeated. The summit was a knifed bevel-edge which we straddled to the highest point. There was no time for relaxation, gazing at scenery, or picture-taking, but only for survival. A bitter and sharp southeast wind whipped our clothes; we immediately descended by rappels.

On arrival at our tent we saw the pond in a stream had frozen solid. The mountains were no longer sleeping in summer drowsiness, but had awakened in cold air to begin the long winter war. Next morning the meadows had vanished under 18 inches of powder snow. Trees and rocks were decked in white. We left in dull, sullen air. The descent to the lake was slippery and treacherous.

Three weeks earlier Jack Schwabland and I had spent Labor Day weekend camped at Snow Lakes. From here the Crags show a matchless splendor of forms derived from the creative interplay of erosion by wind, water, and ice. Though at first glance there is a faint suggestion of mass production, the eye which demands contrasts finds them as the gothic structures change moods with time and weather. As we watched that evening, the line of spires dominating the western sky beyond the upper lake was endlessly various: now radiant in gleaming sun, then tinged pink with evening light; at last the opaque blackness of their forms was penciled in sharp relief against the transparent darkness of the star-pointed night. The gurgling of the outlet stream, the wind in the pines, faded away into sleep.

Shortly after midnight we awoke in a sudden storm and scurried for the shelter of our tarp. The sky occasionally cleared, revealing stars, and from time to time spectral peaks emerged from a confused tangle of hurrying cloud; now and then a violent gust of wind wrenched aside the gray curtain concealing dim rock turrets above. Gradually the east paled, and when dawn burnt on distant snows near Enchantment Lakes, the clouds had miraculously dissolved.

As we struck off up the rockslides our fresh-washed mountain world glistened in the sun. All the many summits cresting the ridge southeast of the lake were unclimbed. But not after that weekend. We found a number of interesting short problems. First was the summit pitch of "The Sentry," a delicate circus act on undiluted exposure, with a shoulder stand atop a knife-edge and then a lasso of the topmost horn. On our best climb, "Rocket Peak," we made our first use of a home-made bolt that contracted when hammered into the drilled hole. Two hummingbirds played darting games about us, making a pretty aerial display.

The top of Rocket gave our first good view of the row upon row of towers and turrets on the southern slopes of 8400-foot McClellan Peak. The nearest ridge we called "Knitting Needles"; beyond was the staccato of crazy "Nightmare Needles." Several were reminiscent of the Guglia d'Amicis in the Dolomites, and eventually the same technique used on that peak—rope-throwing—was employed to reach some of their summits. Others, like "Little Snowpatch" and "Westwind Tower," turned out to be fine combinations of free and direct-aid climbing.

The hillside glowed with incredibly-varied fall color, from the steely green of pines below, to sun-bright heather and grasses on shelving benches, to the rusty rock of the upper rim. But despite the richness, whenever our eyes turned westward they were stopped by the most-celebrated spire of them all, isolated from all others and appearing to have a unique feature: its top was wider than its base! "The Flagpole" demanded an attempt.

In July 1950 Pete Schoening, Phil Sharpe, and I hiked up Ingalls Creek. The forest floor was brightened by the blue and white and yellow of lupine and avalanche lily. More impressive were the creamy blossoms of rhododendron. Everywhere in bloom was kinnikinick, with low-trailing laurel-like leaves. Along the trail we frightened a porcupine; it crawled up a whitebark pine, and then to our surprise fell to the ground with a thud.

170

At Crystal Creek we left the trail and climbed warm sunny slopes north. Goats have worked out a complex but not at all capricious route from one bench to the next; we followed their path with admiration and delight. Dropping packs beside a little lake near timberline, we set off for "Pennant Peak," the mountain which supports The Flagpole. Several hours of pleasant roped climbing brought us to the summit, where we stood amazed, silent and staring. At last Pete said, "Well, shall we take a closer look?" Until now only birds had reached the tip of this solitary rock. We wondered if our equipment was sufficient to reach it too.

To which some of my friends would say, "I can see climbing a mountain like Rainier, but what do you get from scaling a rock needle?" To which I answer, there are those who receive a rich reward climbing peaks that allow a restful frame of mind, with only a rare spark of distant adventure glinting through the long plodding hours, but I find it necessary to keep busy in the hills —even if it is only gathering wood, sorting pitons, or planning future ascents. And to me, the emotional and imaginative benefits of mountaineering are intensified and magnified by the challenge of the unknown.

Alpinism is kinesthetic. It is a "sport," and its attraction therefore depends on the struggle for victories and on the great range of emotions provoked by physical effort. As has often been pointed out, the happiness of the climber comes from the dominion of mind over body, but there is also delight in solving difficult problems, in pitting skill and experience against nature's forces and formations. Certainly the fullest values are obtained when *both* the climb and the victory are the prizes sought.

Achievements come from turmoil, and some are worth the price of pain. Men have often been motivated to seek goals that have no remuneration in themselves and that lie outside any obvious path of "duty." The essence of sport is the duel between the spirit of man and the limitations of matter; the mind must dominate the body. Nowhere is the contrast between apparent peril and actual security more dramatic than in rock climbing.

The Flagpole did not appear to stand very secure. My imagination ran amok with visions of the whole spire toppling over while we were on it. After a complicated traverse, descent, and climb to the base, we examined the great needle with awe. The short, facing edge was at least 75 feet tall, but only here could we see any cracks, and these were thin and intermittent. I climbed a small pedestal and placed a short spoon piton with a thin tip. It held stress, so I snapped in a carabiner, inserted a sling, and went higher. Soon the crack became so poor pitons had no right to be there. I cautioned Pete to be alert for a fall. A knife-blade folded as I hammered, chipping out a small wedge of rock and further diminishing the crack's usefulness. Unnatural strains in my muscles set off the uncontrollable quivering of "sewing-machine leg." Looking up, I could see bolts would now be needed. Dusk was close, so I left the pitons in place and descended the rope on tension.

We rappelled directly down the west wall beneath the spire, leaving a long fixed rope behind. Our camp by the lake was cosy, allowing a much-needed sleep.

In the morning Pete took the first of several alternating leads, placing three bolts before descending for a rest. The pitch proved as difficult as any we had ever done, requiring still more bolts. Higher up I tried to climb a crack past an overhanging block, but decided this way was too risky. I hammered in, sideways, a giant angle piton, and placed a sling—which luckily held my weight. To expedite matters I caught the tip of the block overhead with a short loop of spare rope, and soon was on the summit, which is perhaps 5 feet square. The sheer drop on all sides made me feel I really *was* sitting on a flagpole. Remaining on my knees, I drove a bolt for the rappel. Soon we could turn the spire back to the birds.

12

Steep Rock on Index

The popularity of Index as a view dates from 1893, when the Great Northern Railway began passenger service through the Skykomish valley from Puget Sound to the East. The three peaks of Index, meaning "finger" in local etymology, tower 2500 feet above treeline and 5000 feet above the valley floor. Quite possibly no other large peak in the state, not even the most famous, has been observed close-up by so many people for so many years. True, one can drive on paved road to Austin Pass, Paradise Valley, or Spirit Lake, and admire the rugged heights of Shuksan or Rainier, or the shining slopes of St. Helens, without leaving the car. But in each case the view has been the objective. The nearest, or North Peak of Index, on the other hand, though rising only to a modest 5357-foot altitude, towers so abruptly above a major highway and rail crossing of the Cascades as to be a most spectacular landmark.

Cascade mountain valleys have much in common with the Appalachians. Pioneers make a living off the land or their cattle, working in logging camps or grubbing into the dirt of stump ranches. The older barns and homes are built of native timber and usually roofed with hand-split cedar shakes. In logging headquarters like Sultan and Gold Bar, the lumberjacks keep the beer taps running free on Saturday nights. Index shares the bleak and elemental frontier atmosphere of these foothill towns. It was a brisk mining center in 1898 with over

Author on the Index Town Wall, the Town Crier route. Photo by David Beckstead.

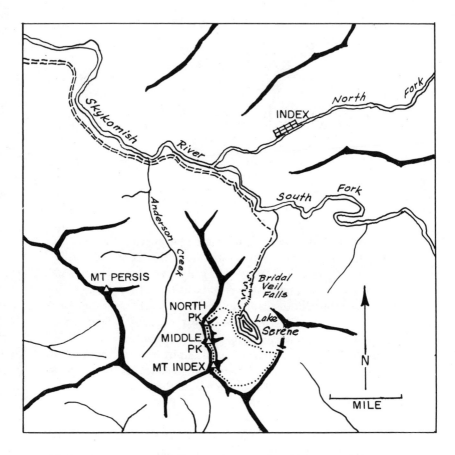

1000 prospectors, and the gateway to the Silver Creek prospecting, which began in 1882 and led to the discovery of Monte Cristo.

From Amos Gunn's tavern miners once offered a reward to any daredevil inclined to risk an ascent of the North Peak. They had no takers. In 1929 Lionel Chute and a companion announced they had reached the summit, but climbing journals took no notice, and little credence would ever have been given their claim had they not placed an identifiable stick on top. Until the second ascent, in 1939, and the finding of the stick—by Otto Trott and Erick Larson—mountaineers generally discredited this first climb. Chute's ascent was an astonishing achievement in view of his relative inexperience in alpine arts and the length and intricacy of the route. He found it necessary to bivouac on the peak, but then so did Trott and many others since. Probably over half of those who have set out for the top have been defeated. Several years after Chute's ascent, there was one well-publicized accident, a long fall and injury to Joe Halwax that necessitated a tricky rescue by local miners. Despite a steady build-up of interest among climbers, only six parties were successful through 1949, though the next summer saw four more. Lionel Chute deserves a salutation not previously given him; he was far ahead of his time.

American mountaineering did not follow the European pattern, and though beginning later, developed its own strong individual flavor and tradition. Americans have led the trend away from elaborate expeditions with guides to informal, self-sufficient groups. And in contrast to many ranges in the world, peaks of the Cascades for the most part have fallen to climbers from nearby cities rather than to men from other nations. Europe generated climbing within a clearly-defined and somewhat restricted social and economic framework, but in the Cascades the early climbers set out for the hills as a result of impulse, without guides, entirely on their own, and relied largely on verve, scrambling, and ingenuity. The use of the rope and other tools was often poorly understood; early-day mass pilgrimages up volcanoes were unique to the Pacific Northwest and Japan.

In 1940 Helmy and I tried the North Peak of Index, but by bearing too far left on the cliffs to the great "hanging brush patch" lost so much time we did not get beyond the "Bowl" in mid-face. Many parties have become confused in this lower area and remember it as a very special sort of experience. On May 16, 1942 Walt Varney and Bob Craig joined us for another attempt on Chute's route. Using nailed boots, we reached the notch on the final ridge, only to be hit by a violent rainstorm. The snowfield in the Bowl was avalanching and for us—with only two axes—very dangerous. On the wet descent, our fingers

The west face of the three peaks of Index, at sunset. Photo by Ed Cooper.

became so numb from the cold we could barely grasp the rope. We were as miserable and soaked as it is possible to be. On July 1, 1945 Helmy and I at last succeeded, leaving the car at 2:15 A.M., reaching the top at 12:30, and returning to the car at 8 P.M. It turned out to be the third ascent, and the first without a night on the peak.

On those trips began my fascination with the North Peak's east face, rising some 2300 feet above talus and 3000 feet above Lake Serene and offering no apparent route. The wall is best seen from the lake in the clear atmosphere of morning, when one can study the slabs in direct sunlight.

Acceptance of the challenge had to await the development of modern "rock engineering," with liberal usage of pitons. It also had to await Tom Campbell's cheery voice on the phone one evening in June of 1941. "Say, Fred, hot weather is here. What do you think of trying the east face this Sunday?" That day's dawn found the two of us, with Jim Crooks, entering the shadow of the river forest.

At the lake, resting from the short but very steep trail (more a ladder of tree roots), we scanned the rock for a line of attack. There seemed only one way to get on the wall, this being the components of a slab gangway running left from the north corner.

Looking up from talus at the base we glimpsed a small tree standing on the face some 500 feet above. What was beyond? No one could tell. Many climbers of the day were stirred by the mystery, a subject of frequent discussion, but as yet no exploration on the wall had been conducted.

In tennis shoes we spent an hour reaching the left extremity of the sloping gangway. The exposure became greater as we mounted; a few pitons were reassuring. By now the sun had climbed above the outline of the main or South Peak to shine directly on our backs. Below, the cool, shimmering lake tortured our parched mouths. The possibility of climbing directly upward was translated with startling abruptness from the abstract to the actual when a 75° trough broke the continuity of the sloping ledge. After climbing part of the trough I led up a knobbed rib, placing all the pitons I could make stick in the scanty cracks; protection was badly needed. Though climbers seek difficult routes, they are generally relieved when difficulties prove less than expected. So it was here, when we found we could "ease up" several rope-lengths.

The self-confidence induced by such precipices is wholly delightful in itself. Even though climbing is not necessarily more dangerous than other sports, the tonic of peril is out of all proportion to the risk. The exquisite relief of safety after danger, the quasi-mystical happiness of moments when the mind has established complete dominion over the body, are part of the answer to "why we climb." Climbing is perhaps the most complete physical sport, demanding continuous coordination of all the faculties. Each difficult ascent is a challenge to physical prowess blended with a peculiarly personal delight in conquest.

Above us, the wall steepened again. We explored several frustrating leads, then examined a shallow chimney with no apparent upward outlet. But, there was a clump of bushes 100 feet higher, a little to the right. Perhaps we could cross to them.

I went up 20 feet and placed some pitons for safety; they did not really seem sound enough to stop a fall, so I took great care crossing a little sill to the bushes. My fingers ached from clinging to tiny holds, but I made it.

That pitch was the crux of the climb, but we needed far more than a Sunday. In a quick review of the 500 feet separating us from the angular transverse ledge that is the dominant feature of the upper face, it appeared this next section would be the ace of trumps. Though we failed to complete the ascent the mission had been valuable. Now all we had to do was figure how to rappel down.

Our trivial success spurred Tom and me to try another exploration on July 19. This time, aided by a bivouac at the foot of the rock and familiarity with the route, by 8 in the morning we reached a point not far from our earlier efforts. To avoid the chimney we considered a wall that led plausibly and directly to the bush clump, first rising gradually from a scree ledge, then in a 30-foot vertical cliff to the overhanging vines.

In 20 minutes I found myself spreadeagled in a shallow V-crack, unable to progress and some distance above my last solid piton. Comfortably perched on the belaying ledge, Tom shook his head slowly and said, "Fred, if there was water ahead you'd get up."

At the moment I needed a physical push, not stimulation. There were no piton cracks at all. My left hand and foot groped uselessly. A trailing branch of vine maple gave me a rather scary idea; it held a momentary test, all I dared make. Balancing my weight between the limber maple and what holds the other hand could find, I rose, hugging the wall for friction, to a lip of rock and burrowed thankfully into a thicket of branches. We had cut our time in half and used only 9 pitons instead of 20.

The remainder of the attempt was anticlimax. Tom came up rapidly and we climbed a number of pitches over continuous downslab, often covered with a thin peel of treacherous moss. Finally a cliff forced us left to a rib bordering a deep canyon culminating above in a cave-like overhang near the transverse ledge. Foreshortening gave a most deceitful impression of these pitches, and now the wall appeared to steepen even more. Progress bogged down so we descended, considering the climb bordering on the unjustifiable.

Early in the summer of 1951 Pete Schoening and I decided to review the route to the rib near mid-face. We felt better equipment and more rigorous preparation would allow a continuation beyond that point. Since the early years of my climbing career I had found that in ascents like this patience and endurance are

The east face of the Index peaks, rising above the cirque of Lake Serene (hidden) and Bridal Veil Falls. On the right is North Peak, the ordinary route partially shadowed and the east-face route in sunshine. Photo by Ed Cooper.

more important than great strength. Good conditioning—much more intensive than one gets in the ordinary course of climbing —is essential to avoid nervous exhaustion. This includes running, which builds resistance to cramps and trains muscles for strains beyond normal use. Sometimes, after work during the week, I would run 1 or 2 hours around Seward Park, Green Lake, or on suburban Seattle roads. In winter, walking up the ski hill to avoid paying the lift ticket provided off-season conditioning, as well as inexpensive skiing.

Several logging spurs had been newly built toward Bridal Veil Falls when we arrived in the vicinity on a June day, and at the second unmarked fork we were confused. Driving mountain roads is not an inadequate introduction to guideless climbing: routefinding can be an intriguing problem. We examined tire tracks and finally decided on a rough bed of stones that seemed to lead to the falls—the "signpost" traditionally used to pick up the unmarked and unmaintained trail to Lake Serene.

After the interval of years, the east face struck me as all new and strange. My vivid memories seemed to have no relation to where we were. Anyone who sits down immediately after returning from a climb and writes a concise statement of the route is surprised by much he has already forgotten, or didn't see in the first place—and how faulty are the descriptions published by others in journals and guidebooks. Honest witnesses in court often give irreconcilable accounts; unless trained, memory is anything but infallible.

Vital questions had to be asked. Could we climb the gray wall directly to the transverse ledge? Or would we be able to follow a line of very steep cracks along the right edge of the vertical rock canyon? Pete climbed with extraordinary skill to the end of a tilted slab; he thought the latter plan offered more hope. But it would be a long, dangerous tour with relentless exposure. Our final plans called for a party of four to cope with the complications of rope-handling and anchorage. To facilitate the next try we left all our spare line anchored to belay points.

On a Saturday in July Pete, with Dick McGowan, "fixed" a route up parts of the lower half of the east face, leaving ropes on the worst passages. This enabled Pete, Dick Berge, Jim Henry, and me to tackle the line of cracks along the canyon very early on Sunday. Twice invisible rocks tore down by us with a droning hum, distressingly close. Pete and Jim were the first rope. Stopped by a holdless section, Pete placed a piton, and with the aid of a nylon-tape sling around a small tree, mounted onto the slab, proceeding here with pious reliance on the edges of the crack, for there was little foot support. Beyond another tree anchorage came the part unanimously voted the hardest. We drove pitons when the crack would support them; more often we hooked tape slings around tiny trees, often growing 2 or 3 feet straight out even on vertical walls.

Exposure was now complete. Looking down the rope the eye could see only the blue lake. It took moral fiber to ignore the void, but fear must not be allowed to captivate the mind. "Be either the hammer or the anvil," Goethe said; we determined to be the hammer.

Hardly any time at all separated late morning from the sinking afternoon sun. We were busy, always. A drink from the canteen and a few squares of chocolate gave new force for a fresh effort on the final cliffs. The slabs leading onto the great transverse ledge—so long remote and unattainable—were broken enough to permit climbing without pitons. Somewhat above the ledge, Berge and I climbed into a crack which looked good as far as we could see—which was only 200 feet. From there a little clump of trees hid a corner; around it, once again a delightful series of unexpected ledges and cracks continued up. A few pitons and tree-slings gave safety on the next three leads; then a shallow crack led to green heather. The evening slant of sunshine so backlighted the slope that not until we came to a heather patch on the final profile of the north ridge did we realize the wall was entirely below us. Waiting for the others, we took off rope and shirts; there was time for a short rest before resuming the way to the summit, a scramble away. Helped by knowledge of the conventional route, we managed to reach the talus in twilight.

In 1950 Pete Schoening and I considered a unique new ascent: a traverse across all three Index peaks. An added incentive was that the Middle Peak was still unclimbed.

Distant views had indicated the best possibility was a high route on or near the crest, but a cloud of anxiety crept into my mind on the summit of North Peak, peering past an intervening gendarme into a deep forbidding gap. We had just completed a warm, pleasant ascent of North Peak in 5 hours, and had at least that many hours of daylight left before we would need to bivouac. We looked far, far down to the curved highway in the valley, and the railway, and the river, but our eyes focused on the knifed ridge of Middle Peak jutting ferociously up from the dark gap. Suspense increased as we rappelled into the gap; a retreat would be hard. The civilized world was below, but we were isolated. All those automobiles and trains couldn't help us if anything went wrong.

Foreshortening had made the 200-foot step above the gap seem almost impossible, but side-lighting now threw its little holds and cracks into proper focus. Belayed by Pete through a piton, I found a reasonable beginning line. Higher I placed two pitons for safety—but halfway in, the upper one folded. When a blank spot baffled me, Pete shouted a suggestion that I get my right foot out on a crack, then pull up to a higher corner. I hurriedly worked out a semblance of his idea, hampered by a bulge in the rock. The next 100 feet went easier, with no need for pitons. Once on the ridge crest we found secure belay spots. The climbing from here to the summit of Middle Peak was exposed, the rock sometimes knifed and fragile. We descended a short distance to a remnant of snow, hoping for water but getting little more than mud, then found a sloping heather patch suitable for bivouac. We roped to a rock anchor: there was a long drop beneath.

Just a few centuries ago only the bravest or most desperate of men dared the torment of a night amid high mountains, objects of worship and fear, a seat for demons and legends, and to the ancients an awful realm between heaven and earth. Terrible

185

folk inhabited the dreaded peaks—not only bandits, who at least were human, but myrmidons, pygmies, fingerlings, devils, ghosts, fairies, and specters. So great was the fear that as late as 1401, when Adam of Usk made a pilgrimage to Rome, he had himself carried blindfolded over St. Gotthard Pass!

On the Middle Peak of Index we welcomed the darkness, which hid the exposure; it also hid from us the uncertainties of the way we would have to travel next morning. By midnight a light fog had formed in the valley but the sky was clear, with neighboring summits penciled in silhouette. The chill gave us insomnia; we passed the long dark hours counting headlights on the highway below and thinking how warm, comfortable, well-fed, un-thirsty, and untroubled were the people within those cars. Eventually the east paled.

An hour after we loosened stiff bones for a start we reached the gap between Middle Peak and South Peak, the 5979-foot summit of Index. A buttress of the South Peak merged into the final face. We studied a series of laminated ledges that seemed to offer the best route. A way up this obstacle had to be found. Once atop the South Peak we would be only a fast scrambling descent from the cool wet waters of Lake Serene.

"Belay on!" Pete called some minutes later, after we had chosen the spot for the initial 100 feet. I followed, hoping.

To describe this north face of South Peak, I can best refer to what others have written about the ordinary route on North Peak, where heather, moss, cedar shrubs, and just plain dirt decorate the way, and where one feels peculiarly isolated from the highway traffic so constantly visible below. What Pete and I went through that morning was the same—but more so.

As we climbed through the mossy rock wall, fog closed off our view of the naked cliffs above, but reaching this final section we saw broken rock leading to the broad summit crown—and to the waters of Lake Serene.

13

The North Wall of Baker

It is remarkable for its beauty of outline, and bears a consider-
able resemblance in this respect to the Jungfrau, the queen of
the Bernese range of the Alps.

Edmund T. Coleman

Soaring a full 7000 feet above a green skirt of forest, a white
cone proportioned in measured symmetry, the perfect dome of
the summit snowcap looming against the sky, it is easy to
understand why Mt. Baker was held in superstitious awe by the
Indians. In Lummi tongue the mountain was "Kulshan," or
"shot at very point." It was their guiding compass and spirit
god, and in legend a fair youth who espoused two wives. One
deserted him, but later became lonely and grew tall from yearn-
ing to look ever northward; as Mt. Rainier, she continues watching. The other went away to be with her island people; Kulshan
had the animals dig a long trench—the Nooksack valley—to
tidewater, so she could visit her.

First notice by Europeans of the peak's existence was on the
map made by the pilot of Manuel Quimper's ship *Princesa Real,*
engaged in exploring the Strait of Juan de Fuca in 1790. The
name which appeared was "La Gran Montana del Carmelo,"
an appellation we can be glad did not last, even though it hon-
ored the Carmelite monks. The name that prevailed was given

Mt. Baker from the north, and the great expanse of the healthy and
advancing Roosevelt and Coleman Glaciers. Aerial photo by Austin Post,
U.S. Geological Survey.

by the English explorer Captain George Vancouver for his mapmaker, Lieutenant Joseph Baker, who sighted it in 1792.

Kulshan, or Baker, rises to 10,750 feet in just 35 miles from tidewater. From the west it stands alone, without rival. Easily seen from most of the Puget Sound region, the Olympic Mountains, and lower British Columbia, Baker displays many moods, often capricious, and is carefully watched by those who have learned, as Lummi people knew, that the peak is a weather prophet: cloudcaps settling onto the summit announce coming storms; the first fresh snow of autumn drops on its slopes, telling of winter's approach. The whitest of the Cascade volcanoes, burdened by one of the heaviest snowfalls in the state, its 12 glaciers are active and some are currently advancing.

Mountains of the west are linked by great fault lines running through the uneasy crust. The 1906 San Francisco earthquake caused avalanches on Baker and exposed lava formations on the Roman Nose and headwalls above the Coleman Glacier. The peak is a monument to ceaseless conflict, with ridges and faces that are mobile and inconstant in the long perspective of geologic time, shaped by the internal forces of creation and the external forces of demolition. A primeval Baker arose just to the west; as the vent shifted, this cone was eroded into the maze of pinnacles now called Black Buttes. In the not-too-distant geologic past explosions radically altered upper features of the present Baker, exploding lava flows for long distances on all sides. The crater on the southeast side of the summit is filled with snow, but internal heat still keeps ridges bare of snow in summer and sometimes the steam and sulfurous fumes from numerous jets and fumeroles along the crater edges build a cloud quite impressive to climbers on the slopes. Generally, though, what is taken for "smoke" is nothing more than banner clouds or wind-driven snow. Despite occasional rumors to the contrary, there have been no eruptions, even minor, in recent decades; the last known volcanic activity was in 1860.

Few peaks are climbed by the men living near them, usually engaged as they are in so stern a battle to gain the necessities of life they seek no further elemental hardships. This, substantially, was the case with the Cascades. Indians ventured to the meadows for huckleberry, deer, and an occasional goat, but never felt the impulse to scale peaks, though they did travel on snow, blackening their faces around the eyes when doing so. Settlers were too busy chopping, slashing, and grubbing to think of mountains in terms of recreation. The prospectors, a special breed never noted for cool logic, were the first to invade the Cascades in force; some of them, drawn by a particularly-intense strain of madness, deliberately climbed ridges and peaks in their search for rich claims.

When the first true mountaineers came to the Cascades, they largely confined their efforts to the volcanoes, the highest and grandest summits yet at the same time offering the fewest technical difficulties. One of the first "sporting" mountaineering expeditions in the Northwest was that by Edmund T. Coleman, an Englishman with experience in the Alps. From his home in Victoria he admired Kulshan, and over several years, on several trips, sought its summit. In 1864 Coleman, Judge Charles Ben Darwin, and a Dr. Brown canoed up the "Skagett" River with Indians, but when they reached the confluence of a stream from the base of the mountain called the "Tukullum" (also called the "Nahcullum" by some Indians but renamed the "Baker" in 1877 by Otto Klement), the "koma" Indians who lived there declined to allow them to proceed. Learning that the natives on the Whatcom side were friendly, Coleman and John Bennett returned in 1866, coming from Victoria to reach close to the summit, only to be blocked by ice girdling the summit dome. In 1868, after canoeing from Victoria to Bellingham Bay, then paddling up the Middle Fork of the Nooksack River with a month's food supply and traversing many miles of wilderness just to reach the mountain, he and three companions were successful. They had spiked boots and "creepers," which had been made for the climb. Still they cut 400 steps where they estimated the summit slope at 60°. His route, via the Coleman Glacier to the saddle above the Black Buttes, is now the most commonly used way to the summit. The difficulty of approach is indicated by one of his summit companions, David Ogilvy, who wrote the "party traveled up the Lummi and Nootsac Rivers by canoe 80 miles, then 20 miles through a desperate country to . . . the foot of the mountain."

That early climbers had ingenuity as well as drive is shown by the August 1892 solo ascent of the steeper northeast side of the mountain by the rancher, miner, and blithe spirit, Joe Morovits, using only a hand ax for support. He climbed the Rainbow Glacier, choosing this steep route by pure chance. At the Cockscomb his partners halted and he continued alone. Two years later he was with a group that pioneered the ridge between the Park and Boulder Glaciers. On his seventh ascent he led The Mountaineers up his "Morovits" route.

Morovits was widely known as the jolly "Hermit of Baker Lake," where he lived alone for 27 years, prospecting, building trails, and running a one-man mine and stamp mill. He created a legend of incredible feats of strength by packing heavy mining gear from Baker City (Concrete) and singlehandedly driving over 1000 feet of tunneling. It was said he customarily carried a 100-pound pack from the store on the Skagit River 32 miles to his homestead. Eventually his ranch became a kind of headquarters for mountaineers seeking guidance.

After the turn of the century the mountain attracted wider interest: Mazamas led by F. H. Kiser climbed via the head of the Mazama Glacier in 1906, claiming they were the first from the north and northeast (for some reason that is not clear they did not acknowledge the earlier solo ascent by Morovits), and in 1908 The Mountaineers made the first "large party" ascent. Three years later 14 local loggers turned up for a "Mt. Baker Marathon," a race timed from Bellingham to summit and return. Contestants traveled by train, horses, wagons, then by foot, any means or route being fair. The contest was staged annually for several years, enlivened by betting excitement and such incidents as the time a train was derailed when it struck a bull.

Nowadays a highway thrusts through Glacier, where scattered clumps of trees give something of a lingering woodland charm

The north wall of Mt. Baker, showing the north ridge first-ascent line. In foreground, green and pleasant ridges. Photo (of unknown date, but old) by Clyde Banks.

to this farthest-upvalley trading center in the Nooksack. The timber industry continues as king here, steadily stripping the green slopes of Baker and its neighbors, ruining the scenic integrity, and it was a logging road built along Glacier Creek to Heliotrope Ridge in 1947 and 1948 that forever destroyed a classic wilderness approach to a Cascade volcano: 10 miles through forest to Kulshan Cabin and then into meadows and onto glaciers streaming from the summit.

The steep northern walls of Baker had been avoided by climbers, not only because there are many other simpler routes, but because of the danger from rockfall and ice avalanches. On the western part of these walls are exposed great overlapping layers of lava, 2–50 feet thick, each layer representing a distinct eruption. Above these is a rim of moving glacier ice. The safest probability seemed to be a snub-nosed ridge dividing the Coleman Glacier headwall and the cascading ice of the Roosevelt Glacier.

Not until a sunny August weekend in 1948 was my urge to explore this route gratified. As is typical of many mountain partnerships, this one was formed one morning by several quick telephone calls. Leaving our respective breakfast dishes undone, Ralph and Dick Widrig, cousins, and I drove to Glacier, where climbers and skiers alike always seem to stop for ice cream or other refreshment. The new logging road wound through dense trees which interlaced to form an evergreen canopy; the rich green gloom of forest was occasionally brightened along the sandy banks of the creek by the white bark of alders and the smooth gray stems of cottonwoods.

My feelings of loss for the old wilderness trail were somewhat relieved by noting that the new logging was being done in relatively small patches, in contrast to the older and enormous clear-cuts in the Nooksack valley. There are three schools of thought about logging in our National Forests. Some think the Forest Service should find every possible way in which the land can be used and, guided by the principle of "multiple-use," extract the maximum amount of every conceivable use; others believe our publicly-owned forests should be used purely to benefit and enrich private enterprise; and there are those who feel our shrinking heritage of wildlands should be held in trust for future recreational and economic needs. My own sympathies have always been with those who seek to preserve and even restore wilderness areas surrounding scenic climaxes, protecting them from short-sighted greed, while conceding the non-climax valleys, lovely as they surely are, to the dreary but perhaps inescapable economics of "multiple-use." It has been pointed out in *The Wild Cascades* that "trees can be grown, and much more efficiently, in many other parts of the Northwest and the nation, but the scenic and recreational values of the North Cascades can be found in no other part of the United States." In the foreword to the book, Justice William O. Douglas, one of the most articulate of wilderness defenders, warns that "our time, in America, is pivotal in regard to wilderness." Our remaining pockets of wildlands are now very small by comparison with frontier days, and it is vital that we recognize what Douglas and many others have stressed: "The wilderness of the North Cascades is a *national* resource of the future, not merely a local commodity to favor local industry."

Kulshan Cabin stands near timberline, and after dropping packs there we walked to the meadows above. Through clumps of dwarfed and flattened mountain hemlocks and alpine firs firmly rooted in rock crevices, we scanned the Coleman Glacier and its crevasse patterns, looking for the simplest route across to the north face of the mountain. The steep wall of blue ice on the upper ridge glistened in the evening sun, giving us something to think about as we walked back down to the cabin through fields of squaw grass, the club-shaped spikes of white flower topping tall scaly stalks.

A dozen chipmunks, the happiest creatures in the woods, scurried about scavenging food tidbits while we prepared dinner over an open fire outside the cabin. Gray jays or "camprobbers," a mischievous lot guilty of no little villainy, kept flitting around our food and equipment even after dark; several times they ate right from Ralph's hand.

195

Except for the lack of nearby snow, this still and mysterious summer evening was identical with another evening the year before, when I had visited here on skis during a winter ascent. Nothing had changed. The icy giant rising from the shadowed valley was faintly alight between the trees, seeming too large by far to be the same peak over whose broad summit I had left tracks of boots and skis on climbs past. But then came full night, and an outburst of stars, and the mountain grew small; the terrestrial faded to insignificance. I thought of Wordsworth's lines:

"His daily teachers had been woods and rills,
  The silence that is in the starry sky,
  The sleep that is among the lonely hills."

We drank tea and told stories quite late—much too late for the task at hand. The stories were so amusing and the firelight so entrancing we simply had no desire for the cabin bunks. When we did, well after midnight, we were kept awake by the pattering of the agile deer mice, a creature of the night and particularly of old cabins and much-used camps.

Sleep was scant because we had vowed to start before dawn, a vow Dick and Ralph had some difficulty getting me to recall. After several pleas to "sleep another half-hour" we finally got underway, without much of a breakfast, and mounted first grassy and then pumiced slopes, arriving at the glacier edge as dawn came. To our right were the Black Buttes, which Edmund Coleman named "Colfax" and "Lincoln" and which historian Charles Easton likened to a Chinese wall, "a solid, homogeneous mass of black basalt. . . . minaretted at the summit." Above was the white wall of the face. We roped and began working through intricate crevasses, aiming for the base of the spur ridge in the center of the face. The stars went out one by one until only the morning star remained.

Suddenly the flat toneless snows at our feet sparkled into a mosaic of glittering light and pearl-grey shadow. There was grace and vitality in the glowing slopes of sun-reflecting crusty

The Black Buttes from slopes of Mt. Baker. Author made the first ascent of the West Butte from the far side, crossing Heliotrope Ridge and Thunder Glacier. Photo by Ed Cooper.

snow—the chill shadows retreated and our bodies relaxed in the golden flood of wine-like warmth. Objectively this view would not change if made accessible without labor, by tramway. "We become what we behold," said Blake. But the view is not the same for the man who pays for beauty in the currency of toil.

Ralph had led us skillfully through the maze, and until awakened by the glory of the alpine sun it was all I could do to plod along behind. They both agreed a little stepkicking would help arouse me, so we reversed ends of the rope and the task soon set sluggish blood circulating. I didn't have to look behind to see how my companions were faring; I could subconsciously feel their presence. Our track led over several large patches of "red snow," colored by an alga which awakens in summer from winter dormancy and apparently is the only living organism able to endure such temperature extremes; in other parts of the world various alga turn the snow brown, green, or yellow.

The snow had become quite frozen, and stepkicking so chilled our feet we put on crampons. An open crevasse briefly barred the way, but so beautiful was the translucent bridge of our crossing we forgave the inconvenience. Warmed by the sun, lava layers close on the right discharged rock pellets and ice blocks, some of which cascaded down the nearby precipice and others on the bleak Roman Wall farther west. It reminded me of a passage from Byron, who described the Grindelwald Glacier "like a frozen hurricane" and when crossing the Scheidegg wrote, "Heard avalanches falling every five minutes nearly—as if God was pelting the Devil down from Heaven with snow balls."

We kept near the crest of the snub-nosed ridge between the Coleman headwall and the Roosevelt and thus were reasonably safe, but that Baker can be a terrible adversary is shown by the 1939 avalanche that swept wet snow off the Roman Wall and on the slope used by most parties, often in similar conditions, killed five members of a Bellingham group.

We looked up to the blue sky, ghostly and insubstantial, and to the very real precipice of snow and ice toward which we were climbing. The atmosphere was charged with color, pools of green, blue, and gold brilliance spilling on foothills, forests, and mountain in a changing kaleidoscope. To the north billowed several dramatic clouds. In the vast silence of dazzling white above 9000 feet we felt closer to the sky than earth. Far below the shining thread of the glacial Nooksack could be traced here and there, running through green forests. In a moment of frank provincialism, we wondered if there could be more beautiful mountains anywhere.

The morning breeze abruptly and completely vanished; the once-exhilarating sun became an oppressive weight. I moistened my very dry mouth with a swallow of canteen water and ate a piece of chocolate. Soon, though, none of us felt any desire to eat—or to climb. During the next half-hour our strength ebbed away until every step was hard labor. We regretted our lack of sleep.

Then the breeze returned, giving Ralph new energy, and his optimism was contagious. Fatigue had made the ice wall seem impossibly distant, though in fact only a few hundred feet above. Soon we saw that to outflank the worst parts we would have to climb its left edge, where the ridge narrows quite sharply. The wall on the right is shorter but more vertical; the ridge, rising at an angle varying between 50° and 65°, looked more feasible.

Himalayan and Andean ice ridges are notorious for sharpness and no edges in the Cascades equal those fragile crests. But here to the left we stared down the longest ice slopes we had seen that summer, and to the right the wall fell away to a steep cliff of rotten lava and black ice. Where the angle increased above 45° Ralph chopped a large stance in the ice, and when he had his belay ready I began chopping a line up the steep ridge, adjusting each blow carefully, shaping each step almost like a work of art. We had soft-steel, barbed ice pitons to protect leads and to anchor belays. For 2 arduous hours I chopped, maintaining a delicate, strained balance on chipped-out handholds. On the second lead, though, we had a bit of luck: a curious small ice cavern large enough for a cold sitting belay. Ralph did all the shivering belaying of those 2 hours; Dick came last, hacking out the pitons as he climbed.

Above the wall the slope angle decreased, but hopes for fast, non-belayed progress were premature. The crest became blue ice covered with loose snow and filmy crusts so variable in depth we could not trust ice-ax belays. We were forced to excavate large stances for body belays, and to scrape away loose material before cutting a step. But despite all problems the ridge was exhilarating, a celestial pathway with only blue sky above.

The covering on the ice became thicker; it was a relief to reach a wall of compact névé. The interminable slope suddenly eased off and we stood on a nearly level ridge crest with the summit visible only a few hundred feet above. A giant bergschrund blocked passage directly ahead to the summit dome, so we made a traverse left between large crevasses toward the exact summit, a little pumice mound peeping through the ice. Ten hours had elapsed since we left the cabin. Knowing the descent via the ordinary Coleman Glacier route would take only a few hours, we relaxed to admire the panorama of islands west, forests around, and glittering mountains east.

Arriving at the logging road next morning, we found a parked truck; perhaps from laziness or perhaps from contempt for the logging, we coasted it several miles down to our car, adding a little spice to our adventure.

Once pioneered, the north wall of Baker was seen in new perspective; direct ascents of the Roosevelt Glacier and the Coleman Glacier headwall have been made, and our route has been frequently repeated.

14

Dolomites in America

"The perpendicular spires of the unclimbed Mt. Liberty Bell across the valley look difficult." So said Herman Ulrichs, writing about his early climbs in the vicinity of Washington Pass, a region that in a coming day of popularity may well be known as the "Dolomites of the West"—not for the rock, which is igneous, but for the resemblance to those famous peaks of the Eastern Alps. Between the head of Lake Chelan and the upper Methow River is an area of pink granitic rock eroded into ridges serrated with fantastically-formed spires, domes, and pinnacles. North of Harts Pass rise the high, rolling peaks of the Pasayten country, principally monstrous heaps of debris—splendid country for the hiker and scrambler but aside from a few exceptions not likely to make the climber sentimental. Even more empty of alpine challenge, though again a heaven for the hillwalker, is the main range to the south, which swings along the Chelan Crest east of the lake and merges with high ridges branching toward the Methow; the unrivalled monarch here is the enormous mass of 8910-foot Mt. Gardner.

Earlier climbs on Kangaroo Ridge etched these granitic peaks in my memory and whetted my appetite for more. In late September of 1946 I returned to the Washington Pass area with two friends, Chuck Welsh and Jerry O'Neil.

Author on a winter ski approach to Mt. Silver Star, with Burgundy Spire in the background. Photo by Mike Borghoff.

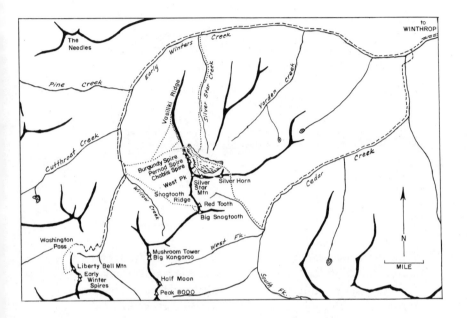

The highway from Wenatchee passes white, yellow, and brown cliffs and then sunburned hills of sagebrush rising above the Columbia River valley, the river itself now drowned by reservoirs behind Rocky Reach and Wells Dams. In wagon-road days travelers took the steamer *City of Ellensburg* up the Columbia to Ives Landing at the mouth of the Methow. Now the gateway to the picturesque Methow valley is Pateros, with its dusty, shady streets. The parched valley always seems to implore vainly the benediction of rain, and only the strip of privileged earth along the meandering river shows lush green clover and groves of black cottonwood whose higher leaves are set in motion by the wind. Though the valley is narrow, often the hills draw back from the gentle slopes or level meadows of alluvial terraces. Here there are orchards, houses, grazing animals, and irrigated fields. Mining in the '90s brought a big boom to the Methow; gold, silver, lead, tungsten, and copper were prospected for and some ore taken out. But today fruit-raising, farming, and dairying are the chief sources of wealth. The trading centers of Twisp and Winthrop take on the appearance of pioneer towns on weekends; it is common to see men riding in from farms and ranches with tanned faces, spurs, Stetson hats, and blue levis. Until just recently Winthrop marked the end of hard-surfaced road. The town is much the same as when Owen Wister lived there among the scenes and people who appeared later in his novel, *The Virginian.* I asked the proprietor of a local hotel to point out where Wister's cabin was. "Nothing has changed much, even the jail by the river there, but we've got running water now," she replied with pride.

The vertical is the keynote of mountain majesty, and behind a long vista of road beyond town the sweeping uplift serves as a foil to emphasize contrast. Approaching the head of the valley, orchards and farms give way to pine forests. Beyond the sign which read "Early Winters Creek" we turned off to the end of a dusty spur road. There the 16-mile trail to Washington Pass began. In glacial times a large body of ice descended the canyon of Early Winters Creek, as noted by Professor I. C. Russell on his probe—perhaps the first by white men—into the valley.

On the trail next day we passed through a most beautiful alp, hundreds of acres of perfect meadow occasionally grazed by flocks of sheep. In a few hours the clearly-cut granite helmet forming Liberty Bell came into full view, a sight that shocked us out of our afternoon trail lethargy. At the pass we camped in a delightful meadow beside a row of spruce trees. A little stream supplied water. We kept close to the fire, for frost soon rimmed every bit of vegetation. The stars—crisp and clear above the dome of Liberty Bell, now in deep, cold shadow—spoke of a perfect morning. Orion's belt and Sirius shone with unnatural brilliance; later, shimmering and colorful Northern Lights streamed over the dark shoulder of Cutthroat Peak. "There is," as St. Augustine said, "a morning and evening in all mortal things." A morning of new adventure was soon to begin, one with lasting memories.

Today people see the same view from their cars. But do they? I think not. The views earned by long hours of toil are more wonderful than those gained in comfort. Scenery the lazy never

205

see seems lovelier than the idle can enjoy. Arnold Lunn emphasizes the close connection between the ascetic and esthetic: "It would puzzle a materialist to explain how frequently the reward of beauty is associated with the discipline of toil, as if nature consciously reserves her noblest effects for those who take some trouble to earn them."

As if it were yesterday I remember awaking to see the first hint of color intrude on darkness. The peak was no longer a shadowy line, but was drawn with sharp precision against velvet sky, and the dawn lit up a plume of silver fog trailing from a ridge.

Liberty Bell first appeared in alpine history in July 1937, when four Sierra Club climbers (Raffi Bedayn, Ken Adam, Ken Davis, Neil Ruge) visited the region. "Our first choice was Mount Liberty Bell, which appeared difficult on all sides," they wrote. Presuming the southerly and highest of the three principal summits of this striking formation was the one intended by the Forest Service map to be "Liberty Bell," they climbed it by the only simple route in the area, at the same time referring to the more challenging-appearing "north peak." My own feeling, since my Kangaroo Ridge climbs, was the descriptive name was meant for this "north peak," which does indeed tower like a bell above Washington Pass. Ultimately, in the course of many conversations through the years, my nomenclature prevailed, with the two southerly peaks (the ones Varney and Crooks raved about after their scouting hike through the pass in 1941) taking on the name "Early Winter Spires."

Since the facing north side of Liberty Bell seemed inaccessible with the equipment we had, we planned to reconnoiter the west side, where gullies carved the rock into towers and steep talus fingers. In 2 hours we were well within the domain of the walls, climbing to a notch on the south side of the final summit, perhaps 400 feet below the virgin peak.

Directly above, the rock was well-broken in cracks and joints, but higher up steepened to smooth slabs; more inviting was a route facing approximately southwest. The first 100 feet followed a pronounced rib to a ledge. The angle then increased, and deciding better climbing could be found elsewhere, we traversed left to a corner. Here Welsh gave me a firm belay as I climbed a short crack to the top of the buttress. While belaying my partners I could see out to Bridge Creek and the forest to the west. It was a perfect morning to enjoy the beauty of creation.

For a short distance easy slabs allowed us to move rapidly toward the summit. When they steepened, as expected, we climbed a narrow overhanging crack, using a piton for safety. A 10-foot finger traverse on a sharp sill ended in a chinning exercise to reach a very flimsy ledge. Blocked from further upward progress I climbed right on its sloping surface, which became continually more slabby and exposed. Two pitons made the belay safer. The holds were sloping the wrong way, but getting my feet on the slabs and lying back with hands pressing firmly downward I was able to delicately climb crabwise to a crack in which I could jam my hands. Then I breathed easier: there was a comfortable ledge for a belay.

After leading the Mummery Crack, Mummery, to prevent the rest of his party from scrambling up with undue facility, thus exposing the Grepon to scorn, judiciously urged them to waste no time and carry their packs. I, too, found this suggestion a material aid in impressing Welsh and O'Neil with due respect for the pitch. One final little step separated us from the summit. With a shoulder stand we managed it in short order. The summit was ours! The climb was just technically right for our mood.

There was a tranquil loveliness in the slow drift of sun-tinted clouds across the blue sky. Softened by distance, the surrounding country spread out below. The eye being unaided by any foreground, all objects at a distance seemed lifted too high. The only sound was the whirring of a mysterious wind eddying around a corner of the enormous precipice below.

The views were outstanding of Silver Star, Cutthroat, Kangaroo Ridge, and Snagtooth Ridge, and of Golden Horn, which Keith

Rankin, Chuck Welsh, and I had "first-ascented" a fortnight ago. Of the nearby possibilities Snagtooth Ridge interested us as good terrain for our remaining time, and 2 days later we sojourned pleasantly on its four highest summits, each a new ascent. Our last night on Early Winters Creek the rain poured down and we enjoyed the luxury of late sleeping. The radio alleviated the monotony of the long drive home through dark towns and the empty night: for 50 miles it was the old Vienna of Mozart, then hours of jazz to keep the driver awake.

Over the 1952 Memorial Day weekend I again visited the soft, pine-covered hills of the Methow, which so much resemble the approach to the Dauphine Alps. Old memories revived. It was all so familiar. Had I ever left?

Since the challenging north peak of Early Winter Spires, adjacent to Liberty Bell, had been climbed by Pete Schoening, Wes Grande, and Dick Widrig in 1950, 8900-foot Silver Star, with its 3-mile ridge of sharp spires, became our objective. We were spurred, too, by the thought of the "spectacular western peak" described by Ulrichs on his first ascent of Silver Star.

The dry, fresh morning air stirred Herb Staley, Joe Hieb, Don Wilde, and me on our hike to camp at the trapper's cabin 11 miles up Early Winters Creek. From timberline next morning we decided to begin scaling the unclimbed towers on the long ridge north of Silver Star. Staley, a modern Lord Byron, engineered the nomenclature: Bacchus, Aphrodite, Ares, and Charon were among the names he bestowed. The changing temper of the weather told us this would be a day of capricious moods; the wind struck our faces maliciously at the col overlooking the glacier cradled into the north slope of Silver Star. Climbing a slope of crusted snow beneath the four upper spires, we marched in cadence to the col separating the summits. It was 7 in the evening.

No memories are more enduring than of moments when a strenuous effort culminates in an unexpected view. The last slopes of the west peak were treacherously-steep, snow-covered

The two Early Winter Spires, on left, and Liberty Bell, the most striking rock formation in the mountains of the Methow River. These east- and north-facing walls offer a host of difficult routes. Photo by Steve Marts.

rock, demanding careful movements and constant belaying. The bizarre overhanging final block required a court e'chelle. But what I recall most poignantly is the austere summit scene: the sinking sun piercing a canopy of level clouds hiding all but a handful of the highest peaks, the billows reflecting purpled sky above a vast sea of fleece, the rainbow of shifting colors fading to a pale yellow—a sunset never to be forgotten.

Time was fleeing with the setting sun. By the time we climbed the main summit and started down the glacier a bright quarter-moon shone over Liberty Bell. While a slight color still lingered on the icy crest of our peak, the ebbing twilight merged imperceptibly into the radiance of the risen moon, and the cloud shadows which had swept up from the valley retreated before a wash of silvery light. Twinkling stars in the eastern sky were beautifully luminous; the enchanting moon, though, diffused its light through thinning clouds, casting a soft glow on the mosaic of slopes and ridges.

A few weeks later I came back with Dick Berge and Wes Grande to do some of the largest spires, numbered from one to four from the south, or in our nomenclature: Chablis, Pernod, Chianti, and Burgundy Spires. The gargantuan slabs of their western faces plummet 1200 feet, and the eastern walls above the glacier tower even more grimly 400 to 800 feet. On first examination, defenses appeared impregnable. Berge, however, expressed faith in a line of fracture cracks on white granodiorite below Chablis Spire. Though the route seemed to verge on the impossible, it turned out to be a delightful belayed climb, and we used only two pitons. The rock was so sound even the most minute holds were sufficient to allow advances. After reaching the exposed tip of Chablis we explored a system of connecting ledges leading north to the notch between Pernod and Chianti Spires. We traced the possibility of a route to the soaring point of Pernod, but after struggling with a slab of granite for 2 hours realized its huge facets would take a full day. Placing two bolts and an assortment of pitons had exhausted our strength; not being anxious to spend the night searching for a route down through the pines we made haste to begin our rappels to the ice.

In early fall I revisited the area to camp at the head of Silver Star Creek. We were partially a new group: Don Wilde, Joe Hieb, Dick McGowan, Art Maki, and myself. The four majestically-proportioned spires rose high above yellowing greens of the deserted meadows. A curtain of orange-flaming larches stood against the background of magical golden rock now whitened with a tracery of fresh snow. Behind our evening campfire transparent shadows were cast by drifting clouds on the vestal loveliness of the glacier snow. Later the wind stirred the branches overhead and the spires were faintly penciled in the night.

Before dawn we crawled from frosty sleeping bags, ate a quick breakfast, and were off for alpine adventure. The air was still. Seldom do rock and snow glisten so brightly as then. In an hour the caress of the sun had comfortably warmed the initial difficult rock stretches. Our route was via the last effort on Pernod Spire. Before 10 we had arrived at the notch and had a lunch of sandwiches and very fresh apples from a Methow orchard. Hieb and Maki elected to try Chianti, the third spire, and we understood their look of tension as they skeptically began a 250-foot rappel down a west-facing couloir. From there they hoped to climb a fork of the gully to the notch beyond the spire; a semblance of a route appeared to lie on that side.

The rest of us set to work on Pernod, and I followed our previous experience to the second bolt. After we assembled on what can be described as a "very inadequate" ledge, and after considerable coaxing by companions, I made a swinging pendulum traverse on a spare rope from the bolt; once started, I was too busy to notice the overhanging exposure. From an awkward position I groped left-handed to a solitary handhold and inched to a steep crack; in 20 feet of nervous movement I arrived at the safety of a cozy platform. It was consoling to see a double-crack leading to a gable 15 feet from the top. McGowan did this 40-foot stretch, using several giant angle pitons. A belay from the gable, not unlike sitting bareback on a horse, gave new protection. Two bolts were needed in the final flawless block; from the highest sling Wilde managed to touch the summit.

Doubts about the success of the other team were dispelled by the sudden appearance of Hieb on the summit ridge of their spire. For several hours the echoes of hammer-ringing had been bouncing around the walls, but we had no idea how high they were. It was amusing to watch them clamber singly to the top of a flawless summit block, a procedure almost identical to ours.

The siege had been a complete success on both fronts, and as the jagged etchings of the spires lengthened their glacier shadows we rappelled down slabby walls to our boots and axes. Stimulated by triumph and chilly air, fleet legs hurried us down the 3 miles of forest along the creek. By midnight we arrived at the car.

Another year brought freshened spirit and muscle. Burgundy, the last unconquered and most imposing of the spires, drew several reconnaissances. In August John Parrott, Mike Hane, and I left the city for a final 3-day attempt. Our new approach via Cedar Creek and a traverse of the Silver Star Glacier to a rock camp provided a much quicker way to the peaks. Since any route on Burgundy from the south notch appeared quite overhanging and hostile, we planned to make the climb via the longer but more-broken north face, which soars 800 feet at a "fascinating" angle before leveling off to the summit spine. Head-on, any route looked like an intense experience, but the profile view suggested a possibility.

We put to good use the few hours of daylight remaining after making camp. We climbed a steep snow gully and 200 feet of small ledges to a previously-established cache. Frowning overhead was a cliff of about 200 feet; of two potential routes we decided on the one to the left. The first lead was up a sloping ledge system where foot-and-hand friction provided the best support. Pitons helped; in fact, quite a few were needed for safety. From the next belay spot the problem was to cross an unfractured slab to a terraced bowl. After a direct approach failed I climbed down 5 feet and frictioned left to a crack, placed pitons until sure one was sound, and then proceeded up to a hold where I could momentarily stop. In 20 feet more there was a small sliver of granite. We tied the rope to it and descended for the day.

Our sleep on the rock outcrop was violently interrupted after midnight by crashing thunder and a cold shower. Morning hopes were dulled by gray cloud wisps, but we set off early on the chance they might scatter. Following the established ropes, we renewed the attack. Mike moved up a line of cracks; but soon the rope ceased to run out. Minutes passed. He was trying to climb an overhanging niche between smooth slabs, a sketchy and inadequate route. With relief we heard the ring of pitons and saw him come into our view again as he used two of these and slings for aid. His prolonged effort on this stretch of scanty holds was exhausting; above, holds seemed to cease altogether. He managed to engineer a meager belay from one good foothold with an angle piton for an anchor.

John followed him up, then climbed through on the next lead. Holding the rope from below I wondered how he would get through the vertical slabs to reach a crack higher to the right. By friction climbing that appeared impossible from below he gained 15 vital feet to another little overhanging niche. Aided by slings and pitons he worked up to a transverse crack. Looking to his right, I saw the crack terminated in an offset fissure. Close behind loomed the bare rocks of the edge of the wall. After an exchange of shouts he assured me it would only take 10 or 15 minutes more, with luck. A line of broken finger holds enabled him to swing agilely to the right. With a protecting piton he then worked delicately to the top of the wall just as Mike loudly warned, "You're out of rope!"

An hour later we explored a granite bowl above the wall. The face narrowed here to slant back into the bowl, then steepened to a pointed spire below the summit. After checking another possibility, discarded as unpromising, we climbed left up a steep but well-fractured wall to a knife-edge arete overlooking the glacier. The sun was out now, but its glorious warmth was almost counteracted by the cool breeze blowing over the edge from the west. We kept our parkas on. It was like Bugaboo climbing at its best: granite rock in glacial surroundings.

The breeze dispelled any possible mid-day sluggishness. I was anxious to get up the squared ridge, if only to keep warm. The route required the usual direct-aid inconveniences: slings, pitons, carabiners, bolts; we even had to lasso a block to get up the exposed final few feet. Now certain the peak's defenses were exhausted, I rigged a solid tension belay while the other two came up by prusik slings on a spare rope. Technique acquired in early years on roofs and bannisters proved its worth on the knifed arete toward the summit spire. By straddling, with a leg over each side, it was possible to move slowly along; at one point it was necessary to stand atop the crest and do a chin-up on an overhang.

One block we bypassed to the left. Now, though, time was running out. Standing in our way was another block, some 40 feet high, apparently holdless. Trusting some way could be found around, we stopped for the day and made long rappels down the route, leaving fixed ropes or carabiner-pulleys in the steepest places. Unfortunately we had no bovou gear with us, so we chose not to stay overnight on the spire.

Block Number Two almost proved our nemesis. The "way around" ended in a flawless wall, and there seemed no chance to traverse out. We could place bolts up the blank face, but that would consume hours. Taking our only other option, we tied a rock to a thin nylon line and John began trying to wing the stone over the tower. After several energetic attempts, amid general amusement, John hit the mark and we were able to pull the line, then a spare rope, over the top.

Each of us had our times of very personal involvement with the route. John's was the most intense as he slowly slid prusik knots up the rope; he couldn't be certain it would stay in place. Nerve tension increased. Finally he clambered safely to the tip, settled down to drill a hole for an anchor bolt, and then continued on, traversing the edge of a tilted flank of the tower and stemming into the open chimney between it and the final tower. From this stemming position, with his back on one wall and feet on the other, he placed another bolt. Then I came up, crossed to the far wall with a sling, and found holds to hoist myself. By placing another bolt I anchored the spare rope so we now had a continuous line strung across the blocks. It was the only safe way. On the summit we mused over the difficulties, and the approximately 30 pitons and 6 bolts. Now we could rest and admire the array of slowly-drifting cumulus.

15

Three Volcanoes

Ye Ice Falls!
Torrents, methinks, that heard a mighty voice,
And stopped at once amid their mightiest plunge!
Motionless torrents! Silent cataracts!
Who made you glorious as the gates of heaven
Beneath the keen full moon.

Hymn Before Sunrise in the Vale of Chamouni
Coleridge

Dormant volcanoes are the best-known aspect of the Cascades. Rainier, tallest of all at 14,410 feet and the most distinctive feature of the range, is the greatest landmark of the Pacific Northwest and by far the largest mountain bulk in the United States outside Alaska. Farther south, contrasting dramatically with the gentle, forested hills that surround them, the three "guardians of the Columbia" rise white and lordly in splendid isolation: 12,307-foot Adams (described in the journals of Lewis and Clark as "perhaps the highest pinnacle in America") is elongated by multiple venting and broadened by erosion differentials; 11,225-foot Hood has a more conical shape marred only by the remains of intermittent eruptions; 9677-foot St. Helens is the prototype of simplicity in volcanic form, with a grace unmatched by the others.

———

Don Gordon crossing a steep ice gut on the Victory Ridge ascent of Mt. Adams. Photo by Fred Beckey.

Adams really is a long ridge, a composite of several great cones and numerous craters; its flanks are vastly irregular, with old glacial scorings and a complex terracing of lava dikes. Sheets of lava once poured out across the land in all directions. The main north-south ridge is comparatively gentle, but as an early mountain writer stated, "on the east and west faces, the cliffs and ice cascades appall even the expert alpinist."

The early climber who knew Adams best, and the first to lead a group up the east side, was C. E. Rusk; in 1921 he used a route via The Castle, between the Klickitat and Rusk Glaciers. Also on the east face, but farther north, is the Wilson Glacier, named by Rusk for the World War president. "The mighty red ridge sandwiched between it and the Rusk Glacier I thought might appropriately bear the name of 'Victory Ridge,' " he wrote in his *Tales of a Western Mountaineer.*

Rusk explored the ridge to 9000 feet, here finding it so "narrow and shattered that it would have been dangerous in the extreme to have attempted further progress." Looking up, "Just to the west, the avalanche-hurling crags of the great precipice loomed, their frowning front crowned by a two-hundred-foot wall of snow. From their northern ramparts the ice-falls of Wilson Glacier plunged wildly downward."

Before 1963 my own experience with Adams consisted of two climbs, each the first ascent of a glacier cascading from the summit to the lava moraines above the belt of whitebark pines: in 1945, the Adams Glacier, largest on the mountain; in 1961, the North Wilson Glacier, a narrow flume of tumbling crevasses. But the real challenge lay where Rusk explored—here was the steepest portion of the great wall and the most direct line to the summit. After a careful study of photos, I felt the climb might be done safely early in the summer on a relatively-cool day—if one hurried. Esthetically, Victory Ridge had exceptional appeal.

I teamed with Don (Claunch) Gordon, who was always in top physical condition, climbed quickly on ice, and was not afraid

—all prerequisites for the undertaking. He was equally interested in the ascent, especially since the appearance in *Summit Magazine* of an article urging the direct route be done.

The evening of July 7, 1963 we bedded down near timberline on the northwest side of the mountain, having hiked in by the usual Killen Creek approach. The night was cool and clear, with glimmering stars. Our plan was to leave early, travel light, and if successful, descend by the north cleaver. We felt that if the climb could be done, we would have to move continually, and in this case extra food and gear would be no help—and if we failed, any added weight would be a burden to bring back.

The north cleaver is a long, long way from the base of Victory Ridge, we found out that morning. Despite a 2 o'clock start, at dawn we were only beneath the Lyman Glacier, still some distance to go. Keeping low to avoid basalt buttresses and crevasse fields, we traversed onward to the South Wilson Glacier. Here we roped and climbed an ice slope, rather than follow Rusk's route up the rotten, red ridge to our left: it was evident why he was cut off—the ridge breaks in a fragile drop-off before continuing onto the upper cliffs, which we planned to reach directly.

In my journal I later wrote: "crossed schrund"; "many stones falling"; "channels into ice face"; "two leads of cutting"; "snow arete on ridge"; "2-hour traversing climb to right." Then we entered the center one of three prominent ice couloirs that sweep up to the final cliff, cutting many steps as we slowly advanced. The way was very steep; most of the time we front-pronged on our crampons. To minimize danger from rockfall we belayed from lateral ledges on the basalt.

Late in the afternoon we reached a strange safety, climbing right up under hanging icicles of the final ice cliff. Staying behind the icicle curtain much of the time, protected by ice and rock pitons and some natural hummocks, we now cut steps leftward for three leads. At last we chopped across a section of blue ice where we could look directly down rotten exposed cliffs

The wide eastern wall of Mt. Adams, showing first-ascent route of Victory Ridge, with the Rusk Glacier on left and Wilson Glaciers on right. Aerial photo by Austin Post, U.S. Geological Survey.

to the Rusk Glacier. An easy 200-foot ice slope tapered toward the true summit.

———

In 1792 members of Captain Vancouver's expedition, sailing up the Columbia River, saw the beautifully-proportioned cone and sculptured faces of Mt. Hood. After the opening in 1845 of the Barlow Road—the first wagon road constructed across the Cascades and an historic immigrant track—the mountain was explored; in 1857 the summit was attained. Now Hood is probably climbed more often than any other American snow peak, usually by the straightforward south-side route.

In 1900 O. C. Yocum built a hotel at Government Camp; later he guided many parties to the summit. The prow-like ridge between the Sandy Glacier and the Little Sandy (Reid) on the west side of the mountain now bears his name. Writing in the 1936 *Mazama* E. L. Darr made this interesting statement: "Yokum (*sic*) Ridge . . . is one of the few rock masses that have defied all attempts to scale it." The problem intrigued me. Stories then circulating indicated Portland climbers had made occasional sorties onto Yocum Ridge and found the rock terribly rotten. An idea occurred to me: why not attempt it under winter conditions? Early in April 1959, Northwest weather turned clear. An interesting trip then evolved. This I wrote in the *American Alpine Journal:*

"As we swung the car up the last few switchbacks to Timberline, Mount Hood stood crystalline clear against the blue sky. There had not been many clear days like this during the present season, and on the chance the weather might not last, it seemed a ripe time for a new ice climb on the mountain. The Austrian, Leopold Scheiblehner, and I had some ski-mountaineering in mind, but after scanning the upper slopes of the mountain, we could not resist the idea of something more complex. We had heard that Yocum Ridge, on the west side, had not been done under winter conditions and just seeing it from the road was a fine lure. At the time, we did not know that the entire ridge and buttress had never been climbed. Since the mock-up in the lodge did not show a dotted route, it aroused our curiosity.

"The date was April 9. At 4 o'clock we had strapped on our packs and were ski-climbing to the Illumination Saddle. Here, at 9000 feet, we pitched my tent in a protected saddle, cooked a quick supper and wondered how cold the night would be. After a winter in nightly comfort, glacier camping seemed a rude shock. It is not hard to oversleep, and we managed this well. But it was only 7 and the sun had not yet reached us. Putting the crampons on, we roped immediately and crossed the saddle to the Reid Glacier. Here we descended and traversed to the lower flanks of Yocum Ridge. The knife-like blades of ice seemed like a nightmare of ice problems instead of a route to the summit. With a covering of ice feathers, not a single rock was visible. The ridge reminded me of a serrated Alaskan one, with fluted ice on the south flank. Getting onto the crest was a toe and ice-pick workout—a strenuous one for the first cramponing of the season. Leo led this, and once on the ridge we alternated the lead. The climbing was easy in some places. In others it was delicate and exposed, and in some places it was unpleasantly difficult and dangerous. Because of the frost and rime formations, the whole surface was often a buildup of frost feathers. An ax belay was often useless, and ice pitons could not be placed. When possible we kept to the wafer-thin crest and hacked out a stance. When crossing the flanks of the fluted walls, we could do little but hope a slip would not occur. Ahead all we could see was the array of glistening towers in the morning sun. Somewhere, 2000 feet above, was the summit of Mount Hood. Both the west and northwest faces of the mountain seemed smooth and gentle in comparison to our picket fence of whiteness. Several of the most treacherous pitches stand out in our minds. A mushrooming tower threatened progress and so Leo decided to try the south flank. After chopping downward and across a groove, he disappeared around a hidden corner. Some 15 minutes later he came into view again, cutting up a gully wall that needed both hand- and footholds. We continued flanking the worst towers just under the crest, being careful to work into tiny belay spots on the ridge or behind

Yocum Ridge of Mt. Hood in winter conditions resembling those of the first ascent. Aerial photo by Ray Atkeson.

towers. Once I chimneyed my way up a 30-foot section of vertical ice, grasping long columns of ice feathers and pulling outwards to keep my balance while kicking and cutting footholds. This required great care, for the wrong slash of the ice ax might have brought the whole chimney wall down. It was a difficult and dangerous place—sometimes I could see daylight through the frost feathers 2 feet under the veneer surface. At one point Leo cut some huge holds over his head and somehow swarmed up a 12-foot overhang. Several times the ridge ran down into notches, and we had to reverse our technique or jump into little ridge platforms. On the final upper buttress a zigzag ice corridor took us past the steepest profile. We climbed right across a fluted flank for one lead and then angled back to the top of the crest. Surprisingly, this section was not as difficult as the lower ridge and in due time we came to the broadening of the ridge, where it merged into the summit slopes. About 1 o'clock we stood on the top, facing a strong, biting wind. Our descent down the normal route led us soon into camp again. Skiing wide open, we raced for the lodge in the afternoon sun."

During half a century, September was the favored month for exploring the northern faces of Rainier. Dora Keen, who probed upward near Ptarmigan Ridge's ice cliffs, said "September seems the best month," probably feeling summer avalanches would be past. Hers was the only serious quest in the early 1900s, though a claim, not generally accepted, was made by a Lee Pickett of a 1905 ascent via Ptarmigan.

Willis Wall is 3600 feet high, a huge precipice of eroded rock capped by ice walls, bounded on the east by Curtis Ridge and on the west by Ptarmigan Ridge, split down the middle by Liberty Ridge.

Ptarmigan Ridge rises from hilly, floral Spray Park to steep slopes of mixed rock and ice. The chief problem was to find a route through great ice ramparts to the gentler slopes below Liberty Cap. In 1933 Hans Grage and two companions climbed to about 11,500 feet, and in the following year Grage and Wolf

Bauer reached the Liberty Cap Glacier at about 12,500 feet. The complete ascent to the summit was made in 1935 by Bauer and Jack Hossack. On all these climbs there was dreadful clatter of September stonefall, though the parties felt safe from ice debris spilling from the hanging glacier between the Carbon and North Mowich Glaciers. "Because anchoring was almost wholly confined to body and ice axe belays, large footholds and frequent knee and hand holds had to be chiseled," Bauer wrote. Cutting was generally done under the bombardment of hissing fragments.

The angular buttress of Liberty Ridge, remnant of a longer spur, gives architectural distinction to the great wall by forming it into a double horseshoe. Avalanches often break off the 300-foot ice cliff at the top, roaring thousands of feet into the depths of the colossal recess, to the floor of the Carbon. On the first successful climb, in September 1935, Ome Daiber, Arnie Campbell, and Will Borrow found "thick layers of igneous rock supported on soft pumice held by frozen moisture"—a structure stable only in cold conditions. At that time of year much chopping was required and they made two bivouacs on the ridge; now the ascent is normally done with a single high camp.

In early August of 1956 John Rupley, Herb Staley, and I decided to consider a new way on the northwest side under midsummer conditions, having learned of other parties that bogged down in June's soft snow. When we drove to Mount Rainier National Park, it had not yet been decided whether we would try to repeat the original Ptarmigan Ridge route or attempt a new climb between that and Liberty Ridge—a direct-as-possible ascent of the Liberty Cap Glacier and its giant ice cliff, one so immense it can plainly be seen from Seattle.

Our start from Mowich Lake was inauspicious: we had to drive back to the Carbon River entrance to check in with the park ranger, though it was our understanding he would be at Mowich. After a late start we plodded up snowfields and cleavers to a depression at about 10,000 feet, not far under the great ice cliff. Three friends who accompanied us planned to return to Mowich the following day, taking our sleeping gear so we could make a lighter summit traverse.

Sleep came in starts and fits amid the night-long noises of falling rock and ice; in the chill, on our beds of sharp stones, we tossed and turned. We could see the Seattle-Tacoma Airport beacon and the faint orange beads of the Lake Washington Floating Bridge. I remember thinking about the ice cliff above. It seemed so menacingly poised.

We started at 4 A.M., perhaps a bit late. However, the timing proved right, for nothing serious fell as we hurried leftward across tilted glazed rock on a steepening ledge. Crampons bit well and there was little need for stepcutting, though the ice grew in angle and hardness as we climbed. We were roped, but moved together, avoiding conversation. We knew speed was our only safety. As we rounded the steepest section—all blue ice where we placed three pitons for protection—a great hanging chunk of ice broke off where we had been 20 minutes before, creating a disaster area. Altogether we were under the ice perhaps 1 hour. For that long we were at the mercy of the gods, or chance, or luck. Sometimes, to do an important climb, one must go beyond the laws of safety and trust the percentages— in short, gamble.

After bearing left some distance we found a way through the ice wall, first by 50 feet of crampon-rock climbing, then by a traverse of a delicate chute. We wove among tottering seracs and debris of an icefall, then suddenly entered a white highway to the upper glacier.

Resting, and feeling some appetite for the first time that morning, we looked about. We could see Rainier's dominance is due not only to height but isolation, rising in an otherwise low portion of the Cascades. It is a world in itself—a giant white colossus, frozen, lonely, and lifeless, without warmth and without mercy. The northern precipices rank with Mont Blanc's greatest flank. Ending our musings, we kept the rope tight, with an open eye for the many crevasses. Only routefinding problems

The northwest side of Mt. Rainier. On the left skyline is Ptarmigan Ridge, broken by the great ice cliff. Left of center is the Mowich Face. In center is Sunset Ridge and to right the Sunset Amphitheater. Photo by Ed Cooper.

lay between us and Liberty Cap, from where we traversed to Columbia Crest, the highest summit, arriving there at 2:30 in the afternoon. As Rupley later pointed out, the climb was the beginning of some good luck in pioneer Northwest climbing; this extended to his automobile-driving the next climbing season when he hit a roadside cliff (while looking at a lovely peak), a deer, and a bear—the luck being his not being injured in any of these episodes.

As one views Rainier's great bulk from Seattle or Tacoma, a wide, smooth wall rises above the North Mowich and Edmunds Glaciers, roughly between Ptarmigan and Sunset Ridges. Climbers called it the "Mowich Face," but as far as I could learn nobody had set foot there. The Edmunds Glacier, just beneath, is the shortest of the 11 main glaciers on the mountain, originating in a shallow cirque at about 11,000 feet, fed by precipitation drifting and avalanching from the steep rocky flanks of the Liberty Cap massif—which is to say, the Mowich Face.

John Rupley, Tom Hornbein, Don (Claunch) Gordon, Herb Staley, and I planned to attempt the face in mid-June 1957. A weekend cleared and we were on our way. From the West Side Road we hiked to Klapatche and St. Andrews Parks, then climbed to the head of Colonnade Ridge to camp—not high, only 8200 feet. Looking up, we could see the Tahoma Glacier tumbling splendidly from a gap in the summit barricade.

We roped at 5 in the morning, climbing breakups of the South Mowich Glacier to reach the base of Sunset Ridge. I remember admiring the narrow chute of the Puyallup Glacier, a maze of crevasses cascading from an upper ice reservoir, then expanding fan-like, sending a portion of its flow to the South Mowich. Our route ascended the lower snow slopes beneath Sunset Ridge, then traversed north onto the upper reaches of the Edmunds. The surface was soft, demanding real effort for progress. Crevasses and a bergschrund forced us to contour to the center of the Edmunds before entering onto the face itself.

Once on the wall the going was better, though much of the surface was crusty ice over powder. Rupley and Claunch were the fittest of our five that day and did the most stepkicking, but we were glad to have plentiful manpower. Except for three ropelengths of very icy surface we climbed in unison. Conditions seemed solid, and stayed that way because a rapidly-approaching storm blotted out the sun. Most of the wall averages perhaps 40°; the upper icy section reaches 50° before rounding off to the crest of upper Sunset Ridge. At 2:30, as mists poured in, we stood atop Liberty Cap.

There was little rejoicing. We were all somewhat tired, and in view of the weather were anxious to get off the mountain in a hurry. But this was not to be. After groping in dense mist for an hour trying to find the correct start toward the Tahoma Glacier —our planned route of descent—we clambered back over the top of Liberty Cap and grimly retraced our steps down the long, long face. The safety and comfort of the green meadow world were immensely far below. We were concerned about losing the way—the whipping wind had obliterated our crampon tracks. I remember concentrating very hard in the search for those telltale punctures, so difficult to distinguish in the mist and wind.

16

Along the 49th Parallel

Only comparatively recently has the white man left his mark in the North Cascades. One of the first real traces was the historic Whatcom Trail. There is a quality of myth about this project, built with funds subscribed in Whatcom for a secure route to join the Fraser Gold Rush of 1858, which drew a multitude of adventurers seeking riches. When settlers along northern Puget Sound asked the federal government for protection from the raiding, hostile Indians, a location for a military post was selected in 1855. By the following summer, when disorders were already largely quelled, Captain George E. Pickett came to establish Fort Bellingham.

By April of 1858 thousands were encamped at Whatcom on Bellingham Bay, awaiting a means of access to the Fraser River mines. Since the gold discoveries were within British territory, Governor Douglas in Victoria felt any profits should accrue to that nation; at the same time he was anxious to see Hudson Bay Company privileges protected. As guardian of British rights on the Fraser he regulated commerce, requiring licenses from the Company—an order backed by gunboats.

Whatcom, hoping to profit from her geographic position and harbor, attempted to wrest from Victoria the supremacy as a shipping point to the mines. For this economic reason, and to avoid the perils of the Fraser Canyon and to evade licenses and

Mt. Slesse from the west, in late sun and clearing winter storm. Aerial photo by Norman Williams, Chilliwack, B.C.

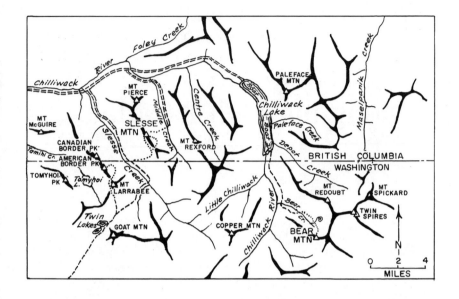

head tax imposed by Governor Douglas, her people tried twice
in 1858 to construct a trail direct to the mines. Both efforts
were largely futile. The plan was to get a trail built through to
the open country beyond the Skagit Range and link it to the old
Hudson Bay Company's Brigade Trail, which went from Hope to
the Thompson River.

Initially the trail from Whatcom was intended to go direct to
Hope via the Nooksack and Chilliwack Rivers, but when the
promoters failed to find a pass through the mountains, they
turned off to a point on the Fraser. High waters and floods in
the lowlands destroyed the route's effectiveness. Captain W. W.
De Lacy, a U.S. Army engineer, undertook to build a second
trail farther inland, along the foot of the mountains from
Sumas Prairie to the Chilliwack River. He then followed the
Boundary Survey trail, which had made use of the Hudson Bay
trail to Chilliwack (Summit) Lake; a ferry-raft was built to
cross the lake lengthwise, but the water barrier eventually made
the route a failure. Here (98 miles on the "Trail") his party
found good horse grass. Blocked by deep snow and high, rough

country beyond the lake, De Lacy tried to turn north to the Fraser-Skagit divide. Next he attempted several crossings to the east from Chuch-chee-hum (Depot) Creek, climbing to two elevations of 5700 feet before finding a circuitous route down Maselpanik Creek and the Kle-sil-kwin to the Skagit; he then followed up it to the Sumallo to join A. C. Anderson's 1846 route, which went up the Skagit and across the divide to eventually join the Brigade Trail. (The trails met near the upper crossing of the Similkameen.) Though a great deal of energy and money was expended in locating the Whatcom Trail, it was never improved or used much; Fraser River boats and the opening of easier ways through the Lillooet country made Whatcom a deserted village.

Long before 1858 the Ch-ihl-KWAY-uhk tribe had some 30 villages along the Chilukweyuk (Chilliwack) River and also houses at the lake. Trail exits went to Hope via Post Creek, Paleface Creek, and Depot Creek. Chief Sapass said a trail went from the head of the lake up the "Klahaihu" (later known as Dolly Varden, then Chilliwack Creek), over the divide and down to the Skagit. Trails also went up Nesakwatch (Middle) and "Senehsey" (Sel-ee-see, later Silesia, then Slesse) Creeks. Some of these various Indian tracks were improved by Hudson Bay Company trappers, who reached Chilliwack Lake at least 5 years before the Boundary Survey.

Prior to 1846 the "Oregon question" was a burning dispute between the United States and Great Britain, with each side claiming mutually-settled land far north and south. That year a treaty was arranged by which the disputed tract was divided; the land boundary line adopted was the present one along the 49th Parallel "between the territories of the United States and those of Her Brittanic Majesty."

Though a British Boundary Survey that year did some mapping toward the Cascades (at least as far as Silesia Creek), not until 10 years later did Congress authorize the appointment of a commission which, with a similar one from Great Britain, was to carry out provisions of this article. Very quickly the field

233

parties saw the inexpedience of marking the entire boundary by cutting, due to the "impracticable nature of the country." It was agreed to ascertain and mark certain points on the line at convenient intervals, these including important stream crossings; vistas were cut only near these fixed points and settlements.

The first survey was completed between 1857 and 1861, with teams from both nations in the field. The American party that began work in 1857 was called the Northwest Boundary Survey, with John G. Parke the chief astronomer and surveyor. The British Commissioner appointed Colonel J. S. Hawkins of the Royal Engineers to determine the line along the 49th Parallel; his party arrived to engage in field work in the summer of 1858, only to encounter many delays because of the gold frenzy. The 1857 camp at Depot Creek gave the stream its present name. By the end of the 1858 season the line had been reconnoitered as far as the Skagit River, crossing the "Skagit Range" above Depot Creek at 4719 feet and the "Hozomeen Range" at 6277 feet. George Gibbs, who served as geologist and interpreter and led the American party on this exploration, noticed that major streams in this "Skagit Range" run through narrow but flat valleys on their upper waters, having a comparatively gentle slope (Dolly Varden Creek a prime example), but that the middle and lower courses are more rapid. The Whatcom Trail (which they encountered) had to be improved to Chilliwack Lake and made practical for pack mules by bridging and corduroying. In 1859 they built boats to cross the 5½-mile waters of the lake, then spent a month of heavy work opening a trail to the Skagit River. A vista was cut at the divide crossing and also at the boundary south of the lake. As the line was often high up on the sides of the peaks, trails had to be built up such side streams as Sen-eh-say and Tum-mea-hai (Tamihi). It proved to be one of the roughest and brushiest borders in the world. The camps used by the survey teams were Camp Sumass, Camp Tum-mea-hai (3 miles above the mouth of Tamihi Creek), Sen-eh-say Station, Ensawkwatch Station, Camp Chiloweyuck, Camp Chuch-che-hum, and Camp Skagit.

In 1859 Henry Custer led a reconnaissance over to the Nooksack River and up tributaries of Dolly Varden Creek. It is known that he reached a minor summit on the divide to the Zakeno (Baker) River. To determine elevations and sketch the topography he ascended a number of vantage points during explorations of the high country around Glacier Peak—the entire "Skagit Range" here was called "Custer Ridge" in subsequent reports. In a trip probably not duplicated before his time by any explorer, he crossed the range to the Skagit by a "Glacier Creek" (Sko-mel-pua-nook), which is now called Little Beaver Creek. He called a peak "of about 9000 feet" at its head "Wailagona-hoist," reporting it was glacier-hung for about 3000 feet at an "angle of 70 degrees." This must have been Mt. Challenger. In his explorations along the high country between the Nooksack and Chilliwack, Custer likely climbed Red (Larrabee) Mountain some time between 1857 and 1860. Its location and height aptly fit a position located and triangulated for a "Put-lush-go-hap Mountain." It is interesting to note that Boundary Survey maps drawn in 1865 show the entire lengths of the Chilliwack and Skagit Rivers quite accurately.

In 1900 it was decided to re-survey the boundary across the Cascades to satisfy the demand for identification of exact positions, made necessary by increased settlement and mining claims. At Silesia Creek, for instance, a stone cairn had been placed at the boundary in 1859, but local misunderstanding had arisen; some early squatters found two sets of stone cairns and more than one vista cut. Though the line was based on the original monuments, a new network of triangulation was established, adding new monuments and vistas. Between 1901 and 1905 trails were cut up Tamihi Creek to the boundary, up Depot, Nesawkwatch, Dolly Varden, and Silesia Creeks. The Chilliwack River was bridged by cedar logs, planed so horses could cross; rafts and a cedar-dugout canoe were again used on the lake.

Right in the footsteps of the boundary surveyors, and sometimes ahead of them, were the miners. They came south from the Fraser into Silesia Creek and over Gold Run Pass into the Nooksack. With the discovery of the Lone Jack ledge of gold quartz in August 1897, the district around Twin Lakes soon was overrun with prospectors; that year up to 500 men were said to be camped there, at "Union City."

The Gargett Brothers ran pack trains from Sumas to mines located high on the west side of Red Mountain, reaching the area via Gold Run Pass and upper Tamihi Creek. But the most famous mine on Red was discovered during a goat-hunting trip on its north side. This became the well-known Boundary–Red Mountain Mine, which opened communication via Silesia Creek to the town of Chilliwack; Canadians obtained a portion of these mines, raised money to open this route, and ran surveys on disputed territory in hopes the boundary line would be established farther south. A dam was built on Silesia Creek for a power site and nearby a mill was constructed; an aerial cable tram conveyed ore from the mine to the stamp mill. In the 1930s, though, the mill was destroyed by fire and avalanche.

The stamp mill at Lone Jack Mine, built in the canyon of Silesia Creek to avoid deep snows, also had an aerial cable tram and power plant. Beginning in 1902 gold was produced, but when the mill had operated 5 years it was destroyed by fire; after a rebuilding, further production, another destruction, this by avalanche, it was rebuilt once more but not operated.

George Otis Smith and Frank C. Calkins, who made a geologic study of the upper Skagit about the turn of the century, published (1904) a reconnaissance map that clearly shows such features as Custer Ridge, "Glacier Creek," and Mt. Hozomeen. In a journal article they said, "So many of the mountain slopes are precipitous that much of the country is practically inaccessible and unknown to the prospectors."

As is frequently the case, the "inaccessibilities" disappeared as time went on (members of the survey climbed Glacier Peak—now Spickard—in 1904), but it is apparent Smith and Calkins did not retrace Custer's tracks. They were content to write, "Looking west from the valley of the Skagit River one sees high peaks with precipitous faces, on whose lower slopes are extensive glaciers, from which flow Beaver and Glacier, or Little Beaver, Creeks."

One reason the early miners and surveyors had so much difficulty penetrating mountains south of the Chilliwack is that the high ridge tops and spur summits drop unusually abruptly to the main drainage valleys, often giving a precipitous relief of 6000 feet or more. In glacial times vast rivers of ice covered the land up to an elevation of about 7000 feet, only the higher peaks rising above—their present jagged summits were plucked into shape by alpine glaciers, while at lower elevations the ice sheets carved domes and planed surfaces both above and below the tree-line.

In submitting his report on the geology of the mountains crossed by the International Boundary at the 49th Parallel, Reginald A. Daly, the Canadian geologist who traversed the border wilderness during field work from 1901 to 1906, wrote of the ice: "These colossal bodies performed rapid geologic work. There is little wonder that the longest of the sheets occurring in the Boundary belt—the Chilliwack Glacier—has produced a long, continuous U-shaped trough, fjord-like in its cross-section." Daly found that "Chilliwack Lake, one of the most beautiful in the cordillera, is held at its level of about 2000 feet above sea by a strong boulder moraine . . . evidently formed during a long halt in the recession of the Chilliwack Glacier. At the outlet a 75-foot notch has been cut through the moraine. Thence the Chilliwack River, on a gradient of nearly 100 feet to the mile, rushes on its torrential way to the Fraser flats." Few early bridges withstood its power. Earlier, George Gibbs had described Chilliwack Lake's waters as "very deep, clear, and transparent, and the views it presents are almost unequalled, even in this region of wild and solitary grandeur."

Daly applied the expressive term "tandem cirques" to the sculptured amphitheatres at the head of Tamihi Creek. He noted that "picturesque lakelets" are common in this region, and that "the effluent glaciers occupying the valleys of Depot, Silver, Middle, Slesse, and Tamihy Creeks have similarly driven back the lateral spurs, greatly steepened the valley walls, and reduced intervening ridges to razor-back profiles for miles." He further described how the descendants of these glaciers are numerous small sheets occupying northerly slopes of the higher massifs, and commented "above the ridges tower pinnacles like Slesse Mountain, Tamihy Mountain, Glacier Peak, and many others which lend their grandeur to the panoramas." In studying the interesting rock of this region, Daly found "Custer gneissic batholith (sheered granodiorite) outcropping at the summit of the Skagit Range. It is cut by the Tertiary Chilliwack batholith of granodiorite, which is genetically connected with a batholith mass named the Slesse diorite." The basin of Chilliwack Lake has been excavated in the Chilliwack batholith; the diorite there is widely exposed and remarkable for its general uniformity in color, texture, and massive structure.

Slesse diorite proved its hardness in one of Canada's worst air disasters. On the night of December 9, 1956, Cascade weather was at its absolute worst: those planes that had to be aloft reported rime ice forming on wings, blind visibility, snow, and severe turbulence in winds of 90 knots. A Trans-Canada Airlines "North Star" with 62 aboard developed an engine fire flying east from Vancouver. Circling back beyond Hope it reported a descent from 19,000 to 13,000 feet, then simply vanished . . . until found in early summer by three climbers near the 7600-foot level of Slesse's east face, south of the summit. The terrific impact had imbedded the front of the plane into the rock, but most of the remains had fallen to the glacier, 2300 feet directly below. When I visited the area some years later the glacier bedrock, outcrops, and moraine outwash were a maze of shattered metal, seat cushions, and fragmentary human remains. I wondered how many fortune-seekers had already been there: according to a claim filed, a Chinese on the craft had $80,000 in cash on his person.

Slesse, from some aspects the most spectacular isolated peak in the Cascades, was called Sel-ee-see (meaning *fang*) by the Indians; some maps used the designation "King George" and in a report of the International Boundary Commission its photo was identified as "Tamihi Mountain." This name, coming from t'ehm-ee-HIY (meaning "deformed") was sometimes also applied to the two American and Canadian Border Peaks, west of Slesse Creek, and to McGuire Mountain. To add to the confusion, on a map drawn about 1899 Red Mountain is identified as "Tomyhoi." The derivation "Tomyhoi" (one story says the name honors a miner of the gold rush days) now shows on American maps, applied to the peak southwest of the Border Peaks and to the U.S. portion of Tamihi Creek. Many of the present names were adopted by the joint Boundary Survey of 1862, but there is still some misunderstanding and spelling variation, each nation holding onto its preferences.

Because of the logical accessibility from the north, the major summits on both sides of the boundary were first climbed by Canadians: Slesse (1927), American Border (1930), Redoubt (1930), Canadian Border (1932), and Rexford (1951). This region was a blank even to the climber-explorer Herman Ulrichs, who admitted he did not know if "there is any interesting climbing there." But though Americans have been late in discovering the spectacle and rugged majesty of these peaks, mastery of the big walls and harder routes has come from stateside. When flying to Chilliwack Lake in 1950, the rapid succession of east and north faces brought me to feverish attention.

Being perhaps the first Washingtonian to climb Slesse by any way, I added spice to my initial ascent in 1952 by doing the first climb of its thumb-like south peak. (The year before, with John Dudra and Dwight Baker, I had completed a "big wall" route in the area, the north face of American Border Peak. Though the face has some exposed snow slopes and treacherous slabs, the view from the valley gives a frightening appearance all out of proportion to its actual difficulty.)

Closer acquaintanceship with Slesse came in 1959 when Ed Cooper, Don (Claunch) Gordon, and I brought nylon ropes and pitons to the high-angled northwest face which rises directly out

239

of a strip of hanging meadows, where we bivouacked on a 30° slope, tied to small trees. In the morning a fog so enveloped the peak we almost but not quite gave up. The route was all free climbing, steep and sound like some of the Teton classics—except for the final hard lead, which we described as a "vertical wall of loose bricks." Several pitches had sections of 5.6 and 5.7. Stumbling down the burnt canyons and windfalls near Slesse Creek on the evening after the climb, we made another weary bivouac.

These climbs on Slesse gave me a proprietary interest in the great east face, which curves around a pronounced pillar to a narrow north wall that rises from a deep chasm, offset from the northwest face and the craggy ridge leading northward to points on the Slesse–Middle Creek divide. Photos were not available, but I knew it must be 2500 feet tall and terribly steep. The polished slabs at its base were at the critical angle for glacier ice; looking down from the summit I recall seeing tottering ice cakes and sections of what must have once been a solid hanging glacier, all clinging to Yosemite-like slabs. "The most magnificent alpine rock wall in the Cascades," I mused in silent tribute.

Before an attempt could be made the base had to be reached with all the equipment needed for a major ascent. This posed problems if one wished to get there in a sane condition—and with companions. Because of the reputedly thick brush in Middle Creek, and the complete disappearance of a trail once cut by the Boundary Survey, I first tried to reach the wall from Twin Lakes, on the American side. During an exploration in November 1957, Don (Claunch) Gordon and I numbed our legs wading the wintry waters of Slesse Creek. Unconsolidated new snow stopped us on the high divide south of Slesse. Later, under summer conditions, Dave Collins and I crossed to the east side —an arduous and somewhat complicated route. On a long descending traverse to the north we kept an eagle eye out for ice blocks that might slide down the slabs from the fragmentary glacier above us, and for any loose currency from the plane wreckage—grim evidence of which lay everywhere.

Our faint hopes of climbing the wall then were soon dispelled. The geologic report had stated that "Slesse diorite was comparatively massive but on the east somewhat metamorphosed by a later batholithic intrusion." As we stood directly beneath the peak, no rockfall gave a sense of urgency to depart. But the upward look was overwhelming; so enormous was the wall we could scarcely concentrate on checking potential routes. It is one thing to admire such a cliff for the beauty, but quite another to feel the emotions related to a projected climb. Taking in the entire dizzy sweep, we thought the most logical route might start where the face corners around the pillar to the north—out of sight and below us. The metamorphosed rock directly above our stance had large, crackless-appearing sections, and seemed tinted with yellow and red. The corner rock was a solid grey hue, looking sounder. The corner, however, began at the very lowest portion of the face—well below the tree-line—and seemed impractical to reach from where we were. A deep, slabbed cirque, dividing buttresses, and the threat of annihilation from sliding seracs stopped us from traversing farther; cliffs below simply dropped off and discouraged a descent to bypass the obstacles.

In July 1963 I finally came to grips with the gargantuan face. Returning from the Bugaboos with Steve Marts, after a successful new climb on Pigeon Spire via the east nose, we left the Trans-Canada Highway at Chilliwack and drove up the valley toward Middle Creek, where I already knew a logging operation was in progress—having made it a point to keep track of any such developments. We learned that a newly-built winding truck road had been put miles up Middle Creek. Our timing was excellent! Not anxious to ruin a good car, we hiked the last grades of the road, which took us to a point in the deep valley directly opposite the east and north faces. Unknown to us, a competent Vancouver party had already been there this summer, to attempt the face. (After all, Slesse is in Canada.) Although there were some individually good technical climbers north of the border, there was a general feeling that when it came to the big walls, they were still dabbling in coloring books while Yosemite and other American climbers were painting masterpieces.

Crossing the creek from a logging slash area, we climbed steep, heavily-timbered ribs, carrying 3 days' dry food, down jackets, a bivouac sack, and technical climbing gear. We were so busy trying to reach timberline that we scarcely studied the face. Nightfall found us clambering around little rock outcrops with stunted evergreens; some tall meadow grass at an uncomfortable angle provided a cool sleeping spot.

In the morning we traversed and climbed to the north, working our way over polished slabs, outcrops, névé, and ice patches to a point near the lowest corner of the northeast pillar. While laboring along the edge of the ice we began to spot litter of aircraft wreckage—first a bright colored object that might have been a string of beads, then pieces of twisted aluminum. Debris was scattered everywhere, including a gear wheel oddly lying atop the ice.

Steve and I agreed the pillar was the logical route, just as indicated by the 1958 reconnaissance. However, with the wild surroundings of fractured glacier, polished white slabs, and the soaring, reddish-tinted wall, nothing appeared *very* logical. Coming against the face, it now seemed steeper than ever. As Wilfred Noyce said in *The Alps,* "In general, the more one looks at a climb from below the more doubtful and dangerous it appears. A climbing problem only 'solves itself' when one has no alternative but to overcome it."

A glacier chasm ruled out a direct approach to the base of the pillar, but an area of slab between seracs led to its clean south edge. We edged our way up and across the exposed slab, trying to avoid the wet spots and the downpours of water from the melting ice above. Remnants of the hanging glacier, with loose pieces as big as automobiles, were perched precariously on slabs. All the while we looked upward for that dreadful sight of moving ice. We hurried!

The north face of Bear Mountain from headwaters of Bear Creek. The summit is right of center, above the white wall of the overhanging "Diamond." The first-ascent route (1967) followed the black buttress immediately to its right. Photo by Alex Bertulis.

Once beyond the firing line we traversed along a ledge to where a crack system made a sensible route-beginning. With a chaos of ice and slabs beneath us and to both sides, we uncoiled ropes and unpacked rucksacks to begin the first pitch. The rock was polished clean, but due to the low altitude there was occasional moss in cracks and sprouts of small evergreens growing from the most illogical perches.

A brutal sound like iron against iron jolted us: a gigantic block broke from its moorings and slid down the granite slab just 100 yards distant. We were safe . . . by perhaps 6 minutes.

We roped up. After an initial open book we climbed left and upwards several short pitches. Steve led three little overhangs in the space of 50 feet, using nylon-tape webbing for the boots when aid was necessary. Then came my "magic carpet"—almost an entire lead on a steep slab wall up a thin vertical ribbon of moss and tiny cedar shrubs. It was a nervous session, quite unprotected. Higher, the pillar fell back temporarily, but still was polished from ancient ice action. The climbing was a tricky series of grooves, corners, and slabs. Once, while leading with a rucksack on my back, I slipped off a fingertip-layback when my hands gave out; a piton stopped a scraping fall. Angered, I re-did it, using some aid, hurrying. By mid-day we reached the one broken area where we could climb Class 3 and 4 for some distance. Here we could carry our packs instead of having to haul them.

Above, we worked through a very steep area, having some routefinding and loose-rock problems. There were some hard individual moves and difficult pitoning. The exposure was getting sensational. Forced to the corner of the pillar and its north side, we found crack systems fortunately continued—often with no alternatives. Here we alternated leads: four long, exposed rope-lengths of free climbing. The rock was firm, but sometimes slippery at mossy spots and in corners. There was no room for error—we were now perhaps halfway up Slesse's great wall, but with no way of accurately discerning what was still in store for us. So far we had simply followed the line of least resistance on the pillar corner: the east face to the left was horrible and seemed to overhang the chaos of glacier beneath; around to the north, a damp eerie wall dropped out of sight into a chasm we knew was ice-filled, bleak, and very steep.

Darkness engulfed us as we reached a comfortable platform. We hammered four solid pitons, tied in with rope anchors, and crawled into our bivouac sack, a nylon envelope that took some of the chill out of the night and cut the wind's effect. To pass time we munched contents of a cloth bag full of "gorp"—raisins, chocolate drops, gum drops, candies, and mixed nuts.

During the bivouac a fog—or was it a cloud?—swallowed us. We seemed to be suspended in mists above the north glacier chasm. Beads of water stood out on the bivouac sack. We did not get wet, but were damp and chilled. Not being able to really sleep, we talked about this new development, and should it continue, what to do? When morning was established all we could see was gray murk; the outlines of the wall faded into white vapor. It was like being on a boat in a dense fog, with no navigation devices and no foghorns.

Steve led a pitch that was short but quite vertical and exacting, then we decided not to risk going on—after all, we had no means of knowing if this was the onset of bad weather, and no way of finding the proper route. Getting lost on such a face was not a thought to savor.

To rappel into ghostly fog, pitch after pitch, losing complete contact with the exact route, requires composure. One needs a capacity to operate calmly under the stresses and intense exposure. I was gravely concerned—it would be a disaster to rappel into the wrong area and pull down the ropes, cutting off upward retreat. Emotional release came like a winning touchdown in the last minute of the game when we discovered one of the little stone cairns we had built along much of the way for just such an eventuality. We had been confused, but now one cairn led to another and the rappels fell in order; we had almost made a dangerous mistake by starting a rappel toward that horrible north chasm. Lower, the fog thinned and the remainder of the descent was no problem; we left the haul line and a spare rope on the "carpet" pitch and on another of the hardest lower sections to speed the next attempt. Wet and dirty, we lowered ourselves to the base slabs.

Unsettled weather and vacation problems delayed the final try until late August. Steve and I felt the isolation of the climb and the hauling and carrying problems indicated a third man. Eric Bjornstad therefore joined us, and proved a strong and spirited addition, willing to undergo the necessary suffering. With the use of a pickup truck we quickly reached the end of the logging road on August 26. A better way through the forest zone and the lower cliffs and ice patches cut the approach time; knowledge made our procedures on the route faster, though it was no easier—in fact, it seemed more exposed than ever. About four pitches below the previous high point we bivouacked. The weather was marvelous; we dozed well.

By mid-morning of the second day we reached our earlier bivouac and picked up some equipment cached there, leaving behind sweaters that rodents had chewed up for nesting. Here Steve found the tricky little vertical pitch even harder than before. Above came a temporary respite, where the pillar bevels back. A snowpatch gave welcome moisture.

Then the angle steepened into the grand final sweep to the summit. This was the climax—the crux region. Steve and I traded leads on three really taxing continuous pitches. Fortunately the rock was excellent, but finding usable cracks for a few pitons proved as tricky as some of the moves. This difficult area went basically free, though it took hours and hours. A 5.8 traverse, a few aid moves, and then a continuously-hard vertical pitch got me to the first good ledge in a long, long, afternoon— just at the turning of darkness. While I was belaying Eric in the inky blackness, slack in the rope told me when he was moving up. Steve elected to spend the night standing in stirrups rather than prusik and clean the pitch in the dark. Eric and I had a good platform and spent a reasonable night, though harassed by a snafflehound which once had the nerve to jump on Eric's back. Despite the fact we sat on our rucksacks, rodents managed to chew up the leather shoulder straps and did their best to work over our boots.

In the shadowed morning we shivered for what seemed half an eternity while Steve cleaned the pitch. Then, in sunlight, we gathered steam, traversing around a corner to the south to find we had completed the serious difficulties the previous evening. A few more pitches, all broken and reasonable climbing, put us on the summit—very, very happy. The beauty queen of North Cascade routes had been done. We had separated myth from reality. Mt. Baker, the Picket Range, and the peaks north of the Fraser valley all glistened in the sun. The length, exposure, and no-escape factors of this route will surely give it increasing fame as a great classic; we used 63 pitons and one bolt on the ascent. The northwest face and a long, tiring scramble along the ridge to the north took us to a couloir that gave descent access into the depths of Middle Creek.

After my visit to Twin Spires I felt no real compulsion to return to that region among the Chilliwack peaks, not even for the fabled north wall of Bear Mountain, whose reputation dates from 1937, when Bill Cox and Will Thompson climbed Redoubt from Bear Lake, the first American climb and second ascent of the peak. A year earlier two fellow members of the George Vancouver Rover Clan (which regrouped as the Ptarmigan Climbing Club), Calder Bressler and Bud Brady, penetrated the Chilliwack country, but were stormed off Redoubt. Thompson and Cox also made an attempt on Glacier Peak (Spickard) but became involved in rock climbing, perhaps not suiting their mood that day, since they certainly could have done the climb; possibly they took as an omen of ill fortune the loss of a silver dollar which spun out of a pack being hauled. Likely also the first climbers to travel up Bear Creek, they had a full view of the great face. Thompson and Calder Bressler, in doing the first ascent of Bear in 1939, felt the north face "overhung for 3000 feet." My guidebook—first published in 1949—added another thousand feet to this estimate. It is easy to understand why climbers discussed the wall in reverent tones.

In the mid-1960s the spirit and technical competence of a new age spurred three ventures to the face. None got far: two bogged down in soft snows while crossing Hannegan Pass with extremely heavy loads; rainy weather diverted the third else-where. A certain laziness came over me at the mere thought of packing the necessary loads over Hannegan, and by this time I fully realized there were other fine walls awaiting in such areas as the Wind Rivers and the Bugaboos—with much less back-packing.

My dormant interest revived, however, when I learned Cana-dian prison inmates, as a rehabilitation project, had been im-proving the road beyond Slesse Creek, and that through their efforts the final portions to Chilliwack Lake might soon be fit for ordinary auto travel.

The Chilliwack River valley is certainly one of the loveliest in the Cascades; sadly, it also gives an acute sense of the fragility of wilderness confronted by domineering man. Entire hillsides have been logged in enormous clear-cuts, and what the Canadi-ans haven't multiply-used they have carelessly wasted—the main and side valleys are a succession of burns, too many and too recent to all be attributed to natural causes. Commercialism, too, is beginning to make its mark, serving the heavy-duty recreationists, any one of whom makes more noise and uses up more wilderness than an entire century of Indians. By contrast, the prison settlements and nursery farms do relatively little to disturb the natural scheme. The old Thurston Ranch, buildings heavy with moss, looks much as shown in a Boundary Survey photo from the days it was an overnight trail post. A sagging two-log bridge leads across the river to the buildings, which are not visible from the main road; one could hope the ranch might be preserved as an historical site.

The prospect of a shorter route to Bear's north face spiced an otherwise dreary weekend in late November 1966. My driving and Eric Bjornstad's urging managed to get a station wagon through the mudholes to Chilliwack Lake. We launched a skiff, but the lateness of the hour and a steady drizzle prompted us to stay as uninvited guests in a tidy cabin by water's edge. (We added our names to a "thank you" note left by others.)

At daybreak we put-putted south until the motor failed to start after a tank refill; 2 miles of rowing kept us warm. The trees showed fresh snow 1500 feet above. We beached the skiff on a sandspit at the south end of the lake and thrashed through willow brush alongside the creek estuary. (On the return hike we discovered the valley trail begins—in any shape for hiking —at some deserted shacks beyond the curve in the estuary.) After finding a section of trail we lost it again, then spent the next half-hour crawling over wet logs and through even wetter brush. When almost ready to abandon the whole pursuit we found a good trail right on the creek bank. Four fast miles later we were at Bear Creek, and soon after discovered that the old "way trail," shown only on some of the earlier Forest Service maps, really did exist. (This is the only occasion I can recall that an out-of-date map assisted in the solution of a climbing problem.) We used the machete often on the 2-mile trail, marking the overgrown portions with colored tape. From its end, before it was time to turn back, I began cutting a path through the brush toward Bear Creek. While rowing down the lake in the cold dark of night we mused on our wintry fortune in having found an apparently good way to the face: research had paid off; some cutting would make it a simple 1-day route. The thought of Bear-seeking climbers struggling over Hannegan Pass was almost humorous. Our little gambit was not publicly discussed, nor were the trail-cutting work parties of late spring.

Not being pressed for time on these trips there was opportunity to admire the magnificent forests of fir and red cedar along Chilliwack Creek, as well as the deep pools under mossy banks. Not far from the lake is a gigantic cedar, really five trees growing out of one super-trunk. The flat valley floor, the gnarled trees with moss-festooned limbs, resemble the Olympic rain forest more than any Cascade valley I can remember. Even the decrepit "Entering the United States" boundary sign, virtually smothered by vines, seemed fitting. It is hoped the Canadians will preserve the primitive nature of the upper end of the lake and the valley beyond.

Rain halted one work party after a path had been slashed through about ½ mile of slide alder and miscellaneous brush along Bear Creek. A kayak paddle up the lake and fine weather gave the impetus to finish the trail-cutting, and to locate a camp near the last spruce trees in the flat portion of the valley. Even when seen from an angle as one pushes up the forested valley, occasional glimpses of the phenomenal face are dazzling. A binocular examination filled me with awe. Facing slightly east of north, it is partly hidden by the curve of its own spurs, and by Redoubt's crowding ramparts on the north—unlike the walls of Slesse, which stand in solitude and can be seen from most compass points.

The rock is Chilliwack granodiorite formed by later recrystallization of Skagit gneiss, at places succeeded by plastic flow. The wall has a relentless beauty, not really esthetic but grimly impressive. Hidden from a distance, hard to approach, seen by few—here is material for a legend. The sinking afternoon sun cast deep shadows on the long battlement, highlighting only spurs and buttresses standing out from the inner wall—or "diamond" as it might be called. The whitish rock of this narrow central wall does indeed overhang, but likely only by about 1000 feet. Below the inner wall is a steep slab, then an ice segment of the basal glacier which cuts into the heart of the mountain. In both directions from the center the face is flanked by wide, continuous cliffs featuring two pronounced buttresses. The black spearlike shape of the right-hand buttress had an elegant, appealing look. Binoculars made the cracks and blank areas on the inner wall appear unpleasant, to understate the case. The support and hauling problems indicated time and manpower probably not available to me that season.

Study through the glasses suggested the black buttress as the likeliest central route to succeed in one push—a strategy I was anxious to employ for many reasons. It appeared difficult but possible; both the glasses and winter aerial photos showed the combinations necessary for a climbing line from the head of the ice apron to the buttress's outside wall, and then directly up its outside edge—a genuine storybook route. I studied alternative areas, as well as the left-hand buttress, whose appeal was diminished by dirty sections. There was no sense of immediacy: one felt more like an explorer than a climber.

With the Bear Creek route slashed and marked, it was now possible to carry a load of gear to the campsite. Jim Sinclair and I did this—in and out in one rather long day—including rowing up half the lake. Beginning the row back, close to midnight, I gave a few "wolf howls." These had been remarkably effective in driving tourists away from a campsite we used earlier in the year at Zion National Park during the Great White Throne face climb.

A lonely voice suddenly came from shore. "Is th-th-thaaat a boat?" We headed in quickly to discover a fisherman camped there, and oriented conversation toward wilderness predators. Poor fishing, mosquitoes, lack of company, and our tired plight prompted him to break camp and tow us back—another lucky stroke.

In July an extremely dry summer was upon us, and it was high time to get on with the climb before these Bear Creek probes became general knowledge. Mark Fielding unexpectedly appeared on the scene; the very mention of Bear fired his mind and we were soon on our way. With the current good weather and my subsequent commitments to climb in Canada, we couldn't wait for other interested companions, unavailable at the moment. We arrived at just the proper time of morning; a kindly fisherman towed us across the lake and into the estuary. This, we felt, was another good omen.

By now the blazes, markers, and slide-alder cuts allowed a fast trip to the cache site, and we arrived early in the afternoon. Taking stock of the food and equipment assembled for a longer push by four climbers, it was apparent we were over-en-trenched. We packed rucksacks and racked the iron on nylon webbing, taking down jackets, a bivouac sack, two ropes, crampons, ice axes, and food for 3 tight days. Sleep came easily that night; with the crystal-clear weather and promise of a hard but reasonably-safe route there was no need for bad dreams. Alone in the area, we planned to climb very carefully and make certain we never really cut off our retreat.

About daybreak we started for the top, 4000 feet above. First we side-stepped and wound through scrub evergreens. Then came steep old moraines followed by hard, hummocked snow. Once onto the steepening névé, our task was to follow the glacier efficiently and aggressively, working left around crevasses and climbing rapidly into the heart of Bear's face.

Where the glacier narrowed to a much-steeper ice apron which ran toward the inner wall, a great schrund blocked the way. We tip-toed over a hole recently filled with ice chunks, listening for fearsome sounds above. Left of the schrund wall was a dirty, polished yellow slab, not really steep but virtually holdless. We climbed it nervously, keeping very near the ice. The pitch was unpleasant—especially with the weight of a rope and rucksack. Returning to the ice we felt more secure, even though there was no place to don crampons. We should have worn them, but continued by kicking in the boot edges hard and occasionally cutting a step. We talked about putting on the claws at the first opportunity, but somehow just kept climbing the rapidly-thinning sheet of ice. We were happy to reach its end, but were immediately confronted with another discomforting situation: steep slabs with a total lack of piton cracks.

We scouted laterally along the tip of the ice sheet, finding no pleasant egress. I tried one spot, didn't like the lack of protection, and came down to attempt another line of holds farther left. I finally mustered the composure to make some hard moves and continue straight upwards, on really unprotected and tricky going, to a point where it was possible to place a runner on a rock horn, then traverse right to a tiny belay ledge. I hauled packs, twice, on the spare rope, then belayed Mark.

Temporarily secure, we surveyed the incredible scene of Bear's great walls from a vantage no man had previously enjoyed. Flanking far to the east, the wall and another buttress looked like a fearfully unpleasant trap with much loose scree on ledges. There is always someone to stretch probability, and with support and time the overhanging and perhaps dangerous inner wall, including its blank sections, cannot be called impossible. However, it did not seem an appealing problem, and in any event we lacked the time, food, bolts, and other equipment, aside from support, required for such an undertaking. Our black buttress, near now and just to the west, and with an aura of safety, almost took on an air of triviality—a relative comparison, of course.

It made us very happy to find good solid holds and a spiral exit to the ramp that promised access to the buttress's outer edge. The inner flanks and the corner that met the "diamond" appeared hostile, poorly cracked, and studded with rows of overhangs. White areas indicated rock break-offs, while the outer edge was black with lichen.

In one or two leads, angling upward to the ramp, we came to a broken area suitable for a needed rest and late breakfast. Then we set out along the ramp, glad to be off the treacherous ice apron and its polished, dirty slabs. To reach a crack-and-chimney system that led up the buttress wall, seemingly a good route to the edge, we first had a short but difficult pitch off the ramp; some hard free climbing and one aid piton took care of the problem. Cracks now guided two continuous Class 5 pitches, and at one point a key traverse led out of trouble; hauling packs instead of carrying them made the climbing enjoyable.

The edge was absolutely sensational. The depths unfolded in front of us, the buttress flanks dropping off sheerly, seemingly infinitely, beneath. Two hard and exposed free pitches, but protected by pitons, brought us to an impasse: the buttress formed a vertical block, perhaps 150 feet high, with flawless, vertical drop-offs on both sides; in the center was a cleft—really a deep chimney—that overhung and flared outward badly at the start. Since Mark was the shorter, I felt he might be able to get inside and jam his way past the overhang. There seemed to be no reliable cracks for direct aid.

Several times Mark slid down a move after struggling up it—very demoralizing and exhausting. Protection was a major problem. The overhanging nature of the crack forced him out; it was impossible to let both hands free. Somehow, after several body-lengths, he managed to get his hands loose and place a piton, but he was certain it was no good. As he squirmed higher and always into a more dangerous place, the odds increased he would fall out of the crack and test my belay. This would be a bad place to get hurt. Somehow he squeezed up farther and placed another piton, plus a sling for aid. It was nearly the last straw—the piton barely held and he was about to fall. Squeezing higher still and gasping for breath, he got his hands loose to insert another piton, clip in a stirrup and work himself as high as possible. The cracks were virtually non-existent, and all on the inside of the chimney, which meant short hammer leverage. Pounding with the side of the hammer to get the needed swing, he was in the process of getting in another piton when the one he was weighting popped out; he was able to hang on to the partly-driven one and use it with a stirrup.

I sent up the bolt kit. There was no other way: he had to place a bolt, hoping all the while that last piton would hold. A fall would certainly zip out the poor iron below. Working almost left-handed as he was, out of the crack, the hole was tough to drill, but the tactic succeeded and gave him a chance to climb higher, find new piton cracks, and struggle up the deep chimney, which flared badly for free climbing. The off-balance pitoning continued difficult. Finally the long pitch ended in some hard free climbing.

The sun was moving faster than we were; we knew our daylight hours were running out. I tried the next pitch two ways, toying with the thin edge of a loose flake in an attempt to make the section go free. Finally I used several aid pitons and climbed out of my slings to where some extremely-exposed free climbing led to the top of a small pedestal. I reached as high as possible, pulled my feet up to a roughness, searching for something to grip; ever so delicately I got my hands overhead to something solid, trusted, and made the pull-up. It seemed overhanging. Now we were on the thinnest part of the edge yet, the corner rearing above with a promise of more difficulties. I hauled the packs and belayed Mark; we then agreed to do only one more pitch and use this last platform for a bivouac unless a better one could be found.

At twilight I was only halfway up the pitch, groping for holds and piton cracks. I tried two ways to the left and one directly up. Both seemed to lead into real trouble, probably requiring bolts. We decided to bivouac while there was still light to organize for the night. Drinking a little water and eating raisins, rye bread, and chocolate, we reflected on our isolation. A few dozen miles away were outposts of civilization, and not much farther, the frenzy of freeways and cities. Yet here, no man-made sound could be heard or light seen—just a blackness with stars, and the fantasy of a dark wall. A precipice usually seems more terrible from above than below. The tingling sense we got looking down the buttress as we strained on our tie-in ropes faded to a drowse. We pulled up jacket-hoods and slept a bit. Soon the bivouac seemed as safe as it really was.

In first morning light I revisited the high point to check a final alternative—a very hairy traverse, with pendulums, to a chimney system one lead to the right of our edge. It appeared the least mechanical of the options, though quite exposed; also there would be a problem returning to the buttress edge if the traverse failed. We weren't able to get a clear view of the last portion of the traverse, where it was imperative to climb high out of the pendulum area and enter the chimney above a giant overhang. The snow-choked chimney looked wet and inhospitable, but leaned back more than the buttress, promising climbability.

We took turns making two consecutive pendulums, abandoning the anchor pitons; inbetween was a tiny "crawl" ledge that helped cut off our retreat. Packs swung across readily on the hauls. Getting into the chimney itself involved a half-pitch of reasonable climbing, without the anticipated problem. Wet rock then gave nasty moments but the next few pitches were simple enough except for tricky spots in a generally quite-exposed area. One chimney "cave" was tough, but above that we were able to carry packs as we climbed either up the chimney or on its left flank, facing the buttress. The final pitch led onto the buttress edge again, near where it flattened into a juncture with the summit ridge.

Beyond a great flat granite slab we looked out to the Pickets, Shuksan, and Baker. Slesse's face knifed the western sky. To the north a little shimmer of blue showed a corner of Chilliwack Lake, where it all started. Keyed as we were to the climb, the sudden end was a surprise. Unroping and leaving gear piled on the slab, we scrambled to Bear's jumbled top.

Chronology of Climbs 1936-1968

The range in which each peak lies is identified in parentheses: for Cascades a "C" is used, and for Olympics an "O"; all other ranges are spelled out, but with the word "range" omitted for simplicity.

First ascents of peaks, faces, buttresses, ridges, or new routes are in italics.

1936:   Boulder (O). Wandered up alone, to worry of parents.

                 Burroughs (C)

1937:   Si (C). With Boy Scout troop.

                 Rose (O)

                 Brothers (O). Scout climb; stayed atop all night.

                 Bretherton (O). Part of a 5-day Scout hike. Also climbed a 6000-foot peak of Mt. Stone.

1938:   Anderson (O). My first glacier climb. Dropped a camera from summit.

                 Chair (C). Incomplete—too terrifying then.

                 Kaleetan (C). Succeeded on this one.

                 Guye (C)

Snoqualmie (C)

Tooth (C). Four of us tied together with 100 feet of ¼-inch rope; gave us a few worried moments.

Sentinel; Wellesley; Claywood (O). Scout climbs.

Olympus (O). Had alpenstock; wore short pants with pajamas beneath for sun protection.

1939: Roosevelt (C)

Castle; Unicorn; Sluiskin (C). Fringing Rainier.

Baker via Boulder Glacier (C). My first volcano—led by Burge Bickford.

Snoqualmie (C)

Columbia (C). Only 7 of 25 made the top in storm.

Triumph (C). Introduced to the rugged North Cascades by Lloyd Anderson.

Despair (C). My first first ascent.

Lundin, west ridge (C)

Sloan (C). Running up big ledges in tennis shoes.

Chair; Bryant; Tooth (C)

Guye, northwest face (C). With Dave Lind; a good rock route.

Grand Teton (Tetons). In a biting wind.

Middle Teton, South Teton, Teewinot, Cloudveil Dome (Tetons)

Nez Perce (Tetons). Interesting rock work in tennis shoes.

Little Big Chief (C). A "bonus" first ascent—we thought it had already been climbed.

Bear's Breast (C). Two goats knocked a volley of rocks on us.

Overcoat (C). *East face.* Four of us in tennis shoes.

Hinman (C)

Baring (C). Impressed with the northeast face.

Shuksan (C). Learned to use crampons.

Three Fingers (C). Saw Northern Lights.

Chikamin (C). Beautiful autumn coloring along Gold Creek.

Huckleberry (C)

1940: Ruth (C). During a 5-day April ski trip; slept in igloo.

Lundin, west ridge (C). One of my favorite early climbs.

Silvertip (C)

Spire Peak (C)

Forbidden (C). Has now become one of the most popular good climbs.

Index (C)

Glacier via Milk Creek (C). Saw a goat on the glacier at 8000 feet.

Dome (C)

Spire Point, *south face* (C)

Blue (Gunsight) (C). Should be called "Gunsight."

Blue (Gunsight), *north peak*. Marvelous granite summit blocks.

Blue (Gunsight), *south peak*

Little Tahoma (C)

Big Four (C). Led Climbing Course trip.

Chimney Rock (C). Second ascent. The first party climbed barefoot on the hardest pitch—Jim Crooks and I used tennis shoes.

Fisher (C)

Arriva (C)

Cutthroat, *north ridge* (Č). Probably second ascent of peak.

McMillan Spire, higher spire (C). Getting there was harder than the climb.

Inspiration (C). Looked really sporting. (It was!)

Challenger (C)

Crooked Thumb (C)

Fury, east peak (C). Second ascent. A fine climb up the hanging glacier.

Luna (C). A dull climb.

Phantom (C). An interesting adventure.

Whatcom (C)

1941:   Index, north peak (C). Third ascent.

Sloan (C). Led Climbing Course trip.

Guye, west face (C). Via *Beckey's Chimney*. I used a shoulder stand, with Helmy as the victim.

Garfield (C). Horrid approach through burnt windfalls.

Leaning Tower of Garfield (C). Did it in November; brush was frosted.

Shuksan (C)

Constance (O)

Cruiser (O). Twice; *new variation on east face*.

Picture Pinnacle (O)

Trylon (O). A fun short climb with a good move.

Skokomish (O)

Rainier via Kautz Glacier (C). Finally got around to doing the Mountain.

Silvertip, Vesper, Sperry (C). Solo.

Del Campo (C)

Gothic (C)

Tooth, *southwest face* (C). Had a fine, exposed lead through the "Flakes."

Twin Spires, Southeast Peak (C). If there is an easy route, we did not see it.

Twin Spires, Northwest Peak (C)

Bear, south face. (C). *New route on upper face.*

Cloudcap (C). Some maps call it "Seahpo." A rugged-looking peak.

Icy (C). Twice.

1942:   Lundin, west ridge (C). Twice.

Si (C). Haystack routes.

Guye, south rib (C). Have always disliked Guye's rock; it has killed a couple of climbers and I took a bad fall once when a piton broke out a chunk of it.

Big Kangaroo (C). Has a crazy summit.

Mushroom Tower (C). Very hard bouldering the way we did it.

Melted Tower (C). In a greedy half-week we bagged all the Kangaroo summits.

The Temple (C). Not by the easiest route.

Little Finger (C)

Half Moon (C). Built giant cairn.

Peak 8100 (C). Above Kangaroo Pass.

The Fin (C)

Tomahawk (C)

South Early Winter Spire, *south ridge* (C)

Munday (B.C. Coast). On skis.

Little Thumb (B.C. Coast)

Waddington, south face. (B.C. Coast). Second ascent of the peak. *New route last 500 feet.* Used felt pullovers on tennis shoes.

B.C. Coast Range summer ski traverse from Waddington to Tiedemann Glacier. Our teen-age success was shocking news to the Canadians, who had made most of the 16 Waddington attempts before the Wiessner-House ascent.

1943:   Quandary (Colorado). With U.S. Army Mountain Troops.

Maroon Bells, *east face of main peak* (Colorado)

1944:   Hayden (Colorado). Ski ascent; set off wind-slab avalanche.

Seneca Rocks (West Virginia). Many short climbs.

1945:   St. Helens (C)

Blum (C)

Index, north peak (C)

Warrior (O). Alone.

Adams via *Adams Glacier* (C). Has since become very popular.

Hagan (C). Also lower summits.

East Wilmon Spire (C). Repeated the climb for a film.

Shuksan, *northeast face—Price Glacier* (C). A marathon traverse the way we did it.

The Triplets, east peak (C)

1946:   Tahquitz Rock (California). Four routes. Cleanest granite I've ever seen.

Higher Cathedral Spire (Yosemite). *First free ascent.* With Charles Wilts.

Lower Brother (Yosemite). *New variation on SW arete.*

Washington Column (Yosemite)

Pulpit Rock (Yosemite). Got poison oak.

Nooksack Tower (C)

Kate's Needle (Alaska). A 4-week expedition to the Stikine Icecap.

Devil's Thumb (Alaska). Hardest climb so far—three summit attempts.

Washington (Oregon Cascades)

South Early Winter Spire (C). The Sierra Club party first climbing it called this spire "Liberty Bell." I redefined the area's nomenclature to its present status.

Liberty Bell (C). A long walk in those days.

Golden Horn (C). A long walk for the amount of true climbing.

Big Snagtooth (C)

Red Tooth, Willow Tooth, Cedar Tooth (C). Eroded granite. Red Tooth proved tricky.

1947:   Temple (C). In the Cashmere Crags.

Temple, *west peak* (C). Renamed "The High Priest."

Monte Cristo (C)

Hozomeen, *south peak* (C). Perseverance paid off.

Baker via Coleman Glacier (C). March ski ascent. Delightful skiing.

Asperity (B.C. Coast). On a 1-month Harvard University expedition.

Tellot (B.C. Coast). Both peaks.

Claw (B.C. Coast). And again for a film.

McCormick (B.C. Coast)

Dentiform (B.C. Coast)

Frontier (B.C. Coast). Northeast of Waddington in a little-known area.

Hermit (B.C. Coast)

Outpost (B.C. Coast)

Pagoda (B.C. Coast). We looked so wild after this expedition we frightened the Indians at Tatla Lake.

1948:   Grand Teton, south face (Tetons). *Beckey Couloir.* Route suggested by Paul Petzoldt, who had tried it.

Warbonnet-Warrior ridge (Wind River). Not prepared for the difficulty of the walls in this region.

Tumwater Tower (C). A surprising discovery.

Tumwater Canyon (C). *Castle Rock's face (Midway Route).*

Splinter Towers (Sawtooth). *The Steeple* and *The Thimble.*

Louis (Canadian Rockies). Worthy of its reputation.

Crescent Spire (Bugaboos)

Bugaboo Spire (Bugaboos). Felt admiration for Conrad Kain doing the gendarme unprotected.

Snowpatch Spire (Bugaboos). Third ascent. With Ralph Widrig and Joe Hieb.

Pigeon Spire, *northeast face* (Bugaboos). Our hardest Bugaboo climb.

Marmolata Spire (Bugaboos)

Sloan, *southwest face* (C)

Baker via *north ridge* (C)

Rocket (C)

The Snags, Gremlin, Arrowhead (C)

The Boxtop (C). One of the best in the Cashmere Crags.

Prusik (C)

Enchantment (C). Solo.

Comet Spire, Lighthouse Tower, Razorback Spire, The Meteor, The Professor (C). From sunset to sundown: a long day's climb into night.

Black Pyramid, The Eagleheads (C)

The Three Musketeers (C). Fun little blocks of granite.

The Dragon Teeth, The Comb, The Hook, Yellowjacket Tower (C)

The Mole (C)

The Duolith (C). Verdict: too many Crag climbs for one season.

1949:
Fishhook Spire (Sawtooth). A Mountaineer group had tried it previously.

Big Baron Spire (Sawtooth). Overhanging bolting on monster summit block.

Red Finger (Sawtooth). Pronounced "unclimbable" by Robert Underhill.

Packrat (Sawtooth)

Grand Aiguille (Sawtooth). Second ascent. We struggled up the chimney used by the Durrance brothers when they attempted the Aiguille and brought it into prominence.

Reward (Sawtooth)

Lower Cathedral Spire (Yosemite)

Tulip Towers (C)

The Dagger (C)

The Chisel (C). Featured photo in Seattle *Times* pictorial section on climbing in the Crags.

Lighthouse Tower (C)

Adams (C). Guided the Iowa Mountaineers.

Baker via Coleman Glacier (C). Climbed in a swim suit.

Organ Pipe (Alaska). On Juneau Icecap Expedition.

Flower Tower (Alaska). On first ski crossing of the Juneau Icecap.

Michael's Sword (Alaska). Looks unbelievable from the Icecap. Our expedition split to simultaneously climb the Sword and Devil's Paw.

Emperor (Alaska)

Couloir (Alaska)

The Antler (Horn Peaks—Alaska). Juneau Icecap.

1950:   *Pennant* (C)

The Flagpole (C). The finest needle in the Crags.

Seal Head, Horizontal Spire (C)

Ostrich Head, Cynical Pinnacle, Fire Spire (C)

Little Snowpatch (C). Made good use of home-made steel bongs.

Windjammer Tower (C)

Westwind Tower (C)

Cascade (C)

Forbidden (C)

Cannonhole Pinnacle (C). In Fifes Peak area.

Middle (C). Flew to Chilliwack Lake, then bivouacked by a fire at timberline. Also climbed a lesser peak to the southwest.

Index, *middle peak* (C). Also *first traverse of the three Index peaks.*

1951:   *April Fool's Tower* (C). On April first, naturally.

Dinosaur Tower, Grand Central Tower (C). Peshastin Pinnacles.

Tumwater Canyon (C). Castle Rock, *Devil's Delight.* Also other new routes.

Inspiration (C). Made climbing film.

Coney Rocks, Lichen Tower (C). Too far up the Ingalls Creek hillside for the amount of climbing.

Spectator Spire (C). Made summit on tyrolean traverse.

Kloochman Fingers, *left Finger* (C)

Index, north peak, *east face* (C). Why doesn't someone repeat this climb?

1952:

The Tooth (C)

The Pleiades (C)

American Border, *north face* (C)

Ingalls (C)

Sahale (C)

Forbidden, *north ridge* (C)

Silver Star, *west peak* (C). Also east peak.

Vasiliki Ridge (C). *Bacchus, Aphrodite, Juno-Jupiter,* and *Ares Towers.*

Chablis Spire (C)

Pernod Spire (C)

The Chessmen (C). *Knight* and *Bishop.*

Fantasia Tower, Crystal Lake Tower (C)

Slesse (C). Impressed with its grand possibilities.

Slesse, *south peak* (C)

Devil's Tower (Wyoming). Second climb of Wiessner's Crack.

Khayyam Tower (Black Hills). Needles are a climber's paradise.

Rubaiyat Tower (Black Hills)

Andrew Tower, Diana Tower, Laureate Tower (Black Hills)

1953:

Lone Finger (C)

Split Tooth, Grey Tooth, Cleft Tooth (C). On Snagtooth Ridge.

Silver Horn (C)

Cirque Tower (C). Traversed across Shuksan's Sulphide Glacier to reach.

Burgundy Spire (C). Hardest of the "wine spires."

Goode, *west tower* (C). On a marathon from Cascade River road, non-stop.

Goode, *northwest face* (C). Relieved the boredom of the up-lake boat trip by locking an occupant in the men's room the entire voyage to Stehekin.

1954: *Window Tower* (C)

April Fool's Tower (C)

McKinley, *northwest buttress* (Alaska). Made film of the ascent, later shown on national TV program, *I Search for Adventure.*

Deborah (Alaska). With Heinrich Harrer and Henry Meybohm. Difficult ice work.

Hunter (Alaska). A classic fast expedition with good weather.

Goode, *northeast face* (C). Viking-type approach, using sailing catamaran on Lake Chelan.

1955: Hood (Oregon Cascades)

Sherpa (C)

Waterfall Column (C). Tumwater Canyon's biggest wall.

The Temple (Kangaroo Ridge), *southeast face* (C)

Concord Tower (C)

Three Feathers (C). Central needle needed some bolts.

Stuart, west ridge (C). Back at car mid-afternoon.

Monte Rosa (Alps). Hard to believe the mass popularity of climbing in Europe.

International Himalayan Expedition to Lhotse. Made ski altitude record to 23,000 feet on Khumbu Glacier.

Lobuje, *south summit* (Nepal)

Langcha (Nepal). Our best climb.

Kangtega IV (Nepal). With Nima Tensing.

Kwangde exploration (Nepal). Discovered one of world's highest lakes.

Kilimanjaro (Africa). My biggest concern was Kikiyu

tribesmen with pierced ears and feather head-dress. (I was alone.)

1956:   *West Black Butte* (C)

Rainier via *Liberty Cap Glacier* (C)

The Temple (Kangaroo Ridge), *south face* (C)

1957:   Tumwater Canyon (C). Six new routes on Castle Rock including *Saints, Canary,* and *Cat Burglar.* New routes on Midnight (*Twin Cracks*) and Rattlesnake (*Viper Crack and variation*) Rocks. Piton Tower, *east face.*

Eldorado (C)

April Fool's Tower (C). *First free ascent.*

The Boxtop (C)

Prusik, *west ridge* (C). The finest of white granite.

The Mole, *east face* (C). Rock not up-to-par for Crags.

Maude, *north face* (C). A really enjoyable snow-and-ice wall.

Rainier via *Mowich Face* (C)

Baker via Coleman Glacier headwall (C). Second ascent.

Huntington–Moose's Tooth Expedition (Alaska). Icy conditions from dry season made Huntington seem a poor risk with our time limit. Reached west ridge.

Barrile (Alaska)

Half Moon, *south face* (C). In October, when the nights are very frosty.

1958:   Jupiter Rock, *east face* (C). *Two new routes.*

Peshastin Pinnacles (C). *Two new routes.*

Snow Creek Wall (C). New routes. *Country Club, White Slabs.*

April Fool's Tower (C)

Cruel Finger (C)

Forbidden, *direct east ridge* (C)

Liberty Bell, *west face* (C). With John Rupley. The new highway should make this a popular technical route.

Baker via *Roosevelt Glacier* (C)

Slesse (C). Consolation ascent after exploring lower east face.

Sherpa, *northeast face* (C)

Golden Horn, *north face* (C)

Argonaut, *north face* (C)

North Early Winter Spire, *north face* (C)

Cutthroat, *south face* (C). A 1½-day round-trip marathon from the end of the Twisp River road.

Inspiration, *east ridge* (C). Summer weather in October.

Sloan, *west face* (C)

1959:   Peshastin Pinnacles (C). *Three new routes.*

West Tumwater Rock (C). *South Nose.*

Midnight Rock (C). *Roller Coaster route.* Like Yosemite climbing.

Snow Creek Wall (C). *King Kong Chimney.* Second lead is flaring chimney overhang.

The Camel, north face (B.C. Coast). In November—a good climb.

Squamish Chief (B.C. Coast). *Squamish Buttress.* First major Squamish route.

Grand Teton, north face (Tetons)

Moran, south buttress (Tetons). Reached summit at sundown.

Owen, *Crescent Arete* (Tetons). Chouinard won wager that we would make it as an Owen-traverse from Jenny Lake and back in one day.

Table, *east face* (Tetons)

Yosemite Peak, *east face* (Tetons)

Hood via *Yocum Ridge* (Oregon Cascades). In winter conditions; probably the best way.

Temple, *east face* (C). Cashmere Crags.

Slesse, *northwest face* (C). Highly recommend the route for steep, exposed free climbing.

Liberty Bell, *north face* (C). One day from Twisp Road and return. With Ed Cooper.

Forbidden, *northwest face* (C). Worth the complicated approach.

Bugaboo Spire, east ridge (Bugaboos). A classic route.

Bugaboo Spire, *direct west face* (Bugaboos). Direct from Warren Glacier to summit.

Snowpatch Spire, *east face* (Bugaboos). Five days—a big one. With Hank Mather.

Snowpatch Spire, west face (Bugaboos). *New route to north summit.* Great chimneys and tough friction pitch.

1960:   Peshastin Pinnacles (C). *Three new routes.*

Snow Creek Wall (C). *Outer Space route.* Unbelievable chickenheads.

Irene's Arete (Tetons)

Symmetry Spire, Jensen Ridge (Tetons). *New variation.*

Squaretop, *northwest face* (Wind River). With Layton Kor, in a 20-hour marathon from the road.

Mitchell, *north face* (Wind River). A great free climb.

Shark's Nose, *north face* (Wind River). Hardest Wind River climb yet.

Shark's Nose, *southwest face* (Wind River). Fantastic rock!

Ingalls (C)

Stuart, *Ice Cliff Glacier headwall* (C). Has been called the "east face" but more properly is the north wall of the east shoulder.

Shuksan, *Nooksack Ridge* (C). Very alpine, but terrible rock.

Index, middle peak, *west face* (C). Too much brush—do not recommend.

Baring, north face (C). *First ascent to final pitch.* A real work project.

1961:   Peshastin Pinnacles (C). *Two new routes.*

Castle Rock (C). *Two new routes.*

Snow Creek Wall (C). White Slabs, *first free ascent; White Fright.*

Chumstick Snag (C). Twice.

St. Helens (C). On skis.

Hood (Oregon Cascades)

Illumination Rock (Oregon Cascades)

Rainier via Liberty Ridge (C). Bivouacked low, then made summit in early afternoon.

Adams via *North Wilson Glacier* (C)

Heyburn (Sawtooth). *First winter ascent.* Skis to final rock.

Heyburn, *north face* (Sawtooth)

Grand Aiguille, *south face* (Sawtooth)

Rotten Monolith (Sawtooth). Clutched up edge of very scary rotten flake.

Silicon Tower, *west face* (Sawtooth)

The Priest (Utah). Three days of work.

Baxter's Pinnacle (Tetons)

Symmetry Spire (Tetons)

Symmetry Crag No. Four, *lower south buttress* (Tetons)

Grand Teton (Tetons). Complete Exum Route.

Little Cottonwood Canyon (Wasatch). Three new routes: *Super Slab, Open Book, Chickenhead Slab.* (Sorry, Utah climbers.)

Temple, north face, *new route* (Wind River). Location of an earlier route uncertain.

Lost Temple (Wind River). Grade IV just to get up it.

Bollinger, *east face* (Wind River)

Papoose Rock (B.C. Coast). *Papoose One.* Bivouacked in the rain.

The Camel, south face, *new route* (B.C. Coast)

Pigeon Spire, *northwest face* (Bugaboos)

South Tower of Howser, *east face* (Bugaboos). Direct up mid-face from the central bergschrund.

South Tower of Howser, *west face* (Bugaboos). One bivouac. A classic climb; with Yvon Chouinard.

Edith Cavell, *north face* (Canadian Rockies). One of Canada's great walls.

Sir Donald, *north face* (Selkirks). Up-tilted quartzite made this a fast, but still serious alpine climb.

1962:

Louis, *west face* (Canadian Rockies)

Patterson, *east buttress* (Canadian Rockies). Buzzed by lightning while on narrow corniced ridge.

Oubliette, *east face* (Canadian Rockies). A classic route line.

Squamish Chief (B.C. Coast). *Upper Angel's Crest.*

Challenger (C)

Challenger, *west peak* (C)

Fury, *north face* (C). Guido Magnone admired it from the air.

Adams via *Victory Ridge on east face* (C)

Snow Creek Wall (C). *Orbit Route.* Will become a classic.

The Monument, *east face* (C)

Dragontail, *west face* (C)

Dragontail North, *north face* (C)

Prusik, *south face* (C). Was first attempted by joint French-American team.

The Mole, west face (C). *New variation.*

Tumwater Tower, *west face* (C)

Peshastin Pinnacles (C). *Two new routes.*

Chumstick Snag (C). Twice.

Midnight Rock (C). *Black Widow Route. Apron Route and variation.*

Wolf's Head, *northeast face* (Wind River). After being snowstormed off the previous year.

Warrior, *east face* (Wind River). One bivouac.

Stroud, *northwest face* (Wind River)

Gannett, *west face* (Wind River). Had a reputation like that of the Eigerwand.

Moran, northeast face, *new route* (Tetons). With Dan Davis.

Lone, *direct west face* (Wasatch). A much talked-about problem in Utah.

Lone, *Question Mark Wall* (Wasatch). A natural mark identifies this sheer face.

Lone, *Flying Buttress* (Wasatch)

La Fiamma (Idaho). A remarkable granite tower.

Damocles Tower (Sawtooth)

Jericho Tower (Sawtooth)

Leaning Tower of Pisa (Sawtooth). A perfect likeness, and a good all-day problem.

Packrat Peak, *north face* (Sawtooth)

Warbonnet Peak, *northeast face* (Sawtooth)

1963:   Constance (O). *First winter ascent.* On crampons from the lake. With Steve Marts.

Three Fingers, south peak (C). *First winter ascent.* A strenuous 1-day achievement considering the trail-breaking.

Twin Sisters, south peak (C). *First winter ascent.*

Sloan (C). *First winter ascent.*

Chumstick Snag, *southwest face* (C)

Snow Creek Wall (C). *Satellite Route, Grand Arch, Umbrella Tree Route.* Outer Space Route, *first free ascent.*

Midnight Rock (C). Roller Coaster Route, *first free ascent.*

Castle Rock (C). Various routes.

Tahquitz Rock (California). Four routes.

Whitney (Sierra)

Day Needle, *east face* (Sierra). One cold September bivouac.

Tehipite Dome, *south face* (Sierra). Almost an expedition. Grade V.

Lower Cathedral Rock, east buttress (Yosemite)

Yosemite Point Buttress (Yosemite)

La Escuela (Yosemite)

Glacier Point Apron (Yosemite)

Royal Arches (Yosemite)

Washington Column direct; North Dome, south face (Yosemite). Both in 1 day, with Herb Swedlund.

Stein's Pillar (Oregon). Second ascent.

Sawtooth Dome, *west face* (Sawtooth). Also known as "Elephant's Perch." One bivouac.

Split Aiguille (Sawtooth). *First direct ascent.*

Ayres Crag No. Five, *south face* (Tetons). Very imposing steepness. Grade IV or V.

Grand Teton, north ridge (Tetons)

Baxter's Pinnacle (Tetons)

Rainier via *South Tahoma Glacier* (C). Annoyed another party which felt it had an exclusive right to the route.

Stuart, north buttress (C). *First complete ascent from base;* one bivouac.

Eisenhower, *Central Buttress south face* (Canadian Rockies)

Crowfoot Peaks, *east face* (Canadian Rockies). Very solid limestone.

Pigeon Spire, *southeast nose* (Bugaboos). One bivouac.

Howser Spire, *west buttress* (Bugaboos). Two nights out.

Slesse, *northeast buttress* (C). Two nights out.

Bennington, *north face* (Canadian Rockies). A steep glacier followed by marvelous quartzite.

Bollinger, *west face* (Wind River)

Pingora, *west face* (Wind River)

Pingora, east face (Wind River). *New route.*

Lizard Head, *east face* (Wind River). Guidebook describes this as a "series of upside-down precipices."

Musembeah, *west face* (Wind River). With Kor—some 5.8 pitches in an icy rainstorm.

Musembeah, *west face of north peak* (Wind River)

Redwall, *east face* (Wind River)

Baptiste Lake Tower (Wind River). Alone.

Bell Towers, Lower Tower, *south face* (Wasatch)

1964:   Castle Rock (C). Angel Route. *First winter ascent* in true winter conditions.

Castle Rock (C). *Rainshadow Route.*

Peshastin Pinnacles (C). *Three new routes.*

Midnight Rock (C). Yellowbird Route. Twice.

Midnight Rock (C). *Nightingale Route, South Ramp.*

Noontime Rock (C). *Gulliver's Travels.*

Snow Creek Wall (C). *Spring Fever Route.*

Snow Creek Wall (C). Champagne Route, Orbit Route.

The Tooth (C). One of my few climbs with a girl.

Stein's Pillar (Oregon). Bjornstad's overloaded car had 14 flat tires.

Squamish Chief (B.C. Coast). *Lower Angel's Crest.*

Ratz (B.C. Coast). American Alpine Club Expedition; climbed two highest peaks on Stikine Icecap.

Tahquitz Rock (California). One route.

Avalanche Spire (Bear's Claw) (Alaska). Second ascent, probably a new route.

Glacier, *north face* (Beartooth Range, Montana). Probably best wall in range.

Bonneville, *west face* (Wind River)

Dragon Head, *east face* (Wind River). With Layton Kor. Grade V.

Pronghorn, *east face* (Wind River). Southeast face is even steeper, but rock unstable.

Haystack, *west face direct* (Wind River). Grade IV— bivouacked on summit.

Spider Peak, *northeast buttress* (Wind River)

1965:   Noontime Rock (C). *Wall Street Route.* Big expanding flakes are the key.

Monte Cristo (C). *First winter ascent.*

Jefferson (Oregon Cascades). Winter ascent. With Don Liska.

Sir Donald (Selkirks). *First winter ascent.*

276

Robson (Canadian Rockies). *First winter ascent.*

Silver Star (C). *First winter ascent.* Snow crystals shimmered in the icy air.

Squamish Chief (B.C. Coast). *Northwest Passage.* Grade VI.

Nightmare Rock (B.C. Coast). *Traumatic Experience Route.*

Papoose Rock (B.C. Coast). *Hallucination Route.* Hardest Papoose route.

Tupper, *south face* (Selkirks). Wanted this one badly.

MacDonald, north face, *new route* (Selkirks). One bivouac. A Canadian party had already 'apparently climbed somewhere on the face—just where, nobody seems to know.

Twa Harpies Expedition (Alaska). Bad windslab and deep powder.

Ball, *northeast buttress* (Canadian Rockies). Wanted the north face, but appears terrible.

Blackhorn West, *north face* (Canadian Rockies). Frightening rockfall.

Bastion, *east face* (Canadian Rockies). Steep snow and ice, then a great rock finish!

Redoubt, *east face* (Canadian Rockies). Three dangerous rock volleys.

Waddington North Face Expedition (B.C. Coast). *New route* up buttress direct from Tiedeman Glacier.

Stiletto, *southwest face* (B.C. Coast). Also second ascent of this fine peak, with Leif Patterson.

Heyburn, east peak, *north buttress* (Sawtooth)

Squaretop, *east face* (Wind River). One bivouac. Did climb amid chilly snow flurries.

Ship Rock, *southwest buttress* (New Mexico). A Grade VI in the desert.

Split Pinnacle, east arete (Yosemite)

Higher Cathedral Spire, south face (Yosemite)

Daff Dome, west face (Yosemite). *New route.*

Rattlesnake Route (Yosemite)

North Early Winter Spire, *west face* (C)

Snow Creek Wall (C). *Hallowe'en Buttress.*

Half Moon, *west face* (C)

Lake Ann Buttress, *south face* (C). A fine face, but beware of the rock.

Easter Tower (C). *Easter Buttress.*

McMillan Spire, *north face* (C). Did higher spire on a 4-day bivouac trek.

Sloan, east face, *new route* (C)

1966: Index Town Wall (C). *Town Crier route.*

The Blockhouse, *south face* (C)

Easter Tower (C). *First free ascent of inside-col route.*

Snow Creek Wall (C). Spring Fever Route, *first free ascent.*

Big Kangaroo, *south face* (C)

The Temple, *northeast face* (C)

South Early Winter Spire, *northwest face* (C)

Goode, *east buttress* (C)

Unicorn (Sierra)

Chimney Rock, *south nose* (Idaho). So narrow it shakes.

Alverstone, *northeast face* (Yukon). Lowell Glacier Expedition to Mt. Kennedy.

Seattle (Alaska). KING-TV expedition. Made film.

Owl Rock (Monument Valley, Arizona)

Echo Tower (Utah)

Grandview Spire (Colorado)

Buffalo Head, *northeast face* (Wind River)

Wolf's Head, *south face* (Wind River). A truly fantastic climb.

Monolith, *northwest face* (Wind River). In 1 day—the marvelous rock saved us.

Musembeah, *northeast buttress* (Wind River)

Lefroy (Canadian Rockies). *First winter ascent.*

Vérendrye, *east face* (Canadian Rockies)

Barbican, *east face* (Canadian Rockies)

Northpost Spire, *north face* (Bugaboos). A big face that is hard to reach.

Squamish Chief (B.C. Coast):
Tantalus Wall. One bivouac. Grade V.
Crescent Ramp. Grade IV.
Western Dihedral. One bivouac. Grade V.
Calculus Crack.
Math Crack. *New variation.*
Bullethead West.
Bullethead Central.
Bullethead East. The Bullethead routes should become classics.

Papoose Rock (B.C. Coast). *Mushroom Route.*

1967:

The Pulpit (Zion Park, Utah). Only two leads, but it overhangs on all sides.

Great White Throne, *northwest face* (Zion Park, Utah). With Galen Rowell and Pat Callis. Every school geography book has an illustration of this face—perhaps the longest sandstone climb in the world.

King-on-a-Throne (Monument Valley, Utah)

Whitney Portal Buttress (Sierra). One bivouac. Grade V.

Overhang Bypass route (Yosemite)

Middle Sister (Monument Valley, Arizona). The local Navajos became restless.

Squamish Chief, *Zodiac Wall* (B.C. Coast). Steepest and hardest route on the Chief.

Squamish Chief, *Unfinished Symphony route* (B.C. Coast) Grade IV.

Squamish Squaw, *Right Wing route* (B.C. Coast)

Gunsight (Blue) (C). North peak, *northwest face;* central peak, *southwest face.* Trouble with high water and black bears.

The Innominate, *east face* (Big Horn Range, Wyoming). Grade IV.

Liberty Bell, *west face via Serpentine Crack* (C)

Bear, *north face* (C)

Bugaboo Spire (Bugaboos)

Snowpatch Spire, west face, *new direct route* (Bugaboos). Beware of the snafflehound! We found a hole eaten through our tent wall.

Continental Tower (Wind River). A nice discovery.

Little Sandy Lake Buttress (Wind River)

Mt. Wilson, *southwest face* (Canadian Rockies)

Dungeon Peak, *east face* (Canadian Rockies). Middle face of the three ramparts above Amethyst Lake.

Devil's Tower, west face, *El Matador route* (Wyoming). There being no place to hide, the call of nature had to be answered in full view of gawking tourists at the parking lot.

1968:   Snow Creek Wall (C). Tempest route, *first free ascent.*

Castle Rock (C). Numerous routes.

Pharaoh's Beard (Yosemite)

Mt. Kimball expedition (Alaska). Snowed out.

Amphitheatre Dome, *north buttress* (Sierra). In Castle Rocks area.

Noname Pyramid, *east face* (Sierra)

University, *northeast face* (Sierra)

Carillon, *east face* (Sierra). In Whitney area. Good granite.

Goldfinger (Sierra). On Sawtooth Ridge.

Impala, *southeast face* (Sierra)

Premiere Buttress (Sierra). At Whitney Portal.

South Early Winter Spire, *direct east buttress* (C)

Hooker, *northeast face* (Canadian Rockies). Between storms.

Pilot Knob, *south face* (Wind River). Above shores of Grave Lake.

Wind River Peak, *north buttress* (Wind River)

Cathedral Peak, *south face* (C). A secluded challenge in the Pasayten Wilderness.